# BETTER CHESS FOR AVERAGE PLAYERS

# BETTER CHESS FOR AVERAGE PLAYERS

## Tim Harding

DOVER PUBLICATIONS, INC.
New York

## Bibliographical Note

This Dover edition, first published in 1996, is an unabridged, corrected and
slightly revised republication of the 1979 corrected printing of the work first
published by Oxford University Press, Oxford, England, 1978, as by "T. D.
Harding." For the Dover edition the author has written a new Preface, made a
number of corrections and provided some additional annotation.

## Library of Congress Cataloging-in-Publication Data

Harding, Tim.
    Better chess for average players / Tim Harding.
        p.    cm.
    Originally published: Oxford: Oxford University Press, 1977. With new
pref.
    ISBN 0-486-29029-8 (pbk.)
    1. Chess.  I. Title.
GV1449.5.H37    1996
794.1'2—dc20                                                   95-38958
                                                               CIP

Manufactured in the United States of America
Dover Publications, Inc., 31 East 2nd Street, Mineola, N.Y. 11501

# Preface to the Dover Edition

It gives me great pleasure to see this book back in print under the distinguished Dover imprint. While I have taken the opportunity to make a few corrections, largely based on readers' letters, I thought it best to leave the text essentially intact. The book was first published in 1978, so some factual statements in the Epilogue about matters of English chess organisation may no longer be up-to-date. Also, happily, few games nowadays suffer premature adjudication and adjourned games are rarer but I do not think the advice given in the book or the reader's enjoyment should be affected. I consider it important that the flavour of the book should be unaltered, so changes have been made only where they definitely improve the book's accuracy and utility for the practical player.

This new edition of *Better Chess for Average Players* is dedicated to my wife and daughters and to women chess players everywhere.

*Tim Harding*

*Dublin*
*January 1996*

# Preface to the First Edition

This book assumes no more knowledge of chess than the moves of the pieces. It is designed both as entertainment and as an instruction course to lead you in gentle stages from first principles up to the standard of a good club team player. Therefore beginners should read the book in order, though experienced club and school players may prefer to skip the first couple of units. Exercises are set at the end of most, though not all, the units, but if you want to derive maximum benefit from the book I recommend that every example should be treated as a puzzle. Study the diagrams before reading what I have to say about them.

*Better Chess* has evolved out of courses of chess coaching which I gave in London between 1973 and 1976 at Catford School and the Sydenham and Forest Hill Evening Institute. I should like to take this opportunity of thanking Adrian Hollis, who read an early draft of the book and made a number of helpful suggestions.

Above all, Adam Hart-Davis must take much of the credit for what is good in this book. As editor, he inspired and guided and goaded me through all stages of the work.

*Dublin*                                                                                          *Tim Harding*
*April 1977*


## AUTHOR'S NOTE

The Midlington Chess Club and their rivals, introduced in Unit 5, are not intended to portray any actual club or chess players. Any resemblance detected by the reader is completely coincidental. Midlington is supposed to be an archetypal club somewhere in the English Midlands, and Harry, Mary, and their friends can be found in almost any town.

# Contents

# Notation

The great majority of the countries of the world use algebraic notation for their chess publications, and this has been an important factor in international chess communication. English- and Spanish-speaking countries have hitherto clung to the descriptive system, but even in these countries there is an increasing tendency for the leading players to prefer algebraic notation, because it is more concise, and because it assists clear, logical thought about the game.

For readers who are not familiar with the algebraic system we give below a game (Charousek—Wollner) in full algebraic, condensed algebraic, and descriptive notation. The main differences are that in algebraic all the squares on the board are identified by a single map-reference system; that pawns are not named, but understood when no piece is named; and that in a capture the captured man is not identified. The system of notation used in this book is condensed algebraic.

| Full algebraic | Condensed algebraic | Descriptive |
|---|---|---|
| 1 e2-e4 e7-e5 | 1 e4 e5 2 d4 exd4 3 c3 dxc3 | 1 P-K4 P-K4 |
| 2 d2-d4 e5xd4 | 4 Bc4 Nf6 5 Nf3 Be5 6 Nxc3 d6 | 2 P-Q4 PxP |
| 3 c2-c3 d4xc3 | 7 0-0 0-0 8 Ng5 h6 9 Nxf7 Rxf7 | 3 P-QB3 PxP |
| 4 Bf1-c4 Ng8-f6 | 10 e5 Ng4 11 e6 Qh4 12 exf7+ | 4 B-QB4 N-KB3 |
| 5 Ng1-f3 Bf8-c5 | Kf8 13 Bf4 Nxf2 14 Qe2 Ng4+ | 5 N-B3 B-B4 |
| 6 Nb1xc3 d7-d6 | 15 Kh1 Bd7 16 Rae1 Nc6 | 6 NxP P-Q3 |
| 7 0-0 0-0 | | 7 0-0 0-0 |
| 8 Nf3-g5 h7-h6 | | 8 N-KN5 P-KR3 |
| 9 Ng5xf7 Rf8xf7 | | 9 NxP RxN |
| 10 e4-e5 Nf6-g4 | | 10 P-K5 N-N5 |
| 11 e5-e6 Qd8-h4 | | 11 P-K6 Q-R5 |
| 12 e6xf7+ Kg8-f8 | | 12 PxRch K-B1 |
| 13 Bc1-f4 Ng4xf2 | | 13 B-B4 NxBP |
| 14 Qd1-e2 Nf2-g4+ | | 14 Q-K2 N-N5ch |
| 15 Kg1-h1 Bc8-d7 | | 15 K-R1 B-Q2 |
| 16 Ra1-e1 Nb8-c6 | | 16 QR-K1 N-QB3 |
| *(see diagram)* | | *(see diagram)* |
| 17 Qe2-e8+ Bxe8 | 17 Qe8+ Rxe8 18 fxe8=Q+ Bxe8 | 17 Q-K8ch RxQ |
| 18 f7xe8(Q)+ Bd7xe8 | 19 Bxd6 mate | 18 PxR(=Q)ch BxQ |
| 19 Bf4xd6 mate | | 19 BxQP mate |

! good move    !! brilliant move    + check    ? bad move    ?? howler

!? double-edged but probably good move    ?! double-edged but probably bad move

♔ K    ♕ Q    ♖ R    ♗ B    ♘ N    ♙ P

# 1. Basics

## UNIT 1    MATERIAL VALUES

### POINT COUNT

The ultimate aim in a chess game is to checkmate your opponent, but only a beginner will allow you to achieve this without a hard struggle. Winning enemy pawns or pieces is an important step towards checkmate. Just as the larger army usually has the advantage in a battle, so in chess the player with extra material is more likely than his opponent to win the game. Although much of the fun of chess lies in finding the exceptions to this rule, the concept of material advantage is fundamental to any understanding of the logic of the chess-board.

You are probably already familiar with the numerical scale of the average values of the pieces. Taking a pawn as the unit, one often says that knights and bishops (the 'minor pieces') are worth three pawns each, a rook five, and the queen nine. The king can't be given a value on this scale, because you can't exchange him for other pieces.

No mechanical system can be of much help to you in evaluating the subtler aspects of your position (much less, even, than point-count systems for bidding in bridge). We'll see some of the exceptions in Unit 30; maybe it would be more precise to call a rook 4½ and a queen 8½.

Nevertheless this 1, 3, 5, 9 rule of thumb should help you avoid elementary errors when exchanging pieces, and at any time the material count will give you some idea of how well or badly you stand. We shall see that many other factors, especially the safety of your king, must be taken into account, but other things being equal an advantage of two or three material points means you should win with correct play. An advantage of one usually means that your opponent has something to worry about, particularly as the endgame draws near.

Why do the pieces have those values? The strength of a piece is a function of its mobility — its speed in crossing the board to the scene of battle, or the number of squares it controls from a good central post. The bishop and knight are considered to be about equal in value because the knight can attack squares of either colour, and this often makes up for its relative sluggishness — especially in blocked positions. However, the two bishops in concert can usually dominate the opponent's two knights — or often bishop and knight; even sometimes rook and knight!

We shall see later on which types of position favour which pieces. For the moment, the main point to bear in mind is that you should not exchange one of your pieces for an opponent's man of lesser value, unless you have a good specific reason for doing so.

### SOME BAD EXCHANGES

By developing your minor pieces before your rooks and queen, you greatly decrease the risk that your opponent may force an unfavourable exchange upon you, and increase your chances of winning material if he is too bold with his major pieces.

Thus a familiar beginners' error is to try to develop the rook first: **1 h4? d5** (see diagram 1.1). Now

'winning the exchange'. See Unit 13.

Early forays with the queen can be still more hazardous. After **1 e4 e5 2 Bc4 Bc5 3 Qh5** is a very old-fashioned move, hoping for 3 . . . Nc6?? 4 Qxf7 mate. Black has a much better reply in **3 . . . Qe7** defending the threatened pawns at f7 and e5), perhaps continuing **4 Nf3 d6 5 Ng5 Nf6** to reach diagram 1.2.

1.1 White to move

1.2 White to move

White cannot proceed with his intended 2 Rh3, for Black would reply 2 . . . Bxh3 winning rook for bishop (a gain of two points) and retaining a superior position. If you are patient, good opportunities for using the rook will arise later in the game, when pawn exchanges have opened a file or two and when some of the minor pieces (the rooks' natural enemies) may also be off the board. By the way, taking a rook for bishop or knight is called

Now 6 Qxf7+ Qxf7 7 Bxf7+ is best, although after 7 . . . Ke7 8 Bc4 h6 9 Nf3 Nxe4 Black regains his pawn with a good position in the centre.

However, from diagram 1.2, White might choose instead the apparently more aggressive move 6 Bxf7+, keeping the queen for an attack that will never be born. This is met by 6 . . . Kd8 7 Qh4 Rf8 8 Bc4 Ng4! 9 0-0 and now White is pole-axed by 9 . . . Rxf2. If 10 Rxf2 Bxf2+ and White loses his queen.

A common error by novices is to exchange bishop and knight for the opponent's rook and pawn by a sequence such as this: **1 e4 e5 2 Nf3 Nc6 3 Bc4 Be7 4 0-0 Nf6 5 Ng5? 0-0 6 Nxf7 Rxf7 7 Bxf7+ Kxf7**.

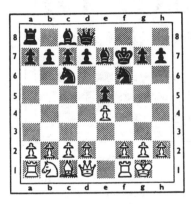

1.3 White to move

Nominally the game is level, since six points have been exchanged for six, but this is one of the cases which suggests that R=4½ rather than 5. In reality, Black has the advantage because he has three pieces in play, whereas all White's developed pieces have disappeared from the board. The black king is not insecure because White has no pieces to attack him with, and after the king has retired to g8 Black can think about bringing out his Q-side pieces and going over to an attack, starting perhaps with . . . d5.

White's extra pawn in such a middle-game situation means much less than the fact that Black has two independent attacking forces (bishop and knight) against White's one — the

king's rook. White should go in for this sort of transaction only in desperation, or if there are definite chances of exploiting the temporarily exposed state of the enemy king.

### DOUBLE ATTACKS

One attacked piece can usually be moved or defended, but a double attack may cost you material. Try, so far as possible, to keep all your pieces and pawns defended by one another. Undefended or 'loose' pieces, even when they are not directly threatened, provide chances for your opponent to find a hidden coup that wins material or inaugurates an attack.

Thus after **1 e4 e5 2 f4 exf4 3 Nf3 Ne7 4 Bc4 d6? 5 0-0 Bg4?** the black bishop on g4 is not guarded.

1.4 White to move

This factor enables White to win a pawn by **6 Bxf7+! Kxf7 7 Ng5+** and **8 Qxg4**, after which Black's homeless king will soon be the source of further agony to him.

White's trick in that example worked because after 7 Ng5+ Black found himself under two simultaneous attacks — the king by White's knight, and the bishop by the white queen — which could not both be parried. Most cases where material is won and lost exemplify this same principle of double attack. We shall look at some special kinds of double attack in units 2 and 3, but here are two more examples:

(a) **1 e4 c5  2 d4 cxd4  3 Nf3 e5  4 Nxe5?? Qa5+** (diagram 1.5), and **5 . . . Qxe5.**

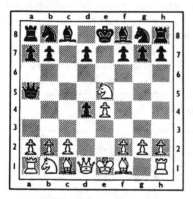

1.5 White to move

(b) **1 e4 e5  2 Nf3 Nf6  3 Nxe5 Nxe4?  4 Qe2 Nd6??  5 Nc6+** (diagram 1.6) **5 . . . Qe7  6 Nxe7** or **5 . . . Be7  6 Nxd8.**

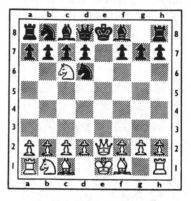

1.6 Black to move

You can see from these that double attacks are very hard to get out of, especially where the king is involved. But in each case, the attack was possible only because Black made a mistake, a blunder, which gave the winner his opportunity.

## HOW TO AVOID BLUNDERS

Blunders occur most often as a result of over-confidence — or its opposite, nervousness, when you are faced with a particularly formidable adversary — or when it is necessary to play very quickly. There is no gilt-edged formula for eliminating blunders from your games; even grandmasters blunder occasionally. But your results will improve, and your enjoyment of the game will grow, if you can cut oversights down to a minimum and so avoid those disheartening days when you spoil a good struggle or have to suffer the cat-and-mouse tactics of an opponent who is two pawns or a piece up.

As you develop your technical grasp and imagination (what strong players call 'sight of the board') you will find you become less prone to fall into double attacks or to leave pieces unprotected. With these beginner's blunders eliminated, you should start thinking about the psychological origins of the real howlers.

It is always advisable to go through a mental checking procedure between deciding on your move and actually making it. 'Sit on your hands!' is an ancient piece of advice, but still wise. We go into greater detail about organizing your thinking in Unit 22.

You have to be particularly conscientious about the last look round the board when you think you are doing well, for that is when over-confidence strikes and error creeps in.

If you do make a blunder, don't play your next move quickly. Rushing will not fool your opponent into thinking that you had expected his move, and you are likely to make the situation worse.

## TRAPS

If you think that your opponent has made a mistake, and that you can win something for nothing — don't be too hasty! Your eagerness to get ahead on material may be your undoing.

Some players are adept at setting traps, playing apparently weak moves that conceal a sting in the tail.

**1 e4 c5 2 Nf3 d6 3 d4 cxd4 4 Nxd4 Nf6 5 Nc3 a6 6 Bg5 e6 7 f4 Qb6** (attacking the white b-pawn) **8 a3!?**

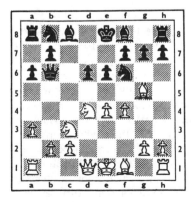

1.7 Black to move

This is not very constructive if Black continues quietly, but if his suspicions are not aroused and he goes 8 . . . Qxb2? then with 9 Na4 the jaws of the trap close around his queen. The lesson here is that when a threat to take material is apparently ignored by your opponent, you should pay special attention to the meaning of his last move. Here the unprepossessing 8 a3 took away the retreat squares a3 and b4 from Black's queen.

Some players take a delight in preparing surprising tactical traps to win material. The danger in this is that they may lose sight of the overall plan of the game, or even make an oversight or miscalculation, and throw away a perfectly good position. The following example of a tactician being hoist with his own petard actually occurred in the 1974 East German Championship.

This position was reached by the apparently innocuous sequence **1 d4 d5 2 c4 c6 3 Nf3 Nf6 4 cd cd 5 Nc3 Nc6 6 Bf4 g6 7 e3 Bg7 8 h3 0-0 9 Be2 Bf5 10 0-0 Ne4 11 Na4 Qa5 12 Rc2 Rac8 13 a3**.

1.8 Black to move

Now Black apparently thought: 'If my knight were not on c6, I could win material by . . . Rxc1; Qxc1 Qxa4'.

The unfortunate man therefore hit on the idea of 13 . . . Nxd4, meeting 14 Nxd4 by 14 . . . Rxc1 15 Qxc1 Qxa4 (gaining a pawn) and answering 14 Rxc8 by 14 . . . Nxe2+ 15 Qxe2 Rxc8 again with the win of a pawn. Can you see the flaw in his reasoning? (The answer is in the solutions at the back of the book.)

### SUMMARY

The final thing to be said at this stage about material advantage is that its benefits are often like those of an insurance policy — only to be felt in the long-term, or in indirect ways. An extra Q-side pawn is rarely of use in an attack on the opponent's king, until late in the ending when it can be turned into a queen. But its existence can draw enemy pieces back into passive defensive posts, or cause the opponent to expend valuable time in capturing it — time which can be turned into an attack or other advantage for you elsewhere on the board. On the other hand, there will be times when you have an attack that is not strong enough to force checkmate, but can be cashed in for an extra pawn or the exchange (rook against minor piece). Sometimes this correct timing of the transformation of a dynamic advantage into a material one (or vice versa) can make all the difference between a draw and a win.

## PUZZLES

Try to solve these puzzles before you go on to the next unit. The solutions are at the back of the book.

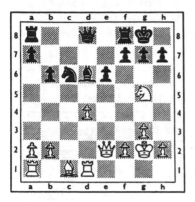

1.9 White to move: How can White win a piece here?

1.10 White to move: The same idea in a more complex setting. White soon wins a piece.

## UNIT 2   FORKS, PINS, AND SKEWERS

### *FORKS*

There are a number of basic tactical devices which win games again and again. To know them, and to recognize when you can use them in both standard and novel settings, is to be armed and ready for the chess battle. To be ignorant of them is to court disaster.

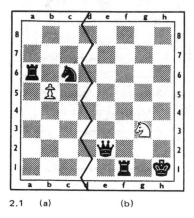

2.1   (a)                    (b)

In a fork a piece or pawn attacks two or more enemy pieces so that one of them is lost. In 2.1(a) the white pawn forks rook and knight.

Knight forks are the most common kind, probably because the knight's agility tends to be under-estimated, even by the strongest players at times. 2.1(b) is a 'family fork' — a particularly nasty affair, where king, queen, and rook are all attacked at once (even two of them would be bad enough).

The following little game, culminating in a fork, has been played many times; even a grandmaster once lost this way. After **1 e4 c5 2 Nf3 d6   3 d4 cxd4   4 Nxd4 Nf6 5 Nc3 a6   6 f4 Qc7   7 Nf3 g6 8 Bd3 Bg7   9 0-0 Nbd7   10 Qe1 e5 11 Qh4 0-0   12 fxe5 dxe5   13 Bh6**

b5  **14 Ng5 Nh5??** (14 ... Bb7 is correct.) **15 Bxg7 Kxg7** (not 15 ... Nxg7? 16 Qxh7 mate)

2.2 Position after 15 ... Kxg7

Now White plays **16 Rxf7+! Rxf7** (16 ... Kg8 17 Rg7+! comes to the same) **17 Ne6+** forking king and queen, and so obtains a decisive material advantage.

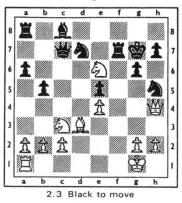

2.3 Black to move

Forks by all the other pieces are also possible.

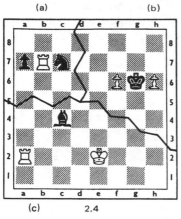

(a)                    (b)

(c)        2.4

Diagram 2.4(a) shows a rook forking knight and pawn; (b) has a king forking two pawns; and (c) shows a bishop forking king and rook. Queen forks are also common, but as the queen is the most valuable piece, it can normally only be used to capture unprotected pieces. So we only speak of a queen fork when it actually leads to a gain of material.

## SKEWERS

This variety of chessic cutlery is also designed for winning enemy pieces. One piece (often the king) is attacked on a diagonal, rank, or file, and is obliged to move out of the way; another piece standing behind is captured instead.

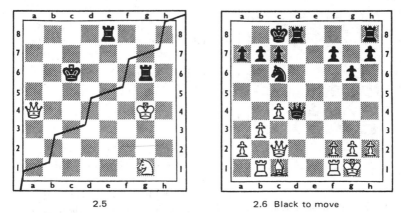

2.5                    2.6  Black to move

In 2.5(a) the queen skewers king and rook; in (b) the rook's skewer wins the white knight. In 2.6, White can win rook for bishop by the skewer 1 Bb2; e.g. 1 . . . Qg4 (1 . . . Qd2? 2 Qxd2 Rxd2 3 Bxh8) 2 Bxh8 etc.

*Forks, pins, and skewers*

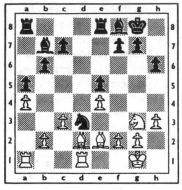

2.7 Black to move

In this position White thought his b-pawn was safe, but he had not seen that Black was ready with a skewer. After 1 . . . Nxb2 2 Rdb1 the knight looked to be lost — but 2 . . . Nd3! 3 Bxd3 Red8 and the skewer of the bishops regained the piece, leaving Black a pawn ahead.

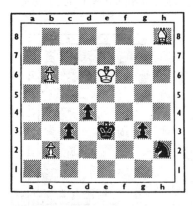

2.8 White to move

Skewers are more common in endgames, especially where pawns are about to be promoted. Diagram 2.8 is a study by Troitzky. White wants to win, but 1 b7 c2 2 b8=Q c1=Q

is not good enough, while if here 2 Bxd4+ Kd3! draws. The point of this is seen in the main variation.

White should play 1 Bxd4+!, forcing 1 . . . Kxd4, and after 2 b7 he will win. Whichever pawn Black queens will be lost rapidly to a skewer.

2.9 Position after 2 b7

Now 2 . . . g2 3 b8=Q g1=Q fails to 4 Qa7+ and 5 Qxg1.

2 . . . c2 is more complicated. White again wins after 3 b8=Q c1=Q 4 Qd8+ Ke4 (4 . . . Kc4 5 Qc8+ is another skewer) 5 Qd5+ Kf4 6 Qf5+ Ke3 7 Qg5+ etc.

## PINS

The pin is probably the most important of the three types of hardware we are examining in this unit. Every pin (see 2.10) involves three essential pieces: the pinning agent, the pinned piece and the 'target', for the sake of which the pinned piece cannot move. In 2.10(a) the pinning agent is the white bishop;

Page 10

the target is the king. The black knight is pinned; it cannot move without exposing the king to check. In 2.10(b) the bishop is pinned by the rook; it can only move at the cost of losing the queen.

(a)

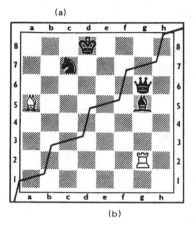

(b)

2.10

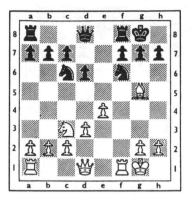

2.11 White to move

Pins and skewers both involve three pieces on a line. The difference is that in a skewer the one in the middle has to move, whereas in a pin the one in the middle can't.

Pins win material immediately only when the pinned piece is worth more than the pinning agent — as when a bishop pins rook on to king. Many pins (like the common pin of a knight by a bishop) never lead directly to a win of material, but the threat to win something and the immobilization can often be equally valuable.

This is because a pinned piece is extremely vulnerable. It can become the focus for the piling up of attacks to breaking point.

White can attack the Nf6 for a third time by 1 Nd5 and so win at least a pawn. Even if it is Black's move, he cannot avoid material and positional losses, because 1 . . . h6 (to break the pin after 2 Bh4 g5) can be met by 2 Bxf6 gxf6 3 Nd5 Kg7 4 Qg4+.

That this debacle was due almost entirely to the pin on the knight can be shown quite simply. In diagram 2.11 place the black queen on d7 instead of d8. Now the knight is free, and after 1 . . . Ne8 White (though he retains a spatial advantage) has no obvious way to break through on the K-side.

This game of Bronstein's shows how deadly pins can be: **1 e4 e5 2 d4 exd4 3 Qxd4 Nc6 4 Qa4 Nf6 5 Nc3 d5** (imprudent, as it creates a self-pin on the Nc6) **6 Bg5** (pins the other knight, and threatens to win it by 7 e5 and 8 exf6) **6 . . . dxe4** See diagram 2.12.

Now came the first fruits of White's pins: **7 Nxe4!** After 7 . . . Nxe4 8 Bxd8 Black would soon

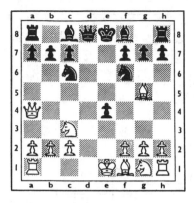

2.12 Position after 6 . . . dxe4

lose. So 7 Nxe4 was met by the counter-pin **7 . . . Qe7**, and then came **8 0-0-0! Qxe4**.

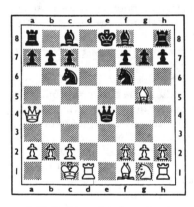

2.13 Position after 8 . . . Qxe4

Black must have thought his opponent had blundered, but he had overlooked a crushing move that exploited White's pins: **9 Rd8+!! Black resigned**, for after 9 . . . Kxd8 (or 9 . . . Ke7) the Nf6 is pinned once more, allowing 10 Qxe4 with no chance of Black recapturing. Note that the pin on the queen's knight

also played its part, by preventing 9 . . . Nxd8.

### THE CROSS-PIN

Even more vicious than the pin is the cross-pin: the case where the focal piece is transfixed in more than one direction. Diagram 2.14 shows a position from an Oxford League game, in which Black set up and exploited a cross-pin by a series of strong moves.

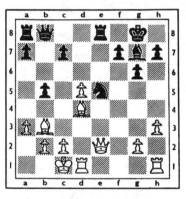

2.14 Black to move

After 1 . . . Nc6! the white queen is under attack from the Re8, and at the same time the Bd4 is attacked by Black's minor pieces. White's self-pinning reply 2 Be3 is the only way to avoid immediate heavy losses, but then comes 2 . . . Bh6, pinning that white bishop against the king as well as the queen. This is a cross-pin.
See diagram 2.15.

If White tries to force the issue now by 3 dxc6, Black wins the queen for rook and bishop by 3 . . . Rxe3! After 4 Qd2 (if 4 Qg4 Re4+

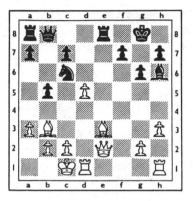

2.15 Position after 2 ... Bh6

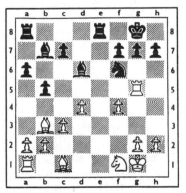

and 5 ... Rxg4) 4 ... Rxh3!
5 Rxh3 Bxd2+ Black would eventually win the game.

So White prefers to defend his bishop by 3 Rd3 Nd4 4 Qf2?
(4 Qd2 would be better) 4 ... Nxb3
5 Rxb3. White now threatens 6 Bxh6, but Black revived the cross-pin by
5 ... Rxe3! 6 Rxe3 Qb6, and the build-up at the focus continued with 7 Rhe1 Re8 8 Kd2.

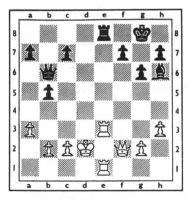

2.16 Position after 8 Kd2

Now 8 ... Qd4+ forced the win of a rook. White resigned.

## COMBINED THEMES

It is not unusual for several tactical themes to be involved in the same material-winning operation. In the next example, a strong pin is supported by the possibility of a fork.

Diagram 2.18 arises after **1 e4 e5 2 Nf3 Nc6 3 Bb5 a6 4 Ba4 Nf6 5 0-0 Be7 6 Re1 b5 7 Bb3 0-0 8 c3 d5 9 exd5 Nxd5 10 Nxe5 Nxe5 11 Rxe5 Bb7 12 d4 Qd7 13 Qh5 Nf6 14 Qf5 Qxf5 15 Rxf5 Be4! 16 Rg5 Bd6** (threatening to win the rook with 17 ... h6) **17 f4 Rfe8 18 Nd2 Bb7! 19 Nf1?** (He stands badly anyway.)

2.17 Position after 19 Nf1?

Now Black plays **19 ... Re1!**
Such pins, which interfere with the opponent's development, can be crippling. White's QB and QR are trapped. The bishop cannot move because of the reply ... Rxa1, and the rook can't get out at all. What is more, the off-side position of White's other rook on g5 means that Black is probably winning already. 20 Re5, giving up the exchange, is relatively

better than what White actually played.

White played **20 Kf2?**, which allowed Black to win material by means of an unusual fork: **20 ... Rxc1! 21 Rxc1 Bxf4** (see diagram 2.18). Now Black picks up a whole rook, which leaves him a piece ahead.

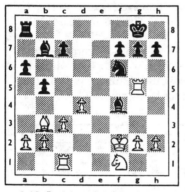

2.18 Position after 21 ... Bxf4

Note that 20 Rg3 would have saved the piece, because with the rook protected Black does no more than regain his pawn by 20 ... Rxc1? 21 Rxc1 Bxf4 22 Re1 Bxg3 23 Nxg3 etc. However, Black can exploit the pin on the QB to win the exchange: 20 ... Bxf4! (instead of ... Rxc1) 21 Bxf4 Rxa1 etc.

So Black's rook was a killer here, but note the supporting role played in the coup by his dark-squared bishop. Black's pin would not have been effective if there had been no other attacking piece available to exploit it. If the rook had been obliged to retreat after Kf2 then the ... Re1 manœuvre would have been a waste of time.

## DEFENCE AGAINST PINS

In games between masters, pins rarely have such dramatic consequences, because strong players are usually quick to take defensive action. The main defensive measures against a pin are:

(a) Interpose a defender between the pinned piece and the target.

(b) Lend additional protection to the pinned piece (without unpinning).

(c) Move the target.

(d) Attack the pinning agent.

Some well-known openings illustrate pins and the appropriate defences. In the Queen's Gambit Declined, a common position is reached after 1 d4 d5 2 c4 e6 3 Nc3 Nf6 4 Bg5, pinning the Nf6.
See diagram 2.19.

Black can use *type a* defence, with 4 ... Be7. He can also try *type b* defence, with 4 ... Nbd7. Note that this type of defence is only partial, since the KN is still pinned: it would be disastrous if White could get a pawn to e5, but he cannot do

2.19 Black to move

so at present. The main point of
*type b* defence is to avoid doubled
pawns (or loss of material) when the
target subsequently moves away
(*type c*) as in the Cambridge Springs
Defence: 5 e3 c6  6 Nf3 Qa5. Note
also a famous trap: 4 . . . Nbd7
5 cxd5 exd5  6 Nxd5 does not win
a pawn, because 6 . . . Nxd5! 7 Bxd8
Bd4+  8 Qd2 Bxd2+  9 Kxd2 Kxd8
leaves Black a piece for a pawn ahead.

2.20 Position after 8 Bg5

*Type d* defence is seen after 1 d4
Nf6  2 c4 g6  3 Nc3 Bg7  4 e4 d6

5 Nf3 0-0  6 Be2 e5  7 d5 Nbd7
8 Bg5 (diagram 2.20).

This move of Petrosian's can be met
by 8 . . . h6  9 Bh4 g5; masters are
still arguing whether the freedom
Black gains by this *type d* unpinning
manœuvre is worth the weaknesses
thus incurred in front of his king.

One special version of *type d* is
worth noting. It is exemplified by
the MacCutcheon Variation of the
French Defence: 1 e4 e6  2 d4 d5
3 Nc3 Nf6  4 Bg5 Bb4  5 e5 (diagram
2.21).

2.21 Black to move

You might think that Black must
lose his pinned knight because of the
pawn attack. The point of the
MacCutcheon, though, is that 5 . . .
h6 ('at the eleventh hour') 6 exf6
(or 6 Bh4 g5) 6 . . . hxg5  7 fxg7
Rg8 gives a complicated game
where Black does not stand badly.

## WHEN ARE PINS USEFUL?

In view of these varied defensive
methods, when is it worth pinning
an opponent's piece? Where it

leads to immediate tactical exploit-
ation, with win of material or
weakening of the kind seen in 2.11,
there is usually little doubt. However, some pins are valuable just
because they restrict the opponent's
options or cause him to lose time.

In the popular modern opening
line 1 Nf3 Nf6 2 c4 c5 3 d4 cxd4
4 Nxd4 e6 5 Nc3 Bb4 the pin enables Black to develop rapidly while
White has to worry about his Q-side
pawns. The longer such pins endure
the better they are; Black would not
mind smashing the white Q-side
pawns, but otherwise is not really
keen to exchange his bishop for a
knight. When *type d* defence is
finally applied, the bishop will often
retreat — unless exchanging keeps
the initiative.

Another useful rule of thumb is
that pins on unprotected pieces are
usually worthwhile — they win at
least one tempo — whereas pins on
well-defended pieces are rarely
worth the trouble, unless you particularly want to exchange off the
piece you are pinning. Then the
pin prevents it running away.

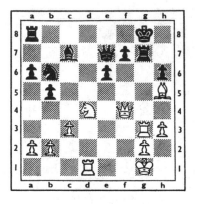

2.22 White to move

2.23 White to move

## PUZZLES

Take a look at diagram 2.22.

White's queen and KR are
skewered by Black's bishop. So
although material is level at the
moment, it looks as if Black is
winning, but is he?

Note that Black's Rg7 is pinned
by White's Rg3. Now try to see how
White can set up a fork, and end
two pawns ahead.

Diagram 2.23 was reached in a
Russian game after 1 e4 e5 2 Nf3
d6 3 Bc4 h6? 4 Nc3 Nc6 5 d4
Bg4 6 dxe5 Nxe5? Black's 5th
move pinned the white KN, and now
by recapturing with the knight on
e5 he thought he was increasing
the pressure against f3. How did
White escape the pin and show that
Black had blundered?

# UNIT 3    CHECKS AND ZWISCHENZUGS

*FORCING MOVES*

The initiative is an important factor in most chess games. The player who is able to keep up a pressure of threats against his opponent is more likely to make progress with his long-range plans. A good defender will naturally prefer to meet short-range threats with moves that fit into a deeper strategy of his own, but this is not always possible, especially when the threats are strong or numerous.

A forcing move is one that restricts the opponent's choice, because of the threat it carries. Sometimes there will be only one legal reply; more commonly there will be several available, but few of them particularly attractive to the defender. Having such a choice often puts the defender under a greater strain than if there were only one possibility, but moves that leave no choice at all ease the attacker's task of calculating ahead.

Forcing moves vary in their degree of compulsion. The moves having the highest degree of compulsion are normally checks, because the requirement to defend the king against checkmate is absolute. A threat to win the queen, say, can in a particular case be more effective, but there is always a possibility that the opponent might find a way of hitting back that enabled him to ignore the threat to his queen.

*TYPES OF CHECK*

Many checks are after all quite innocuous, because perfectly adequate replies are available. This is usually the case when there is a check in a popular opening sequence, such as in the Sicilian (1 e4 c5  2 Nf3 d6 3 Bb5+) or Bogoljubow-Indian (1 d4 Nf6  2 c4 e6  3 Nf3 Bb4+).

Simple checks can be met in one of three ways:

    (a) Capture the checking piece.

    (b) Interpose a piece in front of the king.

    (c) Move the king.

In the case of checks from a knight, only the first and third of these apply, which means that knight checks tend to be more awkward than others unless a capture is possible. Any check which forces the enemy king to relinquish his right to castle is worthy of close attention, as it may lead to a strong attack or at least discoordination in the enemy ranks.

Checks which are combined with another threat can be very difficult to cope with. The most common form is the *discovered check*, where one piece moves away to disclose a check from a rook, bishop, or queen hidden behind. At the same time, the piece that moves away often threatens a piece that cannot be guarded, or takes a pawn, or makes a nuisance of itself in some other way. Diagram 1.6 was an example of a deadly discovered check. Here are a couple more.

3.1 White to move

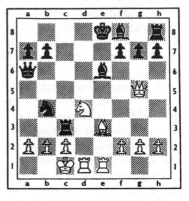

3.2 White to move

In 3.1, White could take the e-pawn with his bishop, giving check, but after 1 Bxe5+ f6 there would be no obvious way to continue the attack. *Do not give check just for the sake of it.*

Given that capturing the e-pawn will open the long diagonal anyway, the future of the Bb2 is assured. One of the other pieces could benefit by reaching the centre, and create stronger threats there than the bishop can.

The most forcing move is 1 Nxe5! The knight threatens to take the queen. Wherever she moves to evade capture, the knight can threaten her again next move, at the same time checking from the bishop. Thus 1 . . . Qd6 2 Nc4+ or 1 . . . Qe7 (or 1 . . . Qd8) 2 Nc6+ followed by taking the queen in each case.

Diagram 3.2 is more complicated. Black seems to have a strong attack, and would mate rapidly after 1bxc3 Qa3+; so White must pull something out of the bag with forcing moves. No check is available except for a sacrifice: 1 Qd8+!! Kxd8 2 Nxe6+.

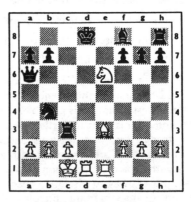

3.3 Position after 2 Nxe6+

White's second move is a special kind of discovered check. As the knight too threatens the king, we call this a *double check*. The only way to deal with a double check is to move the king, which is why double checks are especially to be feared.

Of the three legal moves open to Black, one is hopeless. If 2 . . . Kc8 then 3 Rd8 is checkmate.

Black actually played 2 . . . Ke7, but after 3 Bg5+ (clearing the file and cutting off the retreat to f6) 3 . . . f6 4 Nd8+ (controlling f7) Black resigned. It is mate in two moves after 4 . . . Re3 5 Rxe3+ Qe6 6 Rxe6.

2 . . . Ke8 would have been a more ingenious defence, as 3 Nc7+? Rxc7 and 3 Rd8+ Ke7 4 Bg5+ f6 5 Nc7+ Kxd8 leaves White with nothing. The solution is the other check.

After 2 . . . Ke8 3 Nxg7+! Ke7 (3 . . . Bxg7 4 Bg5+ and 5 Rd8 mate) the double check 4 Bg5 is mate.

## TO CHECK OR NOT TO CHECK?

We have seen that a check can be essential when any other way of seeking counter-play would be too slow. Even then, it is important to take the right check, as some are red herrings.

Checks may be good even if they do not lead to such obvious gains as in the foregoing examples. There may be subtler tactical reasons, or just positional reasons, for taking a check.

Diagram 3.4 was reached after **1 d4 f5  2 Nc3 Nf6  3 Bg5 d5  4 e3 Nbd7  5 Bd3 g6  6 Nf3 Bg7  7 h4!?** when Black tried to go for counter-play by **7 . . . c5!?  8 h5 Qb6?** He overlooked that White could prepare a destructive check.

3.5 Position after 8 . . . Qb6

White played **9 Bxf6! Nxf6** (otherwise 10 Nxd5 follows) **10 Bb5+**, reaching diagram 3.5.

3.5 Position after 10 Bb5+

Black has no good reply to this check. Moving the king is disastrous

(10 . . . Kf8 11 h6 or 10 . . . Kf7 11 Ne5+), but otherwise the d-pawn cannot be guarded. If 10 . . . Bd7 11 Bxd7+ Nxd7 12 Nxd5 Qxb2 (or 12 . . . Qd6 13 dxc5) 12 Nc7+ etc.

Some checks are played to induce a move from the opponent which he would rather not make. An amusing example is this line from the Modern Benoni Defence where first White and then Black 'lose' a move for this reason: **1 d4 Nf6 2 c4 c5 3 d5 e6 4 Nc3 exd5 5 cxd5 d6 6 e4 g6 7 f4 Bg7 8 Bb5+!?**

f3 and h3 by forcing White to play g2-g3.

There are certainly many occasions when it is a mistake to give a check. Arguably, White's 8 Bb5+ in the last example was not a good move — 8 Nf3 would be a reasonable alternative. Many 'obvious' checks can turn out to be howlers.

A check may be bad because it drives the enemy king (or some other piece) where it wants to go, or because it misplaces the checking piece. Or a check may be mistimed, or the wrong check may be given.

3.6 Black to move

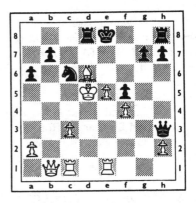

3.7 Black to move

White hopes to cut across Black's development by playing this move rather than simply 8 Bd3. If 8 . . . Nbd7 or 8 . . . Bd7 White may build up an attack with the advance e4-e5.

Black's best reply is **8 . . . Nfd7! 9 Bd3** (otherwise . . . a6 and . . . b5) **9 . . . Qh4+! 10 g3 Qe7**. Rather than go immediately to e7, Black first induces a weakening of the squares

This incredible position occurred in a master game played in 1889. White's king on d5 is not as easy to checkmate as might appear at first sight. Black should have played here 1 . . . Rc8 and if 2 Kc4 g6 3 Kb3 Qxh2 with a material advantage, and the white king still fairly exposed.

As the game went, Black hounded his opponent with checks: 1 . . . Qg2+? 2 Kc4 b5+ 3 Kd3 Qf3+

4 Kc2 Qf2+ 5 Kb3 Rc8 6 Rc2 Qxf4 7 Kb2 Na5 8 Ka1. Now White has at last safeguarded his king, with the help of some gift tempi from Black. Black should still have been able to draw, but in fact lost quickly, his own king being now comparatively the more vulnerable.

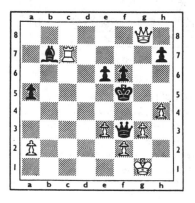

3.8 White to move

This example is more cut-and-dried. White can win this position by 1 g4+! Ke5 (1 . . . Qxg4+ 2 Qxg4+ and 3 Rxb7) 2 Rc5+ Kd6 3 Qf8+ eventually winning the bishop after a series of checks.

Instead, White played 1 Qxh7+??, probably the worst check ever played by a grandmaster! Presumably White thought that next move he would take bishop with rook and it would be all over. So it was, but not in the way he intended.

Only after 1 Qxh7+ was met by 1 . . . Kg4 did White see that either 2 Rxb7 or 2 Qg6+ would be simply met by 2 . . . Kh3 threatening unpreventable mate by Qg2 or Qd1. So White had to resign.

## INTERMEDIATE CHECKS

Unexpected checks are sometimes the key to tactical resources which turn the tables in complicated positions. When one player is obsessed with his plan of attack, which may appear to be going well, he can overlook that his opponent can hit back. Suddenly, an apparently strong threat of his own is ignored, as the opponent instead puts him in check. This may be a 'spite check', easily brushed off, or it may be a killer.

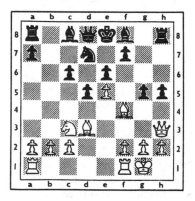

3.9 Position after 12 . . . g5?

Diagram 3.9 arose after 1 e4 c5 2 Nf3 Nc6 3 d4 cxd4 4 Nxd4 Nf6 5 Nc3 e6 6 Bf4 Be7 7 Nxc6 bxc6 8 Bd3 d5 9 e5 Nd7 10 Qg4 Bf8 11 0-0 h5 12 Qh3 g5? Black thought he was driving back the white forces in confusion: if now 13 Bg3 Black wins material by either 13 . . . h4 or 13 . . . g4, while if the bishop retreats to d2, then 13 . . . Nxe5 is good.

However, White played **13 Qxe6+! fxe6 14 Bg6+ Ke7 15 Bxg5+ Nf6**

**16 Bxf6+** followed by **17 Bxd8**, with a winning material advantage.

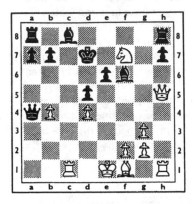

3.10 White to move

White's problem in 3.10 is slightly different. He has promising attack, but 1 Nxh8 might allow perpetual check after 1 . . . Qxb4+ 2 Kd1 (or 2 Ke2 Qb2+) 2 . . . Qb3+. At any rate, White's exposed king would be a serious liability. So White gave up a bishop to give the king a flight square at f1; because the sacrifice was with check, White kept the initiative.

Play went 1 Bb5+! Qxb5 2 Nxh8 Qxb4+ 3 Kf1 Qb5+ (3 . . . Qb2 4 Qf7+ Be7 5 Re1) 4 Qe2 Qxe2+ 5 Kxe2 Bxh8 6 Rxh7+ and White won the game with no trouble at all.

## INTERMEDIATE MOVES

Such moves do not always have to be check to be effective. Intermediate checks are only a special case of the in-between move, or *zwischenzug*.

3.11 Black to move

In this complicated position, Black played 1 . . . Qc7?! and after 2 g3? Qd7 White's weakened K-side was virtually impossible to defend. Yet White could have seized the advantage if he had seen he could play an intermediate move.

After 1 . . . Qc7 the correct move was 2 d5! and if 2 . . . Bxf3 3 d6! cuts off the black queen, before re-capturing the knight. White only saw the variation 3 Rxf3?? Qh2+ 4 Kf1 Qh1+ 5 Ng1 Bh2 which would be a loss for him!

3.12 White to move

Here Black has just played . . . d5, assuming that the knight would have to retreat leaving him with the initiative. White surprised him with a *zwischenzug* that had a neat tactical justification.

White played 1 Bc5! (threatening both Bxf8 and Nd6), with the point that 1 . . . dxe4 2 Bxf8 Qxf8 3 dxe4 would end with White the exchange ahead, thanks to the pin created on the f-file.

Black met 1 Bc5 by 1 . . . Bxe4 (relatively best) 2 dxe4 Rxf1+ 3 Rxf1 dxe4 (since 4 Qxd8 Rxd8 5 Bxe4 Rd2 would not be bad for him). Then 4 Qe3! gave White the initiative.

The moral is that even if your action seems to be forced, look out for an intermediate move that might upset your opponent's plans.

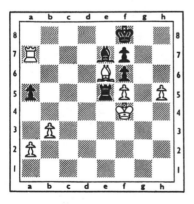

3.13 White to move

The corollary is that sometimes your opponent's moves aren't as

forced as you think! This especially applies when exchanges are being made: there is a tendency to assume that recaptures will automatically be made. This can lead to fatal oversights. In diagram 3.13, White saw that 1 Bc4 Kg7 2 a4 Kh6 3 Bxf7 would not be an easy win, because of the opposite-coloured bishops, so he looked for something better.

Play continued 1 h6?! fxe6 2 Ra8+ Kf7, reaching diagram 3.14.

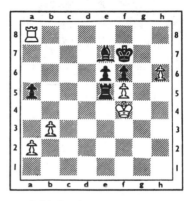

3.14 Position after 2 . . . Kf7

Now if 3 h7 Rxf5+ 4 Ke4 Rh5 5 h8=Q Rxh8 6 Rxh8 Black would probably draw. White played 3 fxe6+?? (planned at move one) assuming that 3 . . . Kxe6 4 h7 Rh5 5 h8=Q Rxh8 6 Rxh8 would follow, with good winning chances for him.

Instead, Black of course played 3 . . . Kg6! (a kind of intermediate move) 4 h7 Kxh7 5 Ra7 Rxe6 6 Rxa5 Kg6 and soon won.

## PUZZLES

Where should White move his king in 3.15 if he wants to avoid perpetual check? Notice the possible pins and counter-pins by the rooks, and try to work out whether 1 Kf1 or 1 Kf2 is correct.

3.16 Black to move

3.15 White to move

One of the uses of checks is to forestall the opponent's attack by making him do something he would rather not do. Diagram 3.16 is an example of this. The position looks rather wild, but Black has a forced win. Can you see what it is?

# UNIT 4   PAWN PLAY

## THE SPECIAL NATURE OF PAWNS

Pawns play an essentially different role from all the other men in a chess game. This is because of the following special characteristics of pawns.

  (a) They can never move backwards;

  (b) They move slowly;

  (c) They are easily blockaded;

  (d) They are promoted if they reach the opponent's back rank;

  (e) There are more of them than there are of the other men.

The dynamic value of pawns (particularly in the ending) follows chiefly from the fourth of these: 'Every corporal carries a marshal's baton in his knapsack' as Napoleon said. In the opening and the middle-game, the other factors are relatively more important.

## STRUCTURE

You have to move some pawns early in the game, otherwise your pieces (knights excepted) could not get into play. But once you move a pawn, it can never go back. This makes pawn moves more committal than most piece moves. Furthermore, because pawns capture in a different direction from the way they make their normal moves, their advance is easily blocked. Mutual pawn blockades as in 4.1(a) are a typical feature of most games.

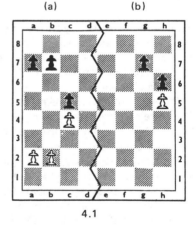

(a)        (b)

4.1

   Blockades of this kind, once they arise, are often a permanent feature of the position. Other types of pawn formation are also important in giving positions certain enduring characteristics. In 4.1(b) the white pawn at h5 prevents its opposite number moving, but also it discourages the black g-pawn from going anywhere: ... g7-g5 being met by h5xg6 *en passant*. This type of 'one pawn holds two' situation can be the basis of a positional

advantage, as can the types of weakness in the pawn structure to be discussed in the next section of this unit.

The fundamental point is that within a dozen moves in most games the
pawns will become locked together to some degree — either loosely as in
4.1(a) where some pawns still have freedom to move, or like 4.2 in a tight

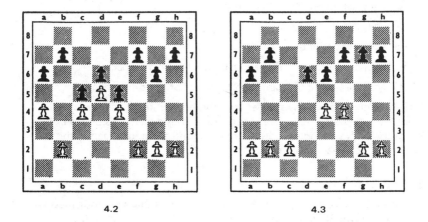

4.2                                          4.3

scrummage which is very hard to dissolve. Even if the pawns have not been
locked in this way, the early pawn exchanges and advances lend a definite
character to the game, in terms of local space advantages, weakened squares,
open and half-open files — as in the typical Scheveningen Sicilian structure
shown in diagram 4.3.

Pieces fit in between the pawns like muscles around a skeleton of bone.
The more rigid the pawn structure, especially around the centre, the more
the possibilities open to the pieces are determined by the skeleton. Each
type of piece is favoured by certain structures and hampered by others.

A knight likes a fairly blocked position, particularly one that provides
him with a supported point near the centre from which enemy pawns cannot chase him away. A bishop prefers open games, or at least one or two
open diagonals of the colour on which he operates. If his pawns are fixed
on his own colour, then he has little to do and becomes what is known as a
'bad bishop'.

In diagram 4.4, White's bishop is
very bad. There is very little for him
to do, and little prospect of his being exchanged. The black bishop is
also rather bad, but not as bad as

the white one. There is a job for
him to do in defending his king
(which is probably on g8), or he
may be exchanged after . . . Bh6
in some cases.

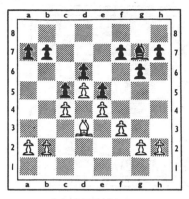

4.4 A bad bishop

Rooks like open or half-open files. A completely open file promises a way of access to the opponent's position, so it is almost always good to double rooks on such a file. Half-open files (ones where your opponent has a pawn but you do not) have a different meaning: they give you the chance of exerting pressure against the enemy pawns. An important feature of position 4.3 is Black's half-open c-file, the basis of his counterplay, while White's half-open d-file helps to maintain his space advantage in the centre.

## ORGANIC WEAKNESSES

Pawns are at their strongest when they stand side by side, or when they are in a chain protecting one another. The more they are advanced, the more there is a risk that they will become exposed to attack by enemy pieces, or to undermining by enemy pawns. Weak pawns are often a serious liability (less so if compen-

sated by the initiative or material advantage), and certain types of weaknesses have to be particularly guarded against.

These are: isolated pawns, doubled pawns and backward pawns, all of which are organic weaknesses in the pawn structure because, once they arise, they are very difficult to get rid of. In the endgame they can prove fatal. In the middle-game they are a worry to the possessor, and a target for the opponent. In 4.5,

4.5 Pawn weaknesses

Black's b-pawn is backward and his e-pawn is isolated. White suffers from an isolated a-pawn, doubled c-pawns and a backward d-pawn.

## ISOLATED PAWNS

Isolated pawns are pawns which cannot be protected by other pawns, because there are none left on the adjacent files. They usually come into being after pawn exchanges in the opening, though they can also develop later on. Here are some typical openings that lead to isolated pawns:

(a) **1 e4 e6 2 d4 d5 3 Nd2 c5 4 exd5 exd5** when White will eventually play dxc5, isolating the black d-pawn.

(b) **1 d4 d5 2 c4 e6 3 Nc3 c5 4 cxd5 exd5 5 Nf3 Nf6 6 g2 Nc6 7 Bg2 Be7 8 0-0 0-0 9 dxc5 Bxc5.**

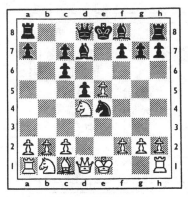

4.7  Isolated a-pawn

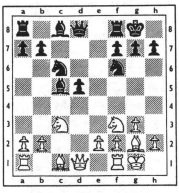

4.6  Isolated queen's pawn

The isolated queen's pawn that arises in these two examples is quite a controversial animal. In theory, it should be weak but it is compensated for by the dynamic factors of space advantage in the centre, adjacent half-open files and support squares for knights; an isolated pawn on the wing would not give so many active chances as one in the centre.

(c) **1 e4 e5 2 Nf3 Nc6 3 Bc4 Nf6 4 d4 exd4 5 e5 Ne4 6 Nxd4 d5 7 Bb5 Bd7 8 Bxc6 bxc6.**
See diagram 4.7.

In position 4.7, Black's a-pawn is isolated, but not weak at the moment; rook's pawns are not so

easy to get at. But in the ending, or if it were advanced to a5 or a4, then the weakness could become serious. At the moment, the doubled pawn on the c-file is at least as great a liability.

It is often a mistake to try to win an isolated pawn. The square in front of the pawn (d4 in diagram 4.6, for example) can be a great asset as a base for a knight (or sometimes a bishop). There is no danger of an enemy pawn chasing it away, and the isolated pawn prevents the opponent exerting pressure down the file. Only in the endgame does the isolated pawn finally fall. Hence grandmaster's Nimzowitsch's formula for dealing with these pawns: 'Restrain, Blockade, Destroy'.

## DOUBLED PAWNS

These only come into being as a result of exchanges, as in 4.7. The trouble with these pawns is chiefly that for all practical purposes they are devalued — Black is virtually a pawn down as there is nothing for the one on c7 to do. If the doubled pawn is isolated or on a half-open file the weakness may be more immediately serious. There are times, though, when doubled pawns may be welcomed for the open lines they give to the pieces. An example of this is the Alekhine Defence variation 1 e4 Nf6 2 e5 Nd5 3 Nc3 Nxc3 4 dxc3 where White obtains a space advantage and open lines with gain of time.

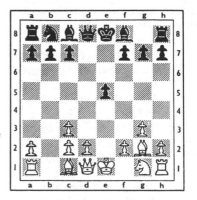

4.9 Position after 6 bxc3

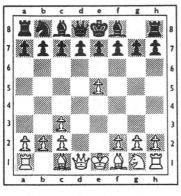

4.8

Another case where the doubled pawn is amply compensated for is the Paulsen line of the Vienna Game. After 1 e4 e5 2 Nc3 Nf6 3 g3 d5 4 exd5 Nxd5 5 Bg2 Nxc3 6 bxc3 White has pressure against b7 (especially after Rb1) and will soon get a pawn majority in the centre. See diagram 4.9.

## BACKWARD PAWNS

Backward pawns are a liability for the same reason as isolated pawns,

except that if they do not stand on half-open files there is less to worry about. Given time, the backward pawn can usually be advanced. The real danger is that the square in front will be occupied by an enemy piece.

Diagram 4.10 arose when after **1 e4 c5 2 Nf3 Nc6 3 d4 cxd4 4 Nxd4 Nf6 5 Nc3 e5 6 Ndb5 h6 7 Nd6+ Bxd6 8 Qxd6 Qe7** Spassky played **9 Nb5!** Black's backward

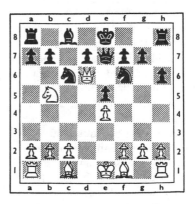

4.10 Position after 9 Nb5!

d-pawn (he should have played 5 . . .
d6 or at least 6 . . . d6.) means that
White has gained control of d6
(and has chances of controlling d5
soon). The pawn itself is not weak
at d7, but it gets in the way of the
bishop. White threatens to win a
rook with Nc7+, and if Black exchanges queens he loses all control
over d5 and d6; e.g. 9 . . . Qxd6
10 Nxd6+ Ke7  11 Nf5+ and
12 Bc4.

Similar questions arise after
1 e4 c5  2 Nf3 Nc6  3 d4 cxd4
4 Nxd4 Nf6  5 Nc3 d6  6 Be2 e5
7 Nb3 (see the next diagram).

**4.11  Black to move**

Diagram 4.11 shows a position
from the Boleslavsky Variation of
the Sicilian, which aims to show that
Black's backward pawn is compensated for by the additional space and
dark-square control that derives from
the pawn at e5. The crux of the
Boleslavsky is the square d5 — if
White can establish a piece there,
then he gets the advantage. But if
a white pawn ends up at d5, it is
not so clear, and if Black achieves
. . . d5 he usually frees his game.

## HANGING PAWNS

Black's pawns in diagram 4.12 are
known as 'hanging pawns'. They are
in effect an isolated pair, which are
always liable to degenerate into a
true isolated pawn although at
present they are not particularly
weak.

**4.12  Hanging pawns**

Hanging pawns on the fourth
rank, as in the diagram, control
quite a lot of space, including those
vital squares in front of them. If the
black pieces can mass behind the
pawns then White may become
cramped and get into difficulties.
Black could get pressure down the
b-file, or on the K-side, or obtain a
useful passed (albeit isolated) d-pawn.

On the other hand, the pawns
may come under fire before Black is
ready, e.g. 1 Bb5 Bb7  2 Qe2 d4?
3 Rd1 Re8  4 exd4 cxd4  5 Bxc6, or
an injudicious advance of one of the
pawns may allow White to blockade
them. This is especially likely if the
hanging pawns do not get to their
optimum position in the first place.
Diagram 4.13 is typical of this.

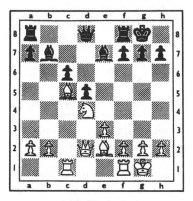

4.13 Blockades

White has two blockades (d4 and c5) instead of just one. The black Bb7 is very bad and the pressure on his a-pawn and c-pawn can only increase. In the long term the d-pawn will be vulnerable.

## CONCLUSION

The number and placing of the pawns has a deep influence on the game. In extreme cases, where there are several weak pawns (such as 4.13) the fight for the pawns and associated weak squares determines the players' strategies completely.

Even in fairly simple situations like 4.4 and 4.7 and 4.8, the pawn structure provides the basis for an understanding of the position. The pawns help to determine which pieces have good prospects and which are restricted; their strength or weakness provides the motive for long-range plans and for various tactical operations. The possibility

of promoting them in the endgame has various influences culminating in the endgame. This is why the 18th Century master André Danican Philidor wrote that 'Pawns are the soul of chess'.

## QUESTIONS

Diagram 4.14 was reached by **1 d4 Nf6 2 c4 c5 3 d5 e6** (the Modern Benoni Defence), **4 Nc3 exd5 5 cxd5 d6 6 e4 g6 7 Be2 Bg7 8 Bg5 0-0 9 Nf3 a6 10 a4 Qa5 11 Bd2 Re8 12 0-0 Qc7 13 Qc2 Bg4 14 h3 Bxf3 15 Bxf3 Nbd7 16 a5.** This is common pawn structure in the Benoni defences. Why does White play 10 a4 and 16 a5?

4.14 Black to move

In the Queen's Gambit Accepted, after **1 d4 d5 2 c4 dxc4 3 Nf3**, Black does not usually try to hold his pawn, but has sometimes played **3 . . . b5?!** What is wrong with that move?

# II. Attack

## UNIT 5   DEVELOPMENT

Most players like to take the initiative and attack their opponent's king. Harry Hacker of the Midlington Chess Club is certainly no exception. He loves open, fighting games almost as much as real draught ale, and his fellow club-members are used to hearing him complain about the rarity of both commodities nowadays.

'Attack is all very well, Harry' said team captain Tom Smith to him after Midlington's latest match, 'but it's no good playing with only one or two pieces. You handicap yourself by not getting all your men out first. That's why you're only rated 1560'.

The British Chess Federation grading list is a sore point with Harry. Every season he plays some lovely attacking games (which he remembers) and some ghastly losses (which he forgets) and never gets a good grading, whereas other club members, like young Johnny Brain for example, play mostly 'boring' games that are drawn on adjudication — but Johnny's rating improves each year, and it's 1810 now.

Harry's latest game on board six for Midlington was a case in point. Although he had Black, he attacked like crazy from the start: **1 e4 e5 2 Nf3 f5  3 Bc4 fxe4  4 Nxe5 Qg5.**

5.1 Position after 4 . . . Qg5

This is one of the sharpest lines of the Latvian Counter-Gambit, an opening which suits Harry's style but certainly has its darker side. Harry is happy to get his queen out early and go marauding on the K-side, but his opponent already has two well-placed minor pieces, which are worth more than Harry's double threat (against the knight and the g-pawn).

Harry's opponent was not panicked into playing defensively, and the game continued **5 d4 Qxg2 6 Qh5+ g6  7 Bf7+ Kd8  8 Bxg6 Qxh1+  9 Ke2.** Harry had still only developed one piece — his queen — but he was satisfied because he was a rook up, and surely his queen was making it hard for White to get the Q-side pieces out?

5.2 Position after 9 Ke2

5.3 Position after 14 Qg5!

Harry thought about playing
9 . . . Qxc1 but finally he decided
on the best move, 9 . . . c6, because
he realized that his king needed a
safe square to run to in case White
gave check with the knight. After
**9 . . . c6  10 Nc3** Harry played
**10 . . . e3**, because he remembered
reading in a chess magazine that
this was the latest Russian improve-
ment. Tom Smith was very unhappy to see Harry moving pawns
when all his pieces were stuck on
the back row, and his fears were
justified.

White thought for half an hour;
with four pieces in play against an
exposed king, he felt sure he must
be winning. Finally he played
**11 Be4 Qg1  12 Bxe3 Qxa1  13 Nf7+
Kc7  14 Qg5!** and went off to get a
cup of coffee. See diagram 5.3.

Harry was worried now. He was
two whole rooks ahead, it's true,
but the threat of Qd8 mate had to
be dealt with, and he had to watch
those white pieces hovering in the

centre. If only there were time for
. . . Qxb2 so that he could get at
White's king!

But it was no good dreaming
about that. Tom and Johnny and
Mary Mashem were all looking at
his position, and he knew he had
to come up with a good idea, for
the team's sake. 14 . . . Be7 looked
horrible because of 15 Bf4+; he
didn't see that 15 . . . d6 16 Bxd6+
Kd7 would have given him chances
of drawing — besides, Harry hates
draws. No, he wanted to escape with
his king and win on material. So it
had to be **14 . . . b6**. See diagram
5.4.

With a smile of satisfaction,
Harry got up from his chair and went
to look at the other games; 'Dull
positional stuff' he noticed. 'What's
happening, Harry?' asked Mary,
who had just made her move on
board two. Harry liked Mary; a
pretty girl in her twenties (Harry,
of course, is middle-aged and
married) and always very polite to

5.4 Position after 14 . . . b6

him — not like that fifteen-year-old Johnny who often made rude remarks about his play!

'Well, Mary, I am two rooks up and he's only got five minutes to play sixteen moves. I expect I'll win on time'. Mary had doubts about that, but murmured something encouraging. 'Sshh' said Harry's opponent; noise is very distracting when you are in time trouble, and perhaps he thought Harry was receiving advice, which of course is against the rules.

But Harry was beyond all help now, though he did not realize it. He expected 15 Qd8+ Kb7 after which his king would be safe.

Suddenly White, after an anxious glance at the minute hand of his clock, played **15 Nb5+!** This was a nasty surprise for Harry; if he took the knight (15 . . . cxb5) then 16 Qd8 would be mate, as the bishop on e4 would cover the b7 square. So Harry played **15 . . . Kb7** and tried not to look worried. But it was no good; it was mate in two and they both knew it. White played **16 Nd8+ Ka6  17 Nc7** and it was all over.

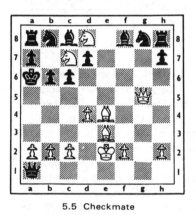

5.5 Checkmate

Harry moved only pawns, his king and his queen throughout the game. The cherished extra rooks never even had a chance to move. Black's premature attack had exposed him to the full force of the concerted action of White's queen and minor pieces.

## SOME DON'Ts

If you want to lose like Harry did, then ignore this list of *Don'ts!* Here is how to allow your opponent a decisive attack:

  (a) Leave your king uncastled.

  (b) Advance pawns in front of your king.

(c) Develop just one or two pieces (including the queen), move them several times, and then exchange them or put them offside. (Harry's queen wasn't much use at a1, was it?)

(d) Make several pawn moves.

(e) Grab material.

If you do these things (or most of them) you stand a good chance of being crushed in under twenty moves.

## CORRECT DEVELOPMENT

The most important rule of development which Harry neglected but his opponent respected is: Bring out Minor Pieces First. In almost all openings which masters play, both players develop both knights and at least one bishop in the first half-dozen moves. Consider these examples:

5.6 Queen's Gambit

5.7 Sicilian Defence

(a) Queen's Gambit: 1 d4 d5 2 c4 e6 3 Nc3 Nf6 4 Bg5 Be7 5 e3 0-0 6 Nf3 Nbd7.

See diagram 5.7.

(b) Sicilian Defence: 1 e4 c5 2 Nf3 Nc6 3 d4 cxd4 4 Nxd4 Nf6 5 Nc3 d6 6 Bg5 Bd7.

See diagram 5.8.

(c) English Opening: 1 c4 e5 2 Nc3 Nc6 3 Nf3 Nf6 4 g3 Bb4 5 Bg2 0-0.

5.8 English Opening

In some openings, one player may delay slightly his Q-side development in order to complete his K-side mobilization, but he will still heed the list of warnings we gave Harry. The Ruy López is an example: 1 e4 e5 2 Nf3 Nc6 3 Bb5 a6 4 Ba4 Nf6 5 0-0 Be7 6 Re1. When White loses in this opening, it can often be traced to neglect of Q-side development, as in example 2.18 above.

5.9 Ruy López

You will notice from these examples that there are no early queen moves, and that the first rook move is usually castling. Pawn moves are kept to the minimum needed to make way for the bishops and to control a fair share of the central area (d4, d5, e5 in particular).

Your overall objective in the opening eight or ten moves should be to:

(a) Control a fair share of the centre.

(b) Move each knight and bishop just once, to an active square.

(c) Castle (usually K-side).

(d) Prepare to challenge one or more open files with your rooks.

If your opponent blunders, or plays a sharp and risky line (like Harry's Latvian Counter-Gambit) you must be adaptable, but should not lose sight of these general principles. Also sometimes (usually if you are Black) you have to be content with some defensive moves at the beginning (e.g. 4 . . . Be7 and 6 . . . Nbd7 in the Queen's Gambit) or you may prefer to accept a watching brief in the centre, hoping to hit back later (as in the Pirc: 1 e4 d6 2 d4 Nf6 3 Nc3 g6), but in these cases too Black makes sure that he has good squares for his minor pieces and a safe home for his king.

White can afford to play a more active role than Black in the opening, because he starts first. But this advantage can easily be frittered away by too many pawn moves or by moving a piece too many times, or by pawn-grabbing. It is often the 'slow' openings which provide the most solid basis for an attack in the middle-game. The early attacks that Harry Hacker loves usually develop only if one player breaks the rules of correct development.

## *CASTLING*

In many openings, one or both of the central files become open quite early, with the result that the kings are exposed. As a rule, the king is safer on the side of the board, and castling makes it easy to get him there, and at the same time to bring a rook towards the centre where it is more likely to have a job to do. In most games between good players, White and Black both castle early on, and usually on the K-side.

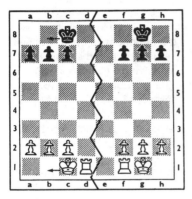

5.10 Castling safety

K-side castling is quicker, because there is one less piece to move out of the way. It is also safer, because in the case of Q-side castling the rook's pawn is not guarded — usually necessitating another king move (Kb1 or, in Black's case, Kb8). However, these differences are only relative, and there are many situations in which Q-side castling is preferable to castling K-side. It is rarely advisable to castle on a side where one's pawns are damaged or missing, or where the opponent is already massing his forces for an attack. But the

cases in which it is preferable not to castle at all are rarer still.

When the players castle on opposite sides (e.g. White on the Q-side and Black on the K-side), especially

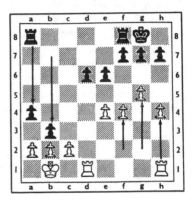

5.11 Pawn storms

sharp positions may arise. This is because both players are able to advance their pawns towards the enemy king without exposing their own king to attack in the process. With both players castled on the same side, such pawn storms are extremely hazardous.

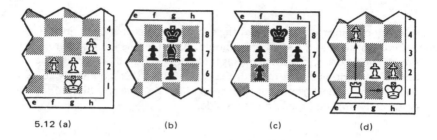

5.12 (a)          (b)          (c)          (d)

Ideally, the pawns in front of the castled king should be kept on their
original squares, as this makes it harder for the opponent to open files and
diagonals, or to obtain knight outposts that will embarrass the king. But
sometimes it is a wise precaution to move one pawn, to guard against
threats of 'back-row' mate'; for this purpose the rook pawn is best (5.12a).

The knight pawn is perhaps the most important of all the castled king's
defenders, and its advance is not advisable unless it is backed up by a
fianchettoed bishop (5.12b). This is a popular way of developing bishops
nowadays, but the weakening of the king's position (should the bishop be
exchanged) must always be borne in mind.

Diagram 12c is a very risky set-up for Black, as the doubling of his f-pawn
has not only devalued his pawns but also exposed his king down the file.
There are occasions when it can be advantageous to tuck the king in the
corner and use the open file for the rooks, but this would presuppose a
superiority of position in the centre and K-side.

Sometimes the f-pawn is needed for attack, as in 12d. In this case, it is
usual to prepare the move f2-f4 by Kg1-h1, to rule out dangerous checks
on the a7-g1 diagonal.

## OPEN LINES

An important factor in obtaining an
effective development is to ensure
that your pieces have clear lines of
action. For bishops, these are diagonals — the longer the better —
and for rooks these are files (and
ranks, if the opponent lets his
position be penetrated). In diagram
5.13 the white bishops are well
placed, but Black's are not. The
black QB is hemmed in by its own
pawns and the KB — potentially a
good piece — has no targets; it will

5.13 Good and bad bishops

only be chased away or captured if Black tries to use it on c5.

5.14 Good open lines

5.15 Knight outposts

Diagram 5.14 is the sort of position Black aims for in the Benko Gambit (1 d4 Nf6 2 c4 c5 3 d5 b5!?). Black is a pawn down, but he has good diagonals for both his bishops, and the a- and b-files for his major pieces. White on the other hand has only found a defensive role for his rooks and KB.

Note also that White in 5.13 and Black in 5.14 have connected their rooks. This is helpful almost always because it improves piece co-ordination.

## OUTPOSTS

Knights don't operate along lines; they are often quite happy with closed positions. What they do want is outposts, and e5 in 5.15 is an excellent outpost. There the knight is established within striking distance of important targets in the enemy position, and cannot be driven away by enemy pawns.

Diagram 5.15 shows four examples of knight outposts. In passing, note that outpost squares can sometimes be used effectively by other pieces too — but it is knights that cannot do without them.

## CO-ORDINATION

When laying out one's pattern of development, it is important to see that the moves do in fact pursue a common aim, and that the pieces and pawns do not end up on squares where they obstruct one another. See diagram 5.16.

A common beginner's error is seen in the sequence 1 e4 e5 2 Nf3 Nf6 3 Bd3? With his third move, White guards his pawn (not strictly necessary here) but blocks the advance of his d-pawn, which in turn means that it is going to be hard to develop the queen's bishop. The move 3 d3 (instead of 3 Bd3), although not strictly an error, is also passive because it condemns

5.16 Position after 3 Bd3?

the white king's bishop to an idle life inside his own pawn chain. A master would play 3 Nxe5, 3 d4 or possibly 3 Nc3 in order to develop the bishop subsequently at c4 or b5 where it puts pressure on Black's position.

One must also give careful thought before developing a knight where it blocks its own bishop. For example, 1 e4 e5 2 Ne2 is not a good opening for White. In example 5.6, however, it is acceptable for Black to play . . . Nbd7, because he intends to develop his queen's bishop by . . . b6 and . . . Bb7. There was never much of a future for that bishop on d7 anyway.

## QUESTIONS

(a) 1 e4 e5 2 Nf3 Qf6?! What is the objection to that move?

(b) Why, in general terms, is 1 g4 a bad opening?

# UNIT 6    THE CENTRE

*THE PAWN CENTRE*

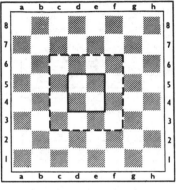

6.1  The centre

Diagram **6.1** shows what most players understand as 'the centre' (the small 2×2 square) and the extended centre of squares adjacent to that true centre. None of those sixteen squares is occupied when a game of chess begins. To control as much of this area as possible is one of the chief aims of positional play, and is also one of the preconditions of a successful attack.

All pieces except the rook increase in mobility as they approach the centre of the chess-board. A piece established in the centre puts pressure on the K-side and Q-side simultaneously, and a pawn in the centre denies central squares to the opponent's pieces. Only the king is unhappily placed in the centre — because of the danger of mating attacks.

In the nineteenth century most players tried to occupy the centre with pawns — the ideal was to have pawns abreast at e4 and d4 (for Black, e5 and d5) with the pieces massed beside and behind the pawn centre. Theory on the centre has quadrupled in sophistication in the last fifty years, since the old dogmas about the centre were first challenged by the 'hypermodern' school, but such a pawn centre still commands respect — if it can be maintained.

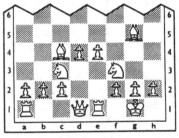

6.2  1880 'Ideal centre'

Diagram **6.2** shows an old-fashioned 'ideal pawn centre' with piece accompaniment. White is well-placed for attack if he can advance the centre pawns and gain more space at the expense of his opponent, whose pieces would then become cramped, or if there are weaknesses in the opponent's position which White's well-posted pieces can attack. But if Black has no particular weaknesses, it will not be too late for him to advance . . . c5, . . . d5, or

. . . e5 after which exchanges of pawns and pieces could lead to equality or even an advantage for Black.

Many popular defences allow White to establish his centre undisturbed, Black's plan being to hit back later by advancing his bishop's pawns or by attacking the centre with his pieces. In most modern openings the flank-developed bishop plays a key role, for potentially it presses down upon the pawn centre and (if the centre collapses) may even set up strong threats in the opposite corner of the board. At the same time, being sheltered behind its knight's pawn, it is not easily exchanged. So both players struggle to achieve the type of pawn structure in the centre which will give scope to their bishops and obstruct those of the opponent.

Typical modern openings of this kind, in which the ideal pawn centre is challenged from the wing, include:

(a) King's Indian Defence: 1 d4 Nf6 2 c4 g6 3 Nc3 Bg7 4 e4 d6 5 Be2 0-0. Black will try for . . . e5 or . . . c5. See diagram 6.3.

(b) Modern Defence: 1 e4 d6 2 d4 g6 3 Nc3 Bg7 4 f4 c6 5 Nf3 Bg4 6 Be3 Qb6. Black's pieces exert pressure on the d-pawn. See diagram 6.4.

(c) Grünfeld Defence: 1 d4 Nf6 2 c4 g6 3 Nc3 d5 4 cxd5 Nxd5 5 e4 Nxc3 6 bxc3 Bg7. Black will find ways to hit back against d4. See diagram 6.5.

Note the flank-developed ('fianchettoed') bishop in each of these examples!

6.3  King's Indian

6.4  Modern Defence

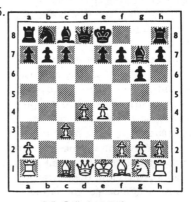

6.5  Grünfeld Defence

## CENTRAL PAWN FORMATIONS

A player who is preparing an attack should pay particular attention to the pawn structure in the centre. Some types of central pawn formation are so static (e.g. 6.6 and 6.7) that the attacker need not fear embarrassing diversions at the critical moment of the attack. In either case, assuming that White has the initiative with his pieces, he has good chances of pressing home his assault without Black being able to create adequate counterplay. Although the d-file is open in 6.7,

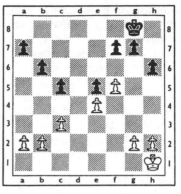

6.7 Fixed centre

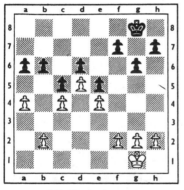

6.6 Blocked centre

if checkmate is not forthcoming quickly enough the defender's pieces may rush in to fill the power vacuum.

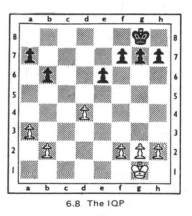

6.8 The IQP

Black cannot necessarily make any use of it, so this type of fixed (though partly open) centre is often as good for the attacker as the completely blocked (6.6) type.

However if the centre is fluid (6.4 or 6.5 for example), White may have to keep his pieces in the centre to forestall counter-attack there. Attacking a castled king almost invariably involves some decentralization of the attacking forces, and

Some types of centre are not so easy to classify. Diagram 6.8 portrays the infamous Isolated Queen Pawn (IQP) structure, which can arise from a variety of openings, e.g. the French and Caro-Kann Defences, the Queen's Gambit Accepted, and the Tarrasch Variation of the Queen's Gambit Declined (see also 4.5). It is well known that, in the hands of a good attacking player, the IQP can favour the attacker, as it provides a base for a knight on e5 and ensures White a space advantage in the centre behind which to mobilize his pieces. But if White is unable to develop strong enough K-side threats he will be condemned to defend the d-pawn in a difficult ending.

Endings with local pawn majorities (see 6.9) almost invariably mean fluid centres with good possibilities of a timely counter-attack. However the attacker can often obtain an advanced passed pawn in addition to his other threats, so a lot depends upon the relative placings of the pieces.

Positions where all central pawns have been exchanged give no cover to the pieces, which are therefore liable to become exchanged, unless one player has a strong initiative. The old 1 e4 e5 openings often lead to an open centre, massive exchanges, and a draw.

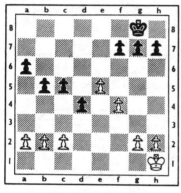

6.9 Fluid centre

## PIECES IN THE CENTRE

A knight, being a short-range piece, is more valuable if it can be established on a central square, protected or shielded by its own pawns. In 6.9 a white knight on e4 and a black knight on d5 would be well-placed. It is even better if the knight cannot be chased away by an enemy pawn, or readily exchanged by an enemy knight or bishop. Black's position in 6.6 would improve if he had a knight on d4, and a knight on d5 in 6.8 would be desirable. But in 6.7 Black has no ideal knight outpost, whereas a white knight on d5, where it dominates Black's dark-squared bishop, could be a killer.

Bishops, on the other hand, can operate best from a distance as long as their diagonals are kept open. However, in all the cases mentioned in the previous paragraph, a bishop would also be usefully placed.

Rooks rarely stand well in the centre until the minor pieces have been exchanged. There is too much danger of losing them for knights or bishops. They are best doubled on an open or half-open file. In 6.7, White wants his rooks at d1 and d2. In 6.8 they could be doubled either on the c-file or one of the centre files (as a preparation for the thrust d4-d5).

Another good arrangement for rooks is side by side on the back row, to support the advance of a pawn majority. In 6.9 White's rooks should stand well at e1 and f1, with the idea of pawn advances to f5 and then e6 or f6. The queen may take the place of a rook in most of these doubling manœuvres, or she may double with a bishop on an open diagonal.

### USING THE SQUARE e5

It is not unusual for a player to base his whole strategy in a game on controlling a particular square in the centre, and using it as a base for operations. In Bird's Opening (1 f4), for example, White aims to control e5 right from the start. The square e5 may also be of use to Black as the following example illustrates.

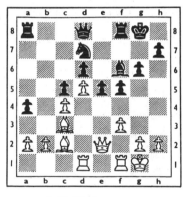

6.10 Black to move

Black (Grandmaster Geller) here enjoys a spatial advantage in the centre and on the K-side. Not seeing any obvious way to utilize his pawn majority, he chose instead an interesting pawn sacrifice with the aim of obtaining maximum activity for his pieces by establishing his knight on e5.

Geller played **1 . . . e4! 2 Bxf6** (if 2 fxe4 Bxc3 weakens White's pawn structure) **2 . . . Qxf6 3 fxe4 f4! 4 Rf2 Ne5.**

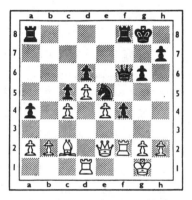

6.11 Position after 4 . . . Ne5

As compensation for the pawn sacrificed, Black has secured exclusive rights to e5. White's extra Q-side pawn has no significance, and the one on e4 restricts the scope of the bishop at d3. Black still has a K-side pawn majority which, in conjunction with the dominating knight, ensures him a strong attack.

The game continued **5 Rdf1 Qh4 6 Bd1 Rf7 7 Qc2 g5 8 Qc3 Raf8 9 h3 h5 10 Be2 g4.** Now White is in despair, trying to repulse the infantry onslaught.

White played **Rxf4** (ingenious,

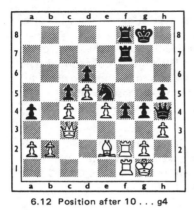

6.12 Position after 10 ... g4

but it fails) **11 ... Rxf4  12 Rxf4 Rxf4  13 g3 Nf3+  14 Kf2 Qxh3 15 gxf4 g3+!  16 Kxf3 g2+  17 Kf2 Qh2!** and **White resigned** as he cannot prevent Black creating a second queen. This game was effectively decided by White's sacrifice at moves 1–4.

## KEY SQUARES

Of course e5 is not the only important central square. Naturally e4 is of equal importance, and both d4 and d5 — though they are further from the K-side — are also excellent bases for attack if control over them can be assured.

Several openings, besides Bird's, are associated with the struggle for particular squares in the centre. Here are some examples:

(a) Nimzo-Indian Defence (1 d4 Nf6  2 c4 e6  3 Nc3 Bb4) — the square e4.

(b) Queen's Indian Defence (1 d4 Nf6  2 c4 e6  3 Nf3 b6) — e4 again.

(c) Larsen's Opening (1 b3) — White fights for e5.

(d) Catalan Opening (1 d4 d5  2 c4 e6  3 g3) — White fights for d5.

(e) Grünfeld Defence (1 d4 Nf6  2 c4 g6  3 Nc3 d5) — Black will try to undermine White's hold on d4, by means of ... Bg7, ... dxc4, ... c5, and sometimes ... e5 or ... Nc6.

Similarly in the Pirc or Modern Defence (1 e4 d6/1 ... g6) Black's primary interest is in the square e5, but this can often extend to d4 or to the whole central area. While in openings like the King's Indian Defence, where the d- and e-files can sometimes be wholly blocked by pawns, the struggle for adjacent squares like c5 and f5 can assume the same importance.

## WHAT DO YOU THINK?

Diagram 6.13 occurred in a game between Midlington's captain, Tom Smith, and Harry Hacker. Harry has just played . . . Rb8 (to guard his bishop) and Tom has replied Rc1. Should Harry take a pawn here by 1 . . . dxc4? (Answer in the back of the book.)

6.13 White to move

# UNIT 7    TARGETS

## *SELECTING THE TARGET*

Successful attacks do not materialize out of thin air. They have to be prepared. We have already seen two of the preconditions for an attack: satisfactory development and control of the centre. This is not enough though — there has to be something to attack. If the opponent has no exploitable weaknesses in his position, then manœuvring rather than attack is appropriate.

Several types of target are possible, and successful attacks usually depend on there being two or three weaknesses which can be threatened. Here are the main types of target:

(a) King exposed in the centre.

(b) Weak squares near the castled king.

(c) Isolated, doubled, and backward pawns.

(d) The enemy queen.

(e) Other exposed enemy pieces.

A strong attack may begin with subsidiary threats to ancillary targets of types c, d, and e, enabling pieces to approach the enemy king with gain of time. In this way, momentum is built up for a mating attack. This procedure can also work in reverse: a feint towards the king, forcing material or positional gains elsewhere on the board.

In some cases, the choice of targets can be almost an accidental matter. An error exposing a piece may enable you to launch an attack sooner than you expected. Attacks early in the middle-game, on the other hand, tend to be determined largely by the nature of the opening.

Thus after 1 e4 c5 2 Nc3 (The Close Sicilian) White has already announced his intention of keeping the centre closed, and trying to break through with a K-side attack before Black can make significant gains on the Q-side. Both players are likely to fianchetto their king's bishops, so already White knows that if he can somehow eliminate the black KB there will be weak squares near the enemy king for him to exploit. Let us see how this works in a concrete example.

## *A CRUSHING ATTACK*

1 e4 c5  2 Nc3 Nc6  3 g3 g6
4 Bg2 Bg7  5 d3 d6  6 Be3 (Spassky
used to play 6 f4 here) 6 . . . e6

7 Nf3 Nd4  8 0-0 Ne7  9 Qd2 0-0
10 Bh6!

7.1 Position after 10 Bh6!

7.2 Position after 19 ... d4

Black hasn't organized his Q-side play quickly enough, so White is able to fulfil the first stage of his program — exchange bishops to create a *type b* target. Black cannot play 10 ... Bxh6 11 Qxh6 Nxc2 because 12 Ng5 forces mate, while 10 ... Nxc2 11 Bxg7 Nxa1 12 Bxf8 is equally fatal.

So Black tried to gain time by **10 ... Nxf3+ 11 Bxf3 Bxh6 12 Qxh6 Nc6**, threatening 13 ... Nd4. White played **13 Bg2 Nd4 14 Qd2**, recentralizing, since the queen alone cannot force mate.

Black's next move, **14 ... b5?** allowed White to get another attacker in place with **15 e5** (threatening 16 Bxa8) **15 ... d5 16 Nd1 Nc6** (forcing White to block his queen) **17 f4 Bb7 18 Nf2 Qe7 19 Ng4 d4** See diagram 7.2.

With the e-pawn and knight in advanced positions, it is clear that the last few moves have aggravated the weakness of the dark squares near Black's king, so that a mating

attack is now a realistic possibility. For this purpose the queen is needed at h6, to mate on the indefensible h7 square. Once this is seen, the concluding breakthrough is not difficult: **20 f5! exf5 21 Rxf5 Nd8** (21 ... h5 is met by 22 Rxh5) **22 Nf6+ Kg7 23 Rh5!**

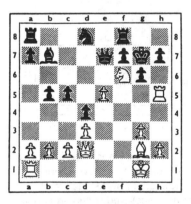

7.3 Position after 23 Rh5!

Mate is now inevitable. The game ended **23 ... gxh5 24 Qg5+ Kh8 25 Qh6 Qxf6 26 Qxf8 mate.**

## EXPOSED ENEMY PIECES

In the last example, Black's king was so poorly defended that subsidiary targets were hardly required. However at move 15 the queen rook played that role.

Many attacks would never get off the ground, but for subsidiary targets. The following short game shows how rapidly threats can escalate if they are not accurately met: **1 e4 c5 2 Nf3 d6 3 d4 cxd4 4 Nxd4 Nf6 5 Nc3 a6 6 Bg5 e6 7 Qd2!?** (an unusual move, to get Black 'out of the book') **7 . . . Be7** (here, or soon, Black should play . . . h6) **8 0-0-0 Qc7 9 Be2 Nbd7 10 f4 b5?** (plausible but wrong) **11 Bxf6!**

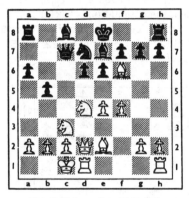

7.4 Position after 11 Bxf6!

This exchange is well-timed, because Black's last move opened weaknesses in his Q-side which would be covered if he was allowed time for . . . b4 or . . . Bb7. If Black recaptures with the bishop, his d-pawn is unguarded and the typical Sicilian sacrifice (11 . . . Bxf6?) 12 Bxb5! axb5 12 Ndxb5 (attack-ing the queen — a *type d* target situation) followed by 13 Nxd6+ gives White three pawns and a strong attack for the knight.

11 . . . Nxf6 also has drawbacks — here the targets are the black knight and the rook on a8. White would reply 12 e5 dxe5 13 fxe5 b4 (or 13 . . . Qxe5 14 Bf3) 14 Ncb5 with complications favouring White, who has the safer king and more pieces in active play. However this might have been preferable to the move Black actually played.

After **11 . . . gxf6** White played **12 f5**, which attacks a new target — the important e6 pawn — and which envisages Nd5 as a reply to . . . e5 or . . . exf5; this outpost square in the centre would be of great value to White. So Black played **12 . . . Ne5** but after **13 fxe6 fxe6** he had to decide what to do with his king in reply to **14 Bh5+**.

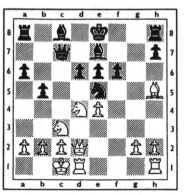

7.5 Position after 14 Bh5+

Interposing the knight is met by Qh6 when White wins at least a pawn, so Black took to the road with **14 ... Kd8**. Now that the king has lost its right to castle, White is certainly justified in looking for a quick mating attack. So he played **15 Nce2 Bf8!? 16 Nf4 Qe7**. Black has managed to defend the vulnerable e6 square, but inevitably in such a porous position there is another way through. **Black resigned** after **17 Qa5+** since next move White will be able to capture the e-pawn after all!

In retrospect, Black should have set a higher value on the safety of his king. His short-run attempts to avoid small material losses and unclear tactical lines only helped White to escalate the scale of his threats.

The next example also shows how an insecure king and an unguarded piece are all it takes to get a lost game. The fatal moment was when, after **1 e4 e5 2 Nf3 Nc6 3 Bc4 Bc5 4 b4 Bxb4 5 c3** (the Evans Gambit) **5 ... Ba5 6 d4 exd4 7 Qb3 Qf6 8 0-0 Nge7 9 cxd4** Black played the plausible but incorrect move **9 ... d6?**

White had a good idea when he saw this move. 'If only there wasn't a black knight on c6, the Qa4+ fork would win that bishop' he thought. Where there's a will, there's (sometimes) a way . . .
**10 Bg5! Qg6 11 d5 Ne5**

'That's the knight out of the way. But I can't win the bishop, because then . . . Nxf3+ and . . . Qxg5 will get it back. Still, his choice is very limited because of that hanging piece . . .'
**12 Nxe5 dxe5** (not 12 . . . Qxg5 13 Nf3 followed by 14 Qa4+ etc.)
**13 Bxe7 Kxe7 14 Qa3+ Kd8**

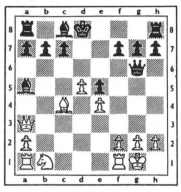

7.7 Position after 14 . . . Kd8

'This cat has nine lives! 15 Qxa5 will lose to 15 . . . Bh3 16 g3 Qxe4! Nevertheless, that loose bishop will be his downfall!'

**15 d6!** Note that this pawn cannot be taken either way because of the reply queen takes bishop, so **15 . . . Bb6 16 dxc7+ Kxc7**. After all that, the bishop has escaped and White is still a pawn down. But White has achieved a lot by this forcing sequence (moves 10 to 16)

7.6 Position after 9 . . . d6?

— he has driven the black king out into a very exposed spot and denied him the time to develop his rooks and QB.

**17 Nc3** was now played, threatening to occupy d5. Black was unable to find a satisfactory defence, and the game ended **17 . . . Be6 18 Nb5+ Kc8 19 Rac1 Bxc4 20 Qe7!** Black here resigned.

One lesson to be learned from these examples is that, when you want to attack the enemy king, you must pay attention to what is happening all over the board, even to apparently accidental circumstances. If you only think about the quarter of the board where the enemy king stands, you may overlook just the detail you need to justify your attack (or to warn you off it). Conversely, if you suspect that your king is about to come under attack, try to make sure that your whole house is in order — lest the decisive blow fall where you least expect it.

## WEAK PAWNS

We have already seen (in Unit 4) that weak pawns are very important entities indeed. Chiefly these are doubled pawns and pawns which are isolated or backward on a half-open file, although any unguarded pawn may be weak in the short term.

The difference between the target pieces we have just discussed and the three main types of weak pawn is this. Pieces are mobile and, given a move or two, an unguarded piece can be moved or protected, which

may be all that is necessary to prevent the enemy attack from being successful.

Pawn weaknesses have much greater permanence, which is why so much positional play is concerned with creating and exploiting weaknesses in the pawn structure.

However in this chapter we are more interested in dynamics. There are ways in which pawn weaknesses can lead to attacks — not on the pawns themselves (though threats to win them may be involved) but on adjacent targets.

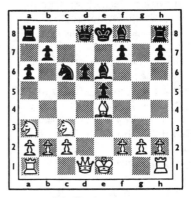

7.8 Black to move

Diagram 7.8 illustrates an important point about backward and isolated pawns. It is often not the weakness of the pawn itself that is significant, but the fact that the squares in front of the pawn can become a base for the opponent's pieces.

Diagram 7.8 arose after **1 e4 c5 2 Nf3 Nc6 3 d4 cxd4 4 Nxd4 Nf6 5 Nc3 e5 6 Ndb5 d6 7 Bg5 a6 8 Bxf6 gxf6 9 Na3 f5 10 exf5 Bxf5 11 Bd3 Be6? 12 Be4.** If only

Black could advance his d-pawn he would free all his pieces, but unfortunately 12 . . . d5 would be an unsound pawn sacrifice. Meanwhile White threatens to instal either his knight or bishop on d5, tying Black up and radiating power in all directions. Whichever way Black goes with his king, he has to reckon with White pieces based at c4, d5, and e4 which both blockade the advance of his pawns (and hence his bishops too) and generate threats on the wings.

7.9 White to move

Another way in which weak pawns can affect the outcome of an attack is that the player who has the weaknesses (whether the attacker or defender) cannot afford to exchange into an endgame where those weaknesses can be exploited. A player who must decide the issue in the middle-game is at a considerable disadvantage when his opponent proposes exchanges of pieces.

### PUZZLES

In 7.9, you will notice that Black's king is needed to defend the queen. If the king could be driven off, then the queen would be a 'hanging piece'. How can this be exploited? See diagram 7.9.

Diagram 7.10 was reached in a master tournament game after **1 e4 c6 2 d4 d5 3 Nd2 dxe4 4 Nxe4 Nd7 5 Bc4 Ngf6 6 Ng5 e6 7 Qe2 Nb6 8 Bd3 h6** (deciding against . . . Qxd4, but Black's idea is at least as unwise as that) **9 N5f3 c5?** (disastrous) **10 dxc5 Nbd7 11 b4 b6 12 Nd4! bxc5.**

7.10 White to move

Now how did White win — in just three moves?

Puzzle 7.11 arises after **1 Nf3 Nf6 2 g3 g6 3 b3 Bg7 4 Bb2 c5 5 Bg2 Nc6 6 0-0 d5 7 d4 cxd4 8 Nxd4 Nxd4 9 Qxd4?** How did Black exploit the vulnerability of White's pieces on the a1–h8 diagonal? You have to find more than one good move to prove that White's ninth move was a mistake.

# UNIT 8  MATING ATTACKS

## MOVING IN FOR THE KILL

In the three previous units we have looked at the three major preconditions
for a successful attack on the king — advantage in the centre (or at least a
static centre), lead in development, and weaknesses in the opponent's
position (of which one at least is in the vicinity of the king). We have already
seen a few examples of mating attacks based on these three advantages.

In this unit we shall assume that you have successfully built up the
momentum of your attack to decisive proportions. The question that
remains is: how to finish him off? Supposedly 'won' positions can still slip
through your fingers if the defence is good and you don't find the most
accurate moves.

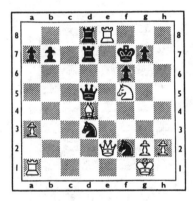

8.1  White to move

8.2  Position after 2 Qh8!!

In this position White (a former
British Champion) could see nothing
better than 1 Rxd8 Rxd8 2 Qe7+
Kg6 3 Qxg7+ Kxf5 4 Qxf6+ and
5 Bxf2 coming out a pawn ahead
with the ending still to play. Can you
see how the game could have been
decided in a few moves by direct
attack?

White can force mate by 1 Qh5+!
g6 2 Qh8!! (see the next diagram).
Only this move wins. Instead 2 Qh7+
leads to a draw after 2 . . . Kxe8
3 Qh8+ etc.

Now White threatens both 3 Qg8
mate and 3 Nh6 mate. The obvious
2 . . . Rxe8 fails to 3 Qg7+ Ke6
4 Qxf6 mate. Black can prolong the
struggle by 2 . . . Nh3+ 3 gxh3
Qxd4+ but it's hopeless for him
after 4 Nxd4 Rxe8 5 Qh7+ and the
skewer wins the rook on d7.

This example shows why the
queen is the strongest piece on the
board. Her strength lies in her ability
to generate threats in three or four
directions at once, and this makes
her particularly valuable in mating

attacks. Note also that the second move in the attack was a 'quiet' move, neither a capture nor a check. Such moves are the hardest to foresee.

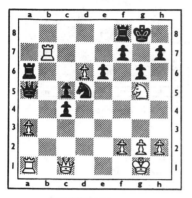

8.3 White to move

In 8.3 Black suffers from weak squares in the vicinity of his king. In particular, notice the square g7 which once housed a fianchettoed bishop. If White's queen — his strongest attacking force — were at h6, Black would be defenceless. White therefore played 1 Nxe6!, clearing the way for the queen, and threatening also to win the exchange (1 . . . Qc3 2 Qxc3 Nxc3 3 Nxf8). Black played 1 . . . fxe6 2 Qh6 (this threatens mate on either g7 or h7) 2 . . . Rf7 but then 3 Rb8+ Rf8 4 Rxf8 was checkmate.

## BACK-ROW MATE

You probably noticed that White's mating attack in the last example was possible only because the black QR had strayed from a8 to a6, leaving the back rank weak. Weak-

ness of the back row features in a wide variety of mating combinations.

Although the queen is featured in most mating attacks, her services can sometimes be dispensed with. The 'back-row' checkmate, using one or both rooks, is perhaps the most typical non-queen mating pattern.

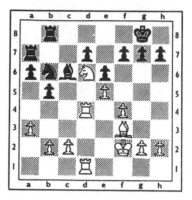

8.4 White to move

In this example, White has built up steady pressure and has just doubled his rooks on the d-file. If it were Black's move, 1 . . . Kf8 or 1 . . . h6 (making a bolt-hole for the king) might enable him to draw eventually. Therefore White must move in immediately for the kill with forcing moves, to allow Black no time to cover his back row.

White played 1 Bxc6! dxc6 2 Nc8! (clearer than 2 Nxb5) with the idea of meeting 2 . . . Rxc8 by 3 Rd8+ Rxd8 4 Rxd8 mate. The threat to the rook on a7 limits Black's choice to 2 . . . Rd7 but after 3 Nxb6 Rxd4 4 Rxd4 he still cannot play 4 . . . Rxb6 because of 5 Rd8 mate, and Black is therefore

permanently a knight down: a hopeless situation.

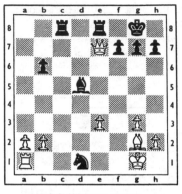

8.6 White to move

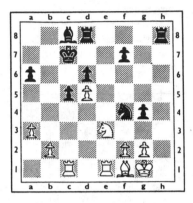

8.5 Black to move

Sometimes 'snap mates' are possible, as the result of blunders rather
than the winner's good play. Position
8.5 occurred in a master tournament
with both players short of time.

Black, who had been struggling
for survival throughout the game,
played 1 . . . Rh5! White, having let
the win slip earlier, was in no state
of mind to see the danger and played
2 Rc4??, doubtless envisaging 2 . . .
Nxd5 3 Nxg4.

However, after 1 . . . Rh5 2 Rc4,
Black played 2 . . . Rdh8 3 f3 g3
and White could not stop mate by
. . . Rh1.

Diagram 8.6 arose in a Karpov–
Spassky game. For his queen, Black
has a rook and knight and is threatening Karpov's queen. If the queen
runs away (e.g. 1 Qb4) Black would
start to conjure up some attack by
1 . . . Bxg2 or 1 . . . Nxe3 threaten-

ing to penetrate with his rooks into
the white position.

Karpov found a move to stop
Black in his tracks. Although it did
not force mate, it used the *threat*
of back-row mate to regain the
initiative.

The move was 1 Rc1!! Now if
1 . . . Rxc1 2 Qxe8 mate or if 1 . . .
Rxe7 2 Rxc8+ and mate next move.
The best Black could do was to
revive his threat to the queen by
1 . . . Rb8, but now that rook was
on a closed file instead of an open
one, which meant it was passively
placed.

In the sequel, the back-row motif
recurred: 1 Rc1 Rb8 2 Qb4 Bxg2
3 Kxg2 Nxe3+ 4 Kg1 Re6 5 Qf4
Rd8 6 Qd4! Rde8 7 Qd7 Ng4
8 Rc8! forcing decisive simplification. Because of the back-row pin,
8 . . . Re1+ leads nowhere: 9 Kg2
R1e2+ 10 Kh3 (not 10 Kf3?? Ne2+)
10 . . . Nf2+ 11 Kh4 R2e4+ 12 g4
Rxg4+ 13 Qxg4 Nxg4 14 Rxe8
mate.

## KING-HUNTS

Sometimes the menaced king makes a run for it. Then it is necessary to pursue him up or across the board, cut him off from any potential refuge and finally weave a mating net.

8.8 Position after 4 Qe3

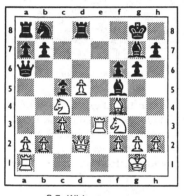

8.7 White to move

Here White has an extra pawn and a lead in development. Moreover Black's move . . . f6 has created a weakness on the white squares which White would like to exploit with his queen.

White ignored the threat to his QN and continued 1 Rae1! Qxc4 2 Re8+ Rxe8 3 Rxe8+ Kf7 4 Qe3. See diagram 8.8.

The threat is Qe7 mate, to which 4 . . . Nc6 is no good defence because of 5 Rxa8. Therefore Black played 4 . . . Bf8, after which the king-hunt got under way in earnest.

White destroyed the last defender by 5 Rxf8+! Kxf8 6 Bd6+ Kg7 7 Qe7+ Kh6 8 Qf8+ Kh5 9 Qxf6 (threatening 10 Qg5 mate) 9 . . . h6. See diagram 8.9.

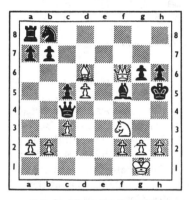

8.9 Position after 9 . . . h6

White's last few moves have been obvious and Black's replies forced. When he made his sacrifices (moves 1 and 5) White probably foresaw this position and assumed that there would be some way to force mate, because the king has been driven into the danger area where the K-side pawns can play a part. Precision is still necessary, though, because White is a rook down.

He played 10 h3! (threatening 11 g4+ Bxg4 12 Qh4 mate) and the reply was 10 . . . Bxh3. It is here that White might go wrong.

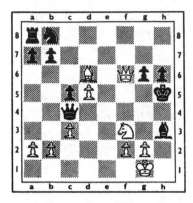

8.10 Position after 10 . . . Bxh3

11 gxh3? is a blunder because of 11 . . . Nd7 and White runs out of steam; 11 g4+ is also useless because of the reply 11 . . . Qxg4+. But 11 Qe5+ is good enough: if then 11 . . . Bf5 12 Qh2+ Kg4 13 Qh4 mate. Black could reply instead 11 . . . g5 12 Qe8+ Kg4 but then 13 Ne5+ wins the queen and decides the game. Finally if 11 . . . Kg4 12 Nh2+ Kh4 13 g3 mate.

White in fact played 11 Bf4, reviving the threat of Qh4 mate, and the game ended 11 . . . g5 12 Qf7+ Kg4 13 Nh2+ (13 Ne5+ also works) 13 . . . Kh4 14 g3 mate.

In this example White could count on success because the enemy king was driven forward. When the king can escape sideways to the shelter of his Q-side (as in Harry Hacker's game in unit 5) the attack may be harder to play.

8.11 Black to move

In exceptional cases, the hunted king may turn into an attacking piece. In diagram 8.11 Black has sacrificed two pieces to drive the enemy king into the open. Now he cut off its retreat by 1 . . . a5!, so that 2 Nxh4? is met by 2 . . . Ne4+ 3 Kc6 Bd5 mate. White has to find a find a flight square for his king, so played 2 Nxc7! Qh5+ 3 Ne5 Nd7+! 4 Kb5 but Black now wins the queen: 4 . . . Qxd1.

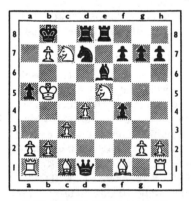

8.12 Position after 4 . . . Qxd1

This isn't the end of it, though, because White can conjure up threats against Black's king and queen! 5 Nxd7+ Kxb7 is one unclear line, but in the game White played 5 Bxf4 Qxa1 6 Ka6 Nxe5 7 Nxe8 threatening mate by Bxe5+ etc.

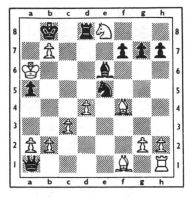

8.13 Position after 7 Nxe8

Which king is in the greater danger? Black now played 7 . . . f6? 8 dxe5 f5 and White won by 9 Be3! (threatening Ba7 mate) 9 . . . Rxe8 10 Bb5! Qxh1 11 Ba7+ Kc7 12 Bc5 Rd8? (12 . . . Bc8! would still force a draw) 13 Ka7! Black resigned as he was faced with inevitable mate.

But shouldn't Black have won, really? Yes, he could have played 7 . . . Rd5! 8 c4 (8 dxe5 Qxb2 is no better) 8 . . . Qxb2 9 cxd5 Qxb7+ 10 Ka5 Qxd5+ and all White's attackers are rapidly polished off by the liberated queen. This resource was overlooked by a British Champion annotating the game — which just goes to show how hard chess can sometimes be!

## THE CASTLED KING

Most of the kings we have so far seen come to grief were either un-castled or driven out into the open from a castled position. However 6.11 and 7.1 have shown ways in which the castled king can be attacked; the next chapter will show more examples, because as a rule sacrifices are needed to strip away the pawn cover to get at the king.

Before looking at sacrifices, though, we must consider those cases where the breakthrough is possible by sheer preponderance of force. In our next example, Black simply piles on the pressure against White's g-pawn until it can no longer be defended; note that this was only possible because White wasted a lot of time in winning material: **1 e4 e5 2 Nf3 Nc6 3 Bc4 Nf6 4 Ng5 d5 5 exd5 Na5 6 Bb5+ c6 7 dxc6 bxc6 8 Qf3 Rb8 9 Bxc6+ Nxc6 10 Qxc6+ Nd7 11 Nf3 Rb6 12 Qe4 Bb7 13 Qe2 Bc5 14 0-0 0-0 15 d3 Rg6 16 Nc3 Qa8!**

8.14 Position after 16 . . . Qa8!

Black's pressure on the g-file, and on the a8-h1 diagonal, will converge on the point g2 — but first the resistance at f3 must be broken down. The game went on **17 Kh1** (to get out of the pin by the rook) **17 . . . f5 18 Be3 Rff6** (envisaging . . . Rxg2 followed by . . . Rg6+ and . . . Bxf3) **19 Bg5 Rxg5! 20 Nxg5 Bxg2+ 21 Kg1 Rg6.**

8.16 White to move

before Black's passed a-pawn becomes a new queen.

The game continued 1 Rf5! a3 2 Rfh5 a2 3 Rxh6 a1=Q+ 4 Kg2 Ra2

8.15 Position after 21 . . . Rg6

Black has accomplished his first objective in destroying all resistance on the long diagonal and the g-file. The rest was easy: **22 Qh5 Nf6 23 Qh4 h6 24 Qc4+ Kh8 25 Qxc5 Rxg5 26 f4 Bh3+ 27 Kf2 Qg2+ 28 Ke3 Ng4 mate.**

Diagram 8.16 shows a somewhat ravaged position. The first wave of White's attack has secured him outposts on the white squares near the enemy king, but the pawn on g6 also helps Black by shielding him from checks down the g-file. The question therefore is whether White can bring enough force to bear at f6 or h6

8.17 Position after 4 . . . Ra2

Black now has an enormous material advantage, but White has the move. So the 'dead hand' of his pinned queen (by controlling g5 and h6) still has the final say: 5 Rh7+ Rxh7 (5 . . . Kxg6 6 R3h6 mate) 6 Rxh7+ Kf8 (or 6 . . . Kxg6 7 Bf5 mate) 7 Rh8+ Kg7 8 Rg8 mate.

## OPPOSITE-SIDE CASTLING

As mentioned in Unit 5, very tense positions can arise when one player castles K-side and the other Q-side. The normal plan in such cases is to storm the enemy king with pawns, in order to exchange off his pawn cover and make way for the pieces to break through. In this type of position, material advantage can be irrelevant. What counts is: who will get his pawns home first (without allowing them to be blockaded)?

8.18 White to move

Positions like this commonly occur with opposite-side castling. How is White to continue? 1 h6 g6 leads nowhere and 1 g6 h6 2 gxf7+ Qxf7 is not much better. Meanwhile Black plans . . . b5 and . . . b4; the 'defending' white knight actually helps Black to gain tempi for his pawn storm — a point worth remembering!

However, White (grandmaster Rubinstein) found a way to force

open the lines on the K-side:
1 Bxh7+! Kxh7 2 g6+ Kg8 (2 . . . fxg6 3 Nxe4 dxe4 4 Ng5+ also wins for White) 3 Nxe4 dxe4 4 h6!

8.19 Position after 4 h6!

Quite a change from the previous diagram! Black's attack has made no headway, but White's battering rams (the g- and h-pawns) are about to bring the king's castle door crashing down. For example, were Black to take the second piece by 4 . . . exf3 White would win by 5 gxf7+ Qxf7 (5 . . . Kxf7 6 Qg6+) 6 hxg7! (threatening Rh8 mate) 6 . . . Qxg7 7 Qh7+ Kf8 8 Qxg7 mate.

4 . . . fxg6 would have been relatively best, although White's attack is powerful enough to win comfortably, starting with 5 Nh4.

Rubinstein's opponent in fact chose 4 . . . f6?, allowing the pretty and instructive finish 5 hxg7! exf3 6 Rh8+ Kxg7 7 Rh7+ Kg8 8 Qf5! c3 9 Rxe7 and Black resigned (9 . . . Rxe7 10 Qxf6 or 9 . . . Bxe7 10 Qe6+).

## Mating attacks

### PUZZLES

This has been a long unit — but an important one. After all, if you mess up the mating attack then you spoil all your good work in the rest of the game.

To finish, here is an easy puzzle — and a second one, not so easy.

8.21  Black to move

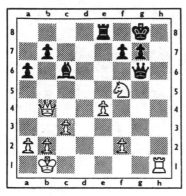

8.20  White to move

Checkmate in two moves! (Not 1 Ne7+? Rxe7! 2 Qxe7 Qxe4+ and Black will win.)

There's a very pretty mate in four. White can avoid that, but he soon loses anyway. How much can you see?

# UNIT 9   QUEEN-SIDE ATTACKS

*HOW JOHNNY WON*

'Johnny played a very nice queen-side attack today' said Tom Smith.

'Queen-side attack?' said Harry; 'That's a contradiction in terms! Attack means going for mate!'

'Not necessarily' said the Club Champion. 'Let's see Johnny's game'.

Johnny Brain's chess-playing style is the complete opposite of Harry's. Sometimes he loses because he's still inexperienced at endings, or because he gives too much weight to what he's read about positional play when he's in a situation where he should be calculating variations. Still, Johnny knows his openings and usually finds the right move quickly as long as his king is not being threatened.

Johnny was Black on board four in the match against Underbury, and the opening moves were **1 e4 g6 2 d4 Bg7 3 c3 d6 4 Nf3 Nf6 5 Nbd2 0-0 6 Bd3 c5 7 0-0 cxd4 8 cxd4 Nc6 9 a3 a5 10 Rb1 Nd7 11 d5 Nce5 12 Bb5 Nxf3+ 13 Qxf3 f5!**

'Good timing, Johnny' said the Champion; 'White should have recaptured with his knight.'

Johnny continued to demonstrate the moves: **14 Bxd7 Bxd7 15 b3 Rc8 16 Bb2 Bxb2 17 Rxb2 Qb6.**

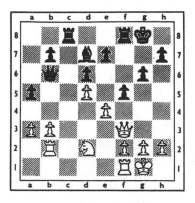

9.1 Position after 17 . . . Qb6

'Call this an attack?'

'Of course, Harry,' said Tom. 'The boy's got the initiative, hasn't he? His . . . a5 move has crippled White's queen-side pawns, and now he is starting to attack them with his pieces. You notice White can't play 18 Nc4 because of 18 . . . Rxc4, thanks to the pin on the b-pawn?'

Johnny spoke up, trying to avoid an argument: 'Now he played **18 Qe3** and I took it.'

With the exchange of queens, Harry inevitably lost interest in any game; the sparks wouldn't fly now. He went off to the bar to order the next round. The rest of the team followed the continuation of Johnny's game.

'After **18 . . . Qxe3 19 fxe3** I played **19 . . . Rc3** making it hard for him to avoid losing a pawn. It went on **20 exf5 Bb5! 21 Re1 gxf5.** His pawns are getting weaker and weaker, though I'm not sure if he's lost yet. I expected 22 e4, but instead he played **22 a4 Bd3 23 b4.**'

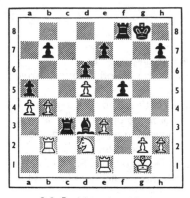

9.2 Position after 23 b4

'I didn't want to take that pawn and let his rook into the game. I felt he was only hanging on thanks to his rook defending everything, so I decided to exchange it, and played **23 . . . Rfc8 24 bxa5 Rc2 25 Rxc2 Rxc2** (see 9.3). Now, although it's an ending and I'm a pawn down, practically all his pawns are targets and I can soon mop them up. For example, if he plays his knight to the queen side, then he can't defend against Be4.'

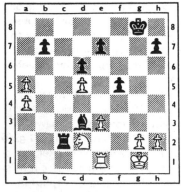

9.3

'So he played **26 Nf3**, I suppose?' inquired Tom.

'Yes, and I replied **26 . . . Be4** anyway; he had to play **27 Rd1** and then I went **27 . . . Rc5** to get my pawn back, and win another. He tried **28 a6 bxa6 29 Kf2** but I won the pawn with **29 . . . Rxd5 30 Rc1 Kg7 31 Rc7 Kf6**. Then it was time to stop. Do you think I'm winning?'

'You'll certainly get a win on adjudication' said the Club Champion. 'You're a good pawn up and your pieces are better placed than his.'

Johnny said it was lucky this was a National Club Championship match — in the local league he would have had to play it on for at least thirty more moves on another day.

'That may be a good thing for the club team, Johnny' said Tom 'but not for your chess. You need endgame practice, and how are our players going to beat the Russians when they can have their games adjudicated after thirty moves half the time, eh? I think you should come and have tea with me tomorrow, since it's Saturday, and see if you can win that position against me.' Everyone thought that was an excellent idea.

Then they started to discuss the Champion's game. But the barman called time.

### RIVAL ATTACKS

Johnny won his game by gaining control of important lines, like the c-file and the a6-f1 diagonal, and using them to infiltrate White's position and attack his pawns.

White tried to stand his ground, but failed. But in some games a Q-side attack is featured in a very different context.

One of the main lines of the King's Indian Defence leads to a situation with a blocked centre where Black attacks on the K-side, trying for mate, while White plays a rival attack on the Q-side in which the main targets are the squares c7 and d6. Because White's objectives seem less tangible than Black's, it might seem that Black has the advantage in such a situation. But what counts is the relative likelihood of the two players succeeding in carrying out their plans. It is not easy to checkmate a properly-defended king, while Q-side attacks can lead to the sudden total collapse of the besieged position. Let us look at an example of this.

After **1 d4 Nf6 2 c4 g6 3 Nc3 Bg7 4 e4 d6 5 Nf3 0-0 6 Be2 e5 7 0-0 Nc6 8 d5 Ne7 9 Ne1 Nd7 10 Nd3 f5 11 Bd2 Nf6 12 f3 f4 13 c5 g5 14 Rc1** a position typical of this variation has arisen. Both players have advanced pawns on the side of the board where they hope to break through, and must now find ways of supporting their pawn storms with pieces. See diagram 9.4.

If Black misjudges the position and tries to continue advancing on the K-side, ignoring White's play, he can lose surprisingly quickly: **14 . . . h5? 15 Nb5 g4? 16 Bb4.** Now Black's d-pawn is hanging. See diagram 9.5.

9.4 Position after 14 Rc1

9.5 Position after 16 Bb4

The simple defensive move **16 . . . Ne8?** loses catastrophically, as White conjures up a decisive passed pawn by 17 Nxc7! dxc5 (17 . . . Nxc7 18 cxd6 is worse) 18 Nxe8 etc.

Therefore **16 . . . dxc5** is necessary, although the position after **17 Bxc5** is clearly favourable to White. For example, 17 . . . a6 can be met by 18 d6 cxd6 19 Nxd6 Nd7 20 Ba3 or 17 . . . gxf3 by 18 Bxf3 with new weaknesses appearing in Black's position in either case. Finally 17 . . . Ne8 allows White to make a mockery of Black's K-side ambitions by 18 fxg4 hxg4 19 Bxg4, or to win a Q-side pawn by 18 Nxa7.

## THE MINORITY ATTACK

In the previous example, White advanced his c-pawn in order to open lines. Another common reason for advancing Q-side pawns is to establish a passed pawn, if one has a majority of pawns on that wing, as in 9.6 where 1 b5 establishes a passed pawn which is going to cause Black some trouble in the near future.

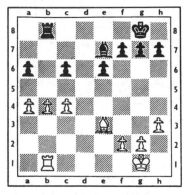

9.6 The pawn majority

Sometimes, though, it pays to advance the Q-side pawns when your opponent has the pawn majority there. The idea is to force pawn exchanges that leave him with one or two backward pawns for your rooks to attack. Though most players know about the Minority Attack in the context of the

Queen's Gambit Declined, Exchange Variation, it is still an idea worth using if the opportunity arises.

The characteristic pawn structure arises after **1 d4 d5 2 c4 e6 3 Nc3 Nf6 4 Bg5 Nbd7 5 cxd5 exd5 6 e3 c6 7 Bd3 Be7 8 Qc2 0-0** (see diagram 9.7). The centre

9.7 Position after 8 . . . 0-0

is static because either e4 by White or c5 by Black would incur an undesirable isolated queen's pawn. Therefore play on the wings is indicated — but Black cannot advance his K-side pawns without exposing his king; already White has some advantages.

Play can continue **9 Nf3 Re8 10 0-0 Nf8 11 Rab1!** (preparing the Minority Attack) **11 . . . Ne4 12 Bxe7 Qxe7 13 b4 Ng6 14 b5** See diagram 9.8.

Black is now certain to have at least a weak c-pawn. He tried to complicate the game by 14 . . . Bg4, but after **15 Bxe4 dxe4 16 Nd2 f5 17 bxc6 bxc6 18 h3 Bh5 19 Qb3+ Kh8 20 Qb7** Black's bishop was

9.8 Position after 14 b5

misplaced and his Q-side pawns in danger.

## PLAY FROM WING TO WING

Further aspects of Q-side attacks will be discussed in later chapters. At this stage there is just one more type of Q-side attack that should be noted: the one that suddenly becomes an attack on the king!

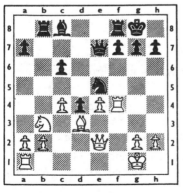

9.9 Black to move

In this position, the following factors are basic to the plans required of the players: the b-file is open for Black; the f-file is open for White; Black has a passed pawn at d4; White's bishop is obstructed by the pawns at c4 and e4, and so is inferior to Black's bishop; the black knight is powerfully placed at e5. White has the 'advantage' of the Q-side pawn majority, but here that means little because it would be so difficult to set in motion. Likewise, White's f-file and slight advantage of K-side mobility are hard to capitalize upon because Black has f7 so solidly defended, and the blockade at e5 cannot be raised by force.

Black's advantages are more tangible, and he consolidates them by 1 ... c5 which at once meets all threats to the passed pawn (Nxd4, or first c5, were in the air) and fixes the potential weakness at c4. It is now possible to see that White's last move, Nd2-b3, was a mistake; he should have played b2-b3 to reduce the pressure on his Q-side pawns. Even now, after 1 Nb3 c5, White could have avoided the worst by carrying out the following manœuvre: 2 Nc1, 3 b3, 4 Bc2, 5 Nd3 which shores up the Q-side and then eliminates the dangerous knight at e5. White may have hoped to carry out this plan a move later, but he found he did not have the time for it ...

After 1 ... c5 White played 2 Raf1? This shows that he had not evaluated the position correctly, because he has no real chance of K-side attack and should have been looking for a sound defensive plan.

After 2 Raf1 Black looked for a target of attack, which would enable him to co-ordinate his main advantages: the b-file pressure, the passed d4 pawn, his strong knight and superior bishop. A weakness in the white camp, within the radius of action of the Ne5, should logically be sought: the pawn at c4!

Therefore Black played 2 ... Be6.

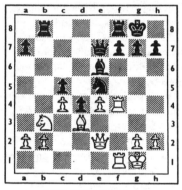

9.10 White to move

Now White cannot play 3 Nc1? because 3 ... Nxd3 wins a pawn (4 Qxd3 Rxb2 or 4 Nxd3 Bxc4) and therefore settled for 3 h3, which prevents an eventual penetration of his position by ... Ne5–g4–e3, but has other drawbacks.

When a target for attack (here the c4 pawn) is correctly selected, one of two consequences should follow. Either the defender will not be able to bring up sufficient reinforcements to hold the threatened point, or in bringing them up he will expose a weakness elsewhere in his position. That is the case here.

After 3 h3, play continued 3 ... Rb4 4 Rc1 Qg5 5 Rff1 Bxh3 (threatening ... Nxd3) 6 Nxc5 Rc8 7 a3 Rb6 8 b4 (to save the piece, White has had to force Black's QR to a good square:) 8 ... Rg6 9 Rc2 Bxg2 and White resigned, because if 10 Qxg2 Qe3+ and 11 ... Rxg2.

## SUMMARY

Let us summarize the lessons of this chapter.

(a) Develop soundly; castle your king into safety and control at least two of the centre squares.

(b) Spot a weak square, or group of such squares, in the opponent's position, preferably in the centre or near his king. Work to establish your pieces in these 'holes' e.g. a knight at c5 or f5, or a bishop at f6 for White.

(c) See what subsidiary threats you can create (e.g. checks, pins, or threats to fork and capture) as these will reduce your opponent's options and help your attack to gain momentum.

(d) When attacking the king, try to find moves that will force your opponent to advance pawns or exchange key defenders, and avoid threats that can be simply parried by bringing over a new defender.

(e) Look for checkmating ideas, either by direct attack or by means of surprising moves and sacrifices. But don't throw all your hard work away on unsound speculations!

(f) If there is no mate, win as much material as you can without jeopardizing your own king or losing the initiative. Two pawns, the exchange, or a piece up should be enough to win comfortably, if those two conditions are satisfied.

(g) If the opponent is tied up, but your immediate threats aren't sufficient to win, bring another piece or pawn into the attack, or improve your position in other ways; then exchange into a favourable endgame.

(h) When attacking on the Q-side, try to create permanent pawn weaknesses in the opponent's position. Then open lines for your pieces to attack those targets.

(i) Keep control of the centre throughout operations on the wings.

## QUESTIONS

Pawn thrusts are quite often the way to expose weaknesses in the enemy camp. Consider 9.11 and 9.12.

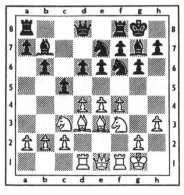
9.11 Black to move

9.12 Black to move

In 9.11, White has an impressive-looking centre. How does Black (to move) punch a big hole in it?

In 9.12, how does Black cash in on the weakness of the doubled white c-pawns?

# III. Sacrifices

## UNIT 10   COMBINATIONS

### WHAT IS A COMBINATION?

In a combination, something extraordinary happens. For a couple of moves — or, in deep combinations, for maybe ten or a dozen moves — material equilibrium and the calm pursuit of small positional objectives are cast aside. There is a surprise move, a flurry of activity, and at the end the game has been decided, or perhaps just some slight advantage has been gained.

Here are a couple of cases where a combination wins material and, probably, the game. In 10.1, White

**5 Nxd4 Bg7  6 Be3 Nf6  7 Bc4 0-0 8 Bb3 Na5?  9 e5! Ne8** Fischer noticed that if he could play his

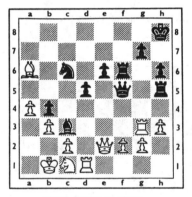

10.1  White to move

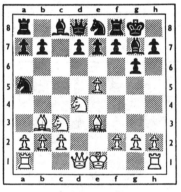

10.2  White to move

can play 1 Rxc3! If Black does not recapture on c3, he will remain a bishop down — but if he does play 1 . . . bxc3 then 2 g4 forks queen and rook. So the Rh5 is lost, and White wins a piece by his combination.

Diagram 10.2 was reached by Bobby Fischer, then only 14 years of age, after the sequence **1 e4 c5 2 Ne2 Nc6  3 Nc3 g6  4 d4 cxd4**

knight from d4 to e6 that the black queen would be attacked and have no safe square to go to (the Be3 would control b6) and the black d-pawn could not take the knight because of the pin down the d-file. The only problem is that the f-pawn could take the knight . . .

Fischer played **10 Bxf7+!!** because if 10 . . . Rxf7 (or 10 . . . Kh8) 11 Ne6 White wins the queen for two pieces — quite enough. **Black resigned**. Couldn't he have played

10.3 Position after 11 . . . Ke6

10 . . . Kxf7 11 Ne6! Kxe6? Here is the second point of Fischer's combination: to save his queen, Black has had to allow his king to be lured into the open. Now 12 Qd5+ Kf5 13 g4+ Kxg4 14 Rg1+ Kh4 (14 . . . Kh3 15 Qg2+ or 14 . . . Kh5 15 Qd1+) 15 Qe4+ Kh3 16 Qg4+ Kxh2 17 Qg3 mate.

Note these characteristics of combinations. First, the surprise move which begins the combination with a (real or apparent) sacrifice of material; often, as in the Fischer example, more than one sacrifice is involved in a combination. Secondly, the forcing nature of the subsequent play: Black was not able to decline the sacrifices or arrange a counterblow. Thirdly, the situation at the end of the forced sequence: either checkmate, or a 'return to normal' but with the difference that Black had lost material.

If the combination is *correct*, the sacrifice that begins it is only a 'pseudo-sacrifice', a loan returned with interest. In the case of a true sacrifice, the consequences are not so easily calculable; material is given up on the basis of intuition or general positional considerations. There are also *unsound* combinations, where the correct defence enables the defender to achieve material or positional advantage — as a result of miscalculation or an ill-judged risk on the part of the player of the combination.

### TWO ASPECTS OF SACRIFICES

In Unit 1 we discussed the relative values of the pieces and pawns, and saw that in normal positions the loss of even one or two material 'points' can lead directly to the loss of the game. But from time to time you will probably reach positions where the normal material values are not as important as some tactical or positional aspects. In such situations, a sacrifice is likely, or even essential.

We speak of a sacrifice when a player makes a move that deliberately allows his opponent to win material (or even forces the material upon him) in order to exploit such abnormal features of the position. Although sacrifices often signal the beginning (or the successful conclusion) of an attack, this is not by any means inevitable, which is why Attack and Sacrifices form separate chapters in this book.

There are two aspects to sacrifices in chess. On the one hand, there is the question of analysis: considering objectively the chess-board consequences of the sacrifice: does it lead to advantage for the sacrificer, to unfathomable complications, or to a demonstrable refutation? On the other hand there are subjective factors, including surprise, bluff and time-trouble.

Few games are decided without the winner at some point playing a good move which his opponent had either overlooked or underestimated, and many sacrifices are hard to see in advance — partly because the chess mind has a tendency to reject without consideration any move which obviously loses material. In normal positions, this is a necessary and time-saving habit (which helps to give humans an advantage over computer players), but it makes it all the more important to recognize the abnormal positions in time and study their peculiarities in the search for the counter-intuitive and therefore (to the opponent) surprising solution. Sometimes a surprise sacrifice will win a game even if it is objectively unsound, and at least in unclear situations the defender will often fail to find the best reply.

## IMAGINATION AND TECHNIQUE

Many tournaments still offer brilliancy prizes, which are awarded to attacking games played with great imaginative flair and capped by some startling sacrifice. Such games, which often find their way into newspaper columns to be admired by the general public, are rarely the games which masters like the best. Many ideas which are surprising to club players are just technique to masters.

Most of us, however hard we studied and practised, could never play with the vision and brilliance of Tal. Much of sacrificial play can be learned, though.

A lot of the secret of good middle-game play is knowing what type of move or plan is good in the type of position you recognize yours to be. This presupposes that you can recognize types of position, according to such factors as the material situation, the pawn structure, and the relative king positions. As your experience grows, the 'look' of a position will become more vivid for you — and you will recognize some of the types of position that call for sacrifices as a matter of technique.

See diagram 10.4.

In diagram 10.4, White is all set for the classical bishop sacrifice (or 'Greek Gift'): 1 Bxh7+! If Black plays 1 . . . Kh8 he will remain a pawn down, but 1 . . . Kxh7 loses immediately to 2 Ng5+ Kg6 (2 . . . Kg8 3 Qh5 Re8 allows mate in five) 3 Qd3+ f5 4 exf6+ Kxf6 5 Rxe6 mate.

10.4 White to move

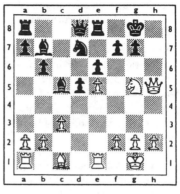

10.5 White to move

beginner might take some time to see the win in diagram 10.5.

In a lightning-chess game, any strong player would play 1 Bxh7+ without pause for calculation, simply on the basis of the look of the position. The most important feature that springs to the eye in diagram 10.4 is that, thanks chiefly to the pawn at e5, Black cannot defend the square h7. Also crucial is White's control of the square g5 — if Black had his bishop at e7 the sacrifice would not work.

Experienced players have seen dozens of these classical sacrifices before, and so have little difficulty in recognising that the necessary preconditions for success are present. If some of the details were different — for example if the white rook were at f1 instead of e1 — they would probably calculate a little before committing themselves, but if short of time would play the sacrifice anyway. They would not, for example, need to satisfy themselves that there would be a checkmate after 2 . . . Kg8, although a

Diagram 10.5 shows the position reached from 10.4 after 1 Bxh7+ Kh8 2 Ng5+ Kg8 3 Qh5 Re8 (the only defence to the threatened Qh7 mate). How long did it take you to see the mate in five moves? Probably you knew already, from seeing similar positions, that a little agility from the queen is all that's needed: 4 Qxf7+ (4 Qh7+ fails to 4 . . . Kf8 5 Qh8+ Ke7 6 Qh4 Rh8! 7 Nh7+ f6 8 exf6+ Nxf6) 4 . . . Kh8 5 Qh5+ Kg8 6 Qh7+ Kf8 7 Qh8+ Ke7 8 Qxg7 mate. This type of mating pattern may have required imagination two hundred years ago, but now it's just technique for most people.

Not all attacks can be played as easily as that one, but you will play few games in which recognition of standard patterns will not help you to some extent. Sometimes the memory of a particular game (your own, or a friend's, or a master game)

will give you a clue, but more often you will just be prompted by your subconscious memory-banks where your brain has collected all kinds of more or less relevant information from the past.

Can you see a resemblance between the positions 10.6 and 10.7, which both arose from the Philidor Defence? A vague memory of White's play in 10.6 prompted the author to find the right solution in the latter example.

10.6 arose in a grandmaster game, after **1 e4 e5  2 Nf3 d6  3 d4 Nf6 4 Nc3 Nbd7  5 Bc4 Be7  6 0-0 c6 7 a4 Qc7  8 Qe2 Nb6.**

10.6 White to move

White (Velimirović) continued **9 dxe5! dxe5** (9 . . . Nxc4? 10 exf6!) **10 Bxf7+!** — a surprising sacrifice which led to a strong attack after **10 . . . Kxf7  11 a5 Nbd7  12 Qc4+ Ke8  13 Ng5 Nf8  14 Rd1 Bd7 15 Be3!** and White went on to win. The game was published all round the world.

Eight years later in a London

League game, an opening indifferently played by both sides reached the position shown in diagram 10.7. Black has just played . . . Rfd8? whereas . . . Rad8 would have equalized.

10.7 White to move

Remembering the grandmaster game White played **1 Bxf7+ Kxf7 2 Qc4+ Ke8  3 Ng5 Nh8** (reaching 10.8). So far Velimirović had done all White's work for him, but now to pursue the attack White had to draw on other aspects of technique, like the pin.

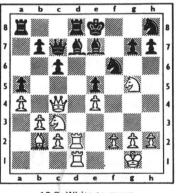

10.8 White to move

Play continued 4 Nb5 Qc8 5 Nd6+ Bxd6 6 Rxd6 b5 7 Qc5 Nf7 reaching another crisis point.

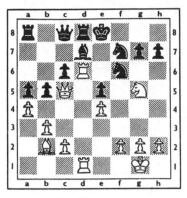

10.9 White to move

White had not foreseen this position when he played 1 Bxf7+; he didn't need to. All he had to see was that the black QR and Q would be idle bystanders. Now, doubtless drawing on some other (this time unidentified) model in the subconscious, White saw the winning sacrifice 8 Rxf6! gxf6 ( 8 . . . Nxg5 9 Rf8 mate) 9 Nxh7, threatening both 10 Nxf6 mate and 10 Qf8 mate. Black resigned after 9 . . . Nd6 10 Qxd6 Kf7 11 Qxf6+.

## MORE ABOUT COMBOS

We have seen that a combination (or 'combo') is a piece of tactical play in which a sacrifice or series of sacrifices enables a player to 'combine' all or several features of the position and gain an advantage. Combinations do not necessarily have anything to do with mating

attacks, although few such attacks will succeed without combinations if the defence is good. Attacking combinations usually work by bringing together some of the basic tactical elements you saw in the early units, and linking them by a sequence of forcing moves, allowing the second player little or no choice. Checks, captures, and big threats are the glue that holds the combination together; a tempo lost by either player can be decisive.

Here are some more examples of combinations. In each case try to guess the surprising move, and the follow-up variations that justify it.

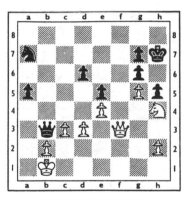

10.10 White to move

White wins two pawns by 1 Nxg6! etc. Black cannot reply 1 . . . Kxg6 because of 2 Qf5 mate. See diagram 10.11.

Thanks to the unguarded rook at a8, White can play 1 Rxd5 exd5 2 Qxd5+ forcing 2 . . . Nf7. Then 3 Nxg6 Rd8 (3 . . . e6 is no better) 4 Qxh5 is followed by Nxf8. Thus White recovers the exchange he

10.11 White to move

10.13 Black to move

sacrificed, and he remains two pawns ahead with an attack.

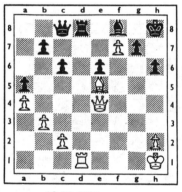

10.12 White to move

White starts with 1 Qg6! — a 'passive sacrifice'; he just leaves the Rd1 to be taken with check! This amazing move was played by grand-master Nimzowitsch.

Black is defenceless against the threat of Qxh6 mate. The checks come to an end after 1 Qg6 Rxd1+ 2 Kg2 Rd2+ (or 2 . . . Rg1+ 3 Kxg1 Bc5+ 4 Kg2) 3 Kh3 and mate is inevitable.

In 10.13, Black has already sacrificed a piece, and he cannot get it back by 1 . . . Rxd2? (hoping for 2 Qxd2?? Nxh3+ and 3 . . . Qxd2) because of 2 Qe8+ Qf8 (2 . . . Kg7? 3 c4+) 3 Qe3 and White will win.

The correct combination is 1 . . . Nxh3+! which launches a mating attack, although some precision is required. White must not play 2 gxh3? because of 2 . . . Qg5+ 3 Kf1 Qg2+ 4 Ke2 Re8+ and the end is nigh.

White therefore tried 2 Kf1 Nf4! (threatens . . . Qh1 mate) 3 Kg1 Bxg2 4 f3 Qh1+ 5 Kf2 Qh2! and now Black's idea was to win the queen by . . . Bh3+, . . . Ng2+ and . . . Nxe1. This forced 6 Ke3. See diagram 10.14.

Here 6 . . . Bh3 looks tempting — it threatens . . . Ng2+ — but White would escape by 7 Qf2 Nd5+ 8 Ke2. Black found the correct solution: 6 . . . Bf1!! and White resigned.

If 7 Qf2 Nd5+ wins the queen, or if 7 Qxf1 Qxd2+ 8 Ke4 f5+ 9 Ke5 Qd6 mate. Finally if 7 Nxf1 Nd5+

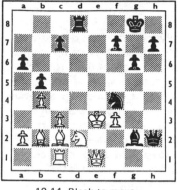

10.14 Black to move

10.15 White to move

8 Kd3 (8 Ke4 f5+) 8 . . . Nxb4+
9 Ke3 Nxc2+ 10 Rxc2 Qxc2 11 Qc1
(both queen and bishop were threatened) 11 . . . Qxc1 12 Bxc1 Rd1
and Black reaches an ending with
the exchange and three pawns ahead!

*PUZZLES*

Here are some more combinations for
you to work on as puzzles. Do not
worry too much if you cannot see
all the variations that are given in
the solutions at the back of the book.
Often the winner himself only saw
the first three or four moves; these
were enough to show him he was on
the right track. See diagram 10.15.
White commences a breakthrough
against the black king with a neat
combination. See diagram 10.16.
White has a nice trick to win (depending on Black's reply) at least a pawn.
See diagram 10.17.
White almost has a checkmate on g7,
but not quite! how can he get through
that wall of defending pawns?

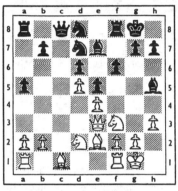

10.16 White to move

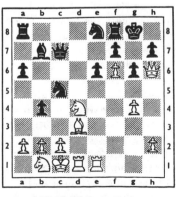

10.17 White to move

## UNIT 11   PAWN SACRIFICES

*GAMBITS*

In Midlington's next match, Harry Hacker had White and his opponent let him play the King's Gambit. What's more, he tried to hang on to the extra pawn. Harry was delighted and, this time, so was team captain Tom Smith.

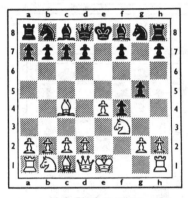

11.1 Black to move

After **1 e4 e5  2 f4 exf4  3 Nf3 g5  4 Bc4** things were shaping up for a real nineteenth-century struggle of the type Harry liked — and by comparison with the disaster of the previous week, it was Harry who had the piece development, his opponent who had the surplus material. (In Unit 12 we shall see how Harry followed up his gambit.)

Though Harry would laugh if you told him so, these old gambits that he likes are a type of positional sacrifice. In return for the pawn or so that the gambiteer gives away, he obtains some open lines and a lead in development which will usually increase if the defender is greedy. But gambits are not combinations: most of them lead to complications whose ramifications could not be exhausted in a lifetime of analysis and games. So not everybody feels at home in gambits. Yet in the hands of players like Harry they score a lot of points at club chess level, and (what is just as important for many of us) they give a lot of fun to the players.

In the King's Gambit, White sacrifices a wing pawn to get a majority of pawns in the centre. This can lead to strong attacks, as we shall see, but in recent years some grandmasters have had success treating the King's Gambit as a purely positional opening. Spassky, for example, won a game that began **1 e4 e5  2 f4 exf4 3 Nf3 h6!?  4 d4 g5  5 g3 fxg3 6 Nc3!? Bg7  7 hxg3 d5** (struggling for air) **8 Nxd5 Bg4  9 Bc4 Nc6 10 Ne3 Qd7  11 c3 0-0-0  12 0-0.**

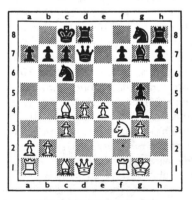

11.2 Position after 12 0-0

White's centre of pawns and minor pieces is unchallengeable. He has only to beat off a K-side demonstration which is doomed to defeat because of White's effective development and extra space. This, and Black's pawn weaknesses, mean that the ending will favour White.

The King's Gambit is not the only such opening to lead to situations where the gambiteer, without necessarily having any exact tactical justification for his sacrifice (against good defence), can get a position in which he has good compensation for his pawn in terms of greater space or mobility, relative king safety and so on. Here are a few examples.

The Morra Gambit against the Sicilian can give Black a lot of trouble. A typical variation is 1 e4 c5 2 d4 cxd4 3 Nf3 Nc6 4 c3 dxc3 5 Nxc3 d6 6 Bc4 e6 7 0-0 Be7 8 Qe2 a6 9 Rd1.

11.3 Morra Gambit

White's QR will soon come to c1, establishing a strong hold on the central files. If Black plays . . . Nf6 too early, White attacks it with Bg5, developing threats against the d6 pawn.

One of the critical lines of the Evans Gambit runs 1 e4 e5 2 Nf3 Nc6 3 Bc4 Bc5 4 b4 Bxb4 5 c3 Ba5 6 d4 d6 7 Qb3 Qd7 8 dxe5 dxe5 9 0-0 Bb6 10 Rd1 Qe7 11 a4.

11.4 Evans Gambit

White's early threats have interfered with Black's development. If 11 . . . Nf6 12 Ba3 and, as the queen cannot go to f6, Black must play 12 . . . Bc5 and White breaks through by 13 Bxc5 Qxc5 14 Bxf7+. Although he is not certain to regain his pawn in the near future, White can look forward to a prolonged initiative based on strong points like the d-file (particularly the d5 square) and the a3–f8 diagonal. Black has to choose his moves with circumspection; 11 . . . Na5 for example is attractive, but would be met by 12 Bxf7+! Qxf7 13 Rd8+! Ke7 14 Bg5+ Nf6 15 Qxf7+ and 16 Rxh8. See 23.3

for a possible continuation after
11 . . . a5.

11.5 Benko Counter-Gambit

The Benko Counter-Gambit is a
popular modern opening. Diagram
11.5 is a typical position from it,
reached by the moves 1 d4 Nf6
2 c4 c5 3 d5 b5 4 cxb5 a6 5 bxa6
Bxa6 6 Nc3 g6 7 Nf3 d6 8 e4 Bxf1
9 Kxf1 Bg7 10 g3 0-0 11 Kg2 Nbd7
12 h3 Qb6. This is the purest kind
of positional gambit. Black has no
immediate threats, but will combine
pressure on the open a- and b-files
with that on the a1–h8 diagonal
and aim to infiltrate gradually on
the weakened Q-side squares. Exchanges, for example of queens and
of a pair of knights, will often lead
to Black's position getting even
better. White on the other hand is
not well placed to create threats in
his sector of the board, the K-side.

## WHY SACRIFICE PAWNS?

There are several reasons why pawns
are popular cannon-fodder — and
not only for gambits. They can get
in the way of our attacking pieces
(if we keep them) or they can create
weaknesses in the enemy's game (if
we give them away). There are subjective factors involved — some
players' judgement becomes warped
if you give them a pawn. They may
underestimate you thereafter, or
they may try too hard to maintain
the extra material.

Pawns are relatively expendable.
There are of course times when a
strong central pawn or advanced
passed pawn will play a crucial role
in a middle-game, but in most cases
an extra pawn will not tell until late
in the endgame. So a good attack,
obtained at the expense of a pawn,
will often regain the sacrificed
material while retaining pressure or
— if the worst comes to the worst —
allow simplification to a drawn
ending. On the other hand if you
sacrifice a piece or the exchange,
and something goes wrong, retri-
bution in the form of a counter-
attack may be very swift.

Finally, opportunities to sacrifice pawns offer themselves
frequently. In particular, the b-
pawn (and to a lesser extent the
a-pawn and f-pawn) can be left unguarded in the opening or early
middle-game, while one is busy
doing more important things. Pawn-
grabbing, particularly by the queen,
often costs time and leads to the
misplacement of pieces; so many
players discipline themselves never
to take such pawns (occasionally
missing chances when they could
get away with it). Although grandmasters like Fischer, Evans, and

Korchnoi are particularly good at taking poisoned pawns and finding ingenious ways of surviving, most players of lesser talent have to be more prudent. But of course if you know that your opponent is a pawn-grabber, you can use this piece of psychology to trap him.

## THE PAWN BREAKTHOUGH

A typical situation requiring a pawn sacrifice is the case where it is necessary to clear pawns out of the way of attacking pieces. Take a look at diagram 11.6. Can you see the breakthrough sacrifice?

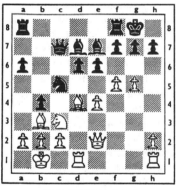

11.6 White to move

White plays 1 g6! He does not fear 1 . . . bxc3 because 2 gxh7+ Kh8 (2 . . . Kxh7 3 Qh5+ etc.) 3 Bxg7+! Kxg7 4 Rhg1+ Kh8 5 Qh5 catches the black king in a mating net. After 5 . . . Nxb3 6 Qh6 or 5 . . . Bf6 6 Qh6 Be5 7 f6 Black could resign.

If, in reply to 1 g6, Black only takes a pawn: 1 . . . hxg6 is met by 2 fxe6! The extra doubled g-pawn

is of little value to Black. White on the other hand had opened attacking lines and could consider opening more by the manœuvre h2-h4-h5. One possible continuation is 2 . . . fxe6 (2 . . . Bxe6 is better) 3 Nd5! and if 3 . . . exd5? 4 Bxc5 dxc5 5 Bxd5+ Kh8 6 Bxa8.

Pawn breakthroughs are typical in positions with opposite-side castling. But they can be used in all kinds of semi-blocked middle-game situations where it is desirable to open lines.

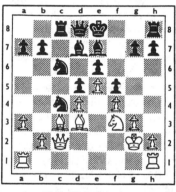

11.7 White to move

In this position White hit upon a sacrificial plan to liberate his 'bad' bishop on c3, which at present is hampered by the fact that all seven white pawns are on dark squares. The sacrifice is possible because Black's king is in the centre, his g-pawn unguarded and most of his pieces passively placed.

White played 1 Bxc4 dxc4 2 d5! exd5 3 e6! Bxe6 4 Bxg7 Rg8 5 Bc3 reaching diagram 11.8.

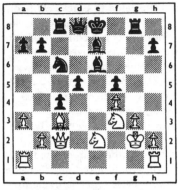

11.8 Position after 5 Bc3

11.9 White to move

Now we can see what White has gained in position in return for the sacrificed pawn. Black's king is deprived of the right to castle, and will soon be under pressure down the opened e-file. White's queen bishop has become a superb piece, thanks to the opening of the long diagonal, while Black's QB has virtually no prospects whatever. Also White's knights threaten to become active, so Black played 5 . . . Bf6 6 Ned4 Nxd4 7 Nxd4 Bxd4 8 Bxd4, but after 8 . . . Kf7 9 Rhe1 Qd6 10 Re5 his position was only getting worse. See diagram 11.9.

In this position, the fight for the centre is beginning after a quiet opening. White's best pieces are his Nc4 and Bh2, but if Black is able to play . . . e5 then the initiative will be lost. The advance e3-e4 would then be calmly met by . . . Nd5-f4, so it is essential to chase away that strong black piece without delay, with 1 e4!

After 1 e4 Nf6 (not 1 . . . Nc7??

2 Qxd8 and 3 Bc7) White is faced with the problem that his e-pawn becomes weak. 2 Bd3 would be a passive continuation, while 2 Qc2 allows Black to win a pawn by the combination 2 . . . Na5! 3 Nxa5 (or 3 Rfd1 Bxe4 4 Rxd8 Bxc2) 3 . . . Bxe4 4 Qa4 bxa5.

But after 1 . . . Nf6 White is able to advance 2 e5, preparing to give away the pawn advantageously. It will be used as a battering ram on e6, to break up the black pawn structure and make the rook on e8 redundant. Black did not like the look of 2 . . . Nd7 (2 . . . Nh5? 3 g4) 3 e6 fxe6 4 Ng5 Nf8 5 Bg4 although this might have been his best chance. Instead he played 2 . . . Nd5. See diagram 11.10.

3 e6 is ineffective now because of the reply 3 . . . f6, so White played 3 Qb3, threatening to pin the knight by Rad1; if Black ever plays . . . e6 then the square d6 will be available for a white knight. Black met 3 Qb3 by 3 . . . Nc7, hoping to instal the knight on e6,

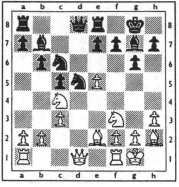

11.10 White to move

but White found a way to force his
pawn through to e6 after all.

White played 4 Ng5 (threatening
5 Nxf7 Kxf7 6 Nd6+) 4 . . . Rf8
5 Rad1 Qe8 (5 . . . Qc8 6 Bg4 e6
7 Nd6) 6 e6 Nxe6 (6 . . . fxe6?
7 Bxc7) 7 Nxe6 fxe6 8 Bg4.

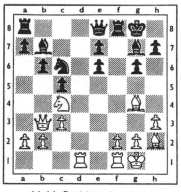

11.11 Position after 8 Bg4

It is now clear that White's
vigorous action in the centre has
completely pre-empted Black's
plans. If Black gives up his e6 pawn
without a fight, he will be left with
a cramped game and a backward

isolated pawn at e6. But after 8 . . .
Nd8 9 Ne5! h5!? (hoping for
10 Rxd8? Rxd8! or 10 Bxe6+?
Nxe6, simplifying prematurely)
10 Be2! (threatening 11 Bb5! among
other things) 10 . . . Bxe5 11 Bxe5
would now weaken Black's position
to an intolerable degree. He panicked
playing 10 . . . Bd5? and was finished
off as we have already seen in 10.11.

A common feature of these examples was that the compensation
for the sacrificed pawn came chiefly
in terms of positional factors – like
opened lines and weakened squares
in the enemy position – rather than
direct threats. It was neither possible
nor necessary for the sacrificer to
calculate all the consequences of his
offer. This is a typical feature of
pawn sacrifices.

*PUZZLES*

Diagram 11.12 arose after **1 d4 Nf6
2 c4 g6 3 Nc3 d5 4 Bf4 Bg7 5 e3
0-0 6 Rc1 c6 7 Nf3 Be6 8 Ng5 Bf5
9 Qb3 Qb6 10 Qxb6 axb6 11 cxd5
Nxd5 12 Nxd5 cxd5 13 a3 Nc6
14 Bb5.**

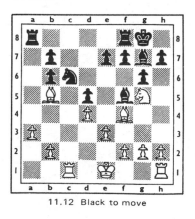

11.12 Black to move

It looks as if the black Q-side pawns are very weak. White would only need a couple of moves (Nf3, 0-0) to establish a clear positional advantage. How did a pawn sacrifice thwart that plan?

Diagram 11.13 shows a position of a type that often occurs in the Sicilian Defence. In this case the opening moves were **1 e4 c5 2 Nf3 d6 3 d4 cxd4 4 Nxd4 Nf6 5 Nc3 a6 6 Bg5 e6 7 f4 Qc7 8 Bd3 Nbd7 9 Qe2 Be7 10 0-0-0 h6 11 Bh4 b5 12 Rhe1.**

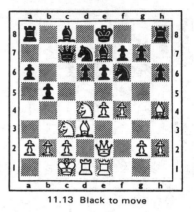

11.13 Black to move

It looks as if White is preparing an attack in the centre by e4-e5. How can Black stop this and give himself good chances, just for a pawn?

# UNIT 12   HEAVY SACRIFICES

*THE ELEMENT OF RISK*

To be a pawn down, or the exchange for a pawn down, is often not too serious. So sacrifices of one material point can often be played without calculating deeply, if the positional compensation seems adequate. But what if you are considering sacrificing a piece, or even a rook, or your queen? In such cases there is undeniably a risk of losing on material, so that before embarking on a heavy sacrifice you will usually want to assure yourself that you will indeed force mate or regain the sacrificed material. Of course it is not always possible to analyse positions to exhaustion (it partly depends on your skill and experience), and a point comes where you have to assess the risk involved.

There are in fact two kinds of risk. The first kind comes where you think your sacrifice is sound in all variations, but the risk remains that you have made a miscalculation. The deciding factor here is your confidence in your own powers. The second kind of risk is where you cannot prove the sacrifice sound, at least against the time-limit, and judgement of complicated positions (plus probably a gamble on subjective factors like the opponent's time-trouble) is crucial.

A few pragmatic guidelines are all that can help you here, apart from your own calculations and experience. First, do not sacrifice in good positions unless you are convinced that your advantage will otherwise disappear. Secondly, have confidence in your calculation of variations where the lines are short or where your threats have a high degree of compulsion — checks, threats of mate, or to win a rook or queen for example. Long variations, and situations where the opponent may ignore your threats in favour of sacrificing for counter-play, are the times when error may creep into your calculations (especially if you are inclined to optimism).

On the other hand, there will be occasions when you will rightly feel that you must sacrifice, even if the consequences are not clear. Sometimes a sacrifice is the only consistent continuation of your strategy, and chickening out will lead to your losing the initiative. On other occasions, you simply have the worst of it so you prefer to set your opponent a few problems rather than go down without a fight. This is the only situation where it may be justified to play a sacrifice which works only if the opponent blunders.

Some heavy sacrifices really involve no risk at all. These are the breakthrough combinations where the outcome is easily calculable. Here are a couple of examples.

In 12.1 Black wins by 1 . . . Nxe4 and, whichever way White recaptures, 2 . . . Rxg2. If 2 fxe4, for example; 2 . . . Rxg2! 3 Rxg2 (3 Qd3 Rxg1+ 4 Bxg1 Rg3 etc.) 3 . . . Qxh3+ 4 Rh2 (or 4 Kg1 Qxg2 mate) 4 . . . Qf1+

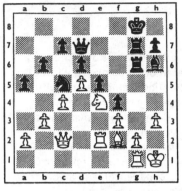

12.1 Black to move

5 Bg1 Rxg1 mate. In this case, it was not hard to verify that White had no defence. Moreover, with no g-pawn available to prise open White's barricades, Black could be sure that a sacrifice on g2 or h3 would be the only possible way to win.

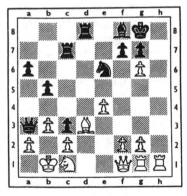

12.2 White to move

In the case of 12.2, Dr. Johnson's dictum applies: 'The knowledge that

he is to be hanged in a fortnight concentrates a man's mind wonderfully.'

White is threatened with unstoppable mate on b2, so all he need consider are checks: 1 Rh8+! Kxh8 2 Rh1+ Kg8 3 Rh8+ Kxh8 4 Qh1+ Kg8 5 Qh7 mate.

Some chess problems involve the idea of an 'interference' sacrifice, and occasionally interferences crop up in actual game positions.

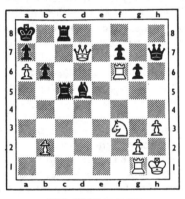

12.3 White to move

In 12.3, White wins by 1 Rc6!, which threatens both Qb7 mate and Qxc8 mate. If Black captures the white rook with either of his own rooks, then 2 Qb7 mate. If the bishop takes the rook, then 2 Qxc8 mate.

This combination relies on the detail that the black rooks' mutual defence, and the bishop's defence of b7 intersect at one square: c6. By giving up a piece on that square, White destroys the co-ordination of the black forces; suddenly they interfere with one another.

## HARRY STRIKES!

Another class of heavy sacrifices is those sacrifices of one or more pieces for a strong attack on the king, which cannot be called combinations because they do not lead to clear-cut gains in the same way as the foregoing examples.

Harry Hacker's game for Midlington against Barmouth began, as we saw in Unit 11, as a King's Gambit: **1 e4 e5 2 f4 exf4 3 Nf3 g5 4 Bc4.** Black now spurned the developing move 4 . . . Bg7, and played **4 . . . g4.** This attacked the Nf3, but Harry was glad to sacrifice it. He played **5 0-0 gxf3 6 Qxf3** giving him three pieces in play against Black's none.

12.4 Position after 6 Qf3

Harry's opponent replied **6 . . . Qf6,** threatening 7 . . . Qd4+ and 8 . . . Qxc4, but Harry thought only of getting at that black king, and so he went berserk: **7 e5 Qxe5 8 Bxf7+** ('That's got him in the open!') **8 . . . Kxf7 9 d4 Qxd4+ 10 Kh1.**

12.5 Position after 10 Kh1

Black, two pieces and a pawn up now, was not sure whether he was winning or losing. Harry had played those 'insane' moves with such confidence. It was undeniable that the black king would have some anxious moments before it could find safety. The Barmouth player eventually settled on **10 . . . Qf6,** reckoning that it would be necessary sooner or later.

Harry contained his excitement long enough to play a few calm developing moves: **11 Bxf4 Bg7 12 Nc3,** threatening to win some of his material back by 13 Nd5. 12 . . . c6 did not look like a defence, because of 13 Ne4 Qf5 14 Nd6+, so Black played **12 . . . Ne7** to keep d6 under the control of his c-pawn. Harry played **13 Nd5** anyway: it was important to play with threats before more defenders came out. See diagram 12.6.

Now Black saw that 13 . . . Qf5 would fail to 14 Nxe7 Kxe7 15 Bd6+ followed by the loss of his queen. So he quickly played **13 . . . Nxd5**

12.6 Position after 13 Nd5

**14 Qxd5+ Qe6 15 Bd2+ Kg8** and
breathed a sigh of relief; his queen
was safe now.

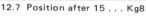

12.7 Position after 15 . . . Kg8

Harry stared at the position as
he stirred his coffee. Surely his attack
could not come to a dead stop so
easily? Last week he had been two
rooks up, and lost, so this week, two
pieces down he ought to win, if
there were any justice! But his
attack would disappear if he exchanged queens, and 16 Qg5 (which
he almost played) did not seem to
work after 16 . . . h6. Well, maybe
he could play that as a last resort,

but was there nothing better?

Suddenly he realized it: 'I haven't
sacrificed enough yet!' Triumphantly,
he played **16 Rae1!**, bringing his last
undeveloped piece into play. Black,
he reckoned, must now lose his
queen for rook and still face a strong
attack.

Harry's opponent did not see it
the same way. He blinked and
picked up his queen, and then
suddenly went red, and put the piece
back on its square. 'Touch and move'
Harry reminded him. In the league,
as in all serious chess, once you've
touched a piece, you have to move
it if you can.

In the end Black reconciled himself to **16 . . . Qxd5** and Harry
played **17 Re8**. 'Check' he said, a bit
too loudly; everyone hushed at him.
Black played **17 . . . Bf8**, the only
legal move. He did not like the look
of 18 Rexf8+ Kg7 19 Bc3+ and all
that, but he wasn't going to give up
yet. To his surprise, Harry did not
take the bishop but carried on thinking about the position.

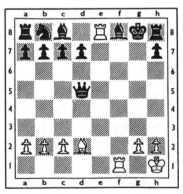

12.8 Position after 17 . . . Bf8

Finally, Harry played it, the cruellest cut of all: **18 Bh6!** Black looked around for a swindle; he couldn't bear to lose in under twenty moves. He played **18 ... Qf7** as nonchalantly as he could, hoping for Rxf7. But Harry played **19 Rxf8+! Qxf8 20 Rxf8 mate** and the drinks were on him that night.

*COMPLICATIONS*

Certain types of tactical situation are very hard to analyse. They often arise as a result of a speculative sacrifice by one player, leading to a situation where both players develop new threats so that many pieces may be *en prise* (free to be taken) at the same time; checks, mate threats, and threats to promote passed pawns may also come into it. Situations with unbalanced material (rook against bishop, say, or queen against rook and knight) are sometimes of this kind, and more unusual material situations (like two rooks against three minor pieces) can be disorient- ing even to the strongest players.

When you don't know whether you are winning or not in a compli- cated situation you have to rely a lot on instinct. The distinction be- tween sacrificing and losing material can become blurred. Then you just have to concentrate on spotting the threats and finding the best moves, wherever they lead you.

Diagram 12.9 arose after **1 e4 d6 2 d4 Nf6 3 Nc3 g6 4 f4 Bg7 5 Nf3 0-0 6 Bd3 Nc6 7 h3 Nb4 8 0-0 b6**

**9 Qe2 Nxd3 10 Qxd3 c5 11 d5 Ne8 12 g4!? Nc7 13 a4 e6 14 f5!?**

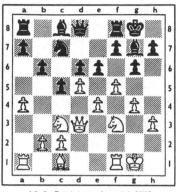

12.9 Position after 14 f5!?

Things are beginning to hot up. Let us follow the play without comment for a while, until it gets really wild: **14 ... exf5 15 gxf5 gxf5 16 exf5 Qf6 17 Ne4 Qxf5 18 Nfg5 Qg6** (not 18 ... Qxd5?? 19 Nf6+ Bxf6 20 Qxh7 mate) **19 Rf2.**

12.10 Position after 19 Rf2

The Club Champion, playing Black, was rather taken aback by White's aggressive play. First he was offered a pawn, and now a piece —

but he could see that 19 . . . f5 might be risky because of 20 Rg2 fxe4 21 Nxe4 with strong threats like Bh6. Yet he found it hard to believe that he had made any error to justify this attack by his opponent.

After deep thought, he decided that the right plan was to allow White to win material, so long as it led to Black getting a counter-attack along those lines towards the white king. All very well in theory; but he also had to guess what exactly was White's intention. There were so many possible threats and sacrifices!

The Champion took a last look and then played **19 . . . h6!? 20 Rg2 Bf5**. He confessed afterwards that he was a bit worried about 21 Qf1, but White actually played **21 Ne6**.

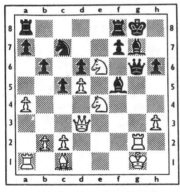

12.11 Position after 21 Ne6

The players had to reach move thirty, with only a couple of minutes each in hand, so long had the difficult decisions of the last few moves taken them. Like a flash, the Club Champion played **21 . . . fxe6! 22 Rxg6 Bxg6**, keep-

ing the pin on White's other knight so that 23 dxe6 would fail to 23 . . . d5. White had to waste a tempo on **23 Qe2.**

There seemed so many attacking possibilities, and so little time to decide between them. Backing his instincts, the Club Champion played **23 . . . exd5 24 Nxd6 Rad8.** If he could win that knight, he would be ahead on material, or if the knight went away to b5, then . . . Rde8 would be certain to give a winning attack. But White chose **25 Qe7**, protecting the knight and setting up threats of his own.

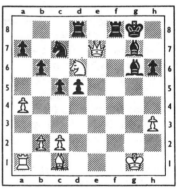

12.12 Position after 25 Qe7

The Champ couldn't consider a passive move like . . . Na6, so he played **25 . . . Bd4+ 26 Kg2 Rf2+ 27 Kg3 Rdf8**, seeing that White dare not take the knight (28 Qxc7? Be5+ 29 Kh4 Rg2 and 30 . . . Bf6+). White smelled a rat, so he played **28 Bxh6 R8f3+ 29 Kg4** leaving his opponent two moves to play in a minute in this very complicated position.

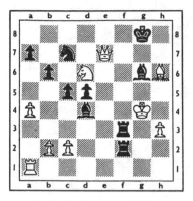

12.13 Position after 29 Kg4

The situation seemed desperate; all the Midlington team were looking on with pained expressions. Johnny Brain was biting his nails. Harry tried to work out the variations: what about 29 . . . Bxb2? No, White would just play 30 Re1 and it would be curtains. No good checks; no time to save the knight, and down on material already — hopeless. He looked away; this wasn't the kind of sacrificial game Harry could understand.

Mary stood on a chair to see over the shoulders of the other spectators. Gosh, his flag is teetering on the brink!

Tom Smith alone did not abandon hope. If anyone could find a way out, the Champ could. They all called him that, because nobody could pronounce his name; it was rumoured that he was once champion of Lithuania (or was it Estonia?) which, together with his appalling accent, gave him all the charisma of a Soviet master. All the members of the club had learned a lot from him.

The Champ had an idea, and he checked it as quickly as he could. The adrenalin was flowing, so he could see the board with unusual clarity, despite the complexity of the position, the whispers of the spectators and the tobacco smoke. 'I have one piece off-side' he thought 'I must get it into action somehow'. With seconds to spare, he played **29 . . . Ne8!!**

White kept his composure somehow. He had just enough time to see that 30 Nxe8 would lose to 30 . . . Bf5+ (e.g. 31 Kh4 Rxh3+ 32 Kg5 Rg3+ 33 Kh4 Rg4+ 34 Kh3 Rg7+ winning the queen). If he could stop that Nf6 check, maybe he would still win on time, so he played **30 Bg5**, but like a shot the reply came back: **30 . . . Ng7!**

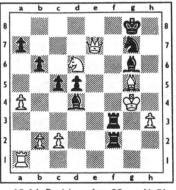

12.14 Position after 30 . . . Ng7!

White sealed a move, but resigned after the Champ convinced him that Black had an easy win in every variation. It wasn't worth travelling twenty miles again just to lose quickly, and there just wasn't an adequate answer to the threat of . . . Bh5+ followed by . . . Rh2. He had sealed 31 Qd8+, but the reply would be 31 ... Kh7 32 Rg1 Bh5+ 33 Kh4 Rh2 34 Rg3 Bf2 winning lots of material.

'Maybe 30 Ra3 would have been stronger?' he asked.

'No' said the Champion, who was a man of few words, few English words anyway. He set up the position and showed how 30 Ra3 would have lost to 30 ... Nf6+ 31 Kh4 Nh5 32 Rxf3 (or 32 Ne8 Rf7!) 32 ... Rxf3 33 Qd8+ Kh7 34 Bg5 Bf2+ 35 Kg4 Rg3+ 36 Kh4 Rg2 mate.

'You saw all that in under a minute?' asked Johnny with evident admiration.

'Sometimes one is lucky' was all he'd say.

12.16 White to move

In 12.16 White must sacrifice two pieces to press home the attack against Black's king. How does he do it?

## PUZZLES

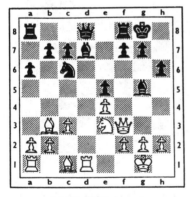

12.15 White to move

How did White break through after 1 Nf5! Bxc1?

# UNIT 13   EXCHANGE SACRIFICES

*'THE EXCHANGE'*

A player who wins his opponent's rook for a knight or bishop is said to 'win the exchange'. To lose (or give up) a rook for a minor piece is to lose (or sacrifice) the exchange. This is not a great sacrifice, since the exchange is worth less than a piece.

There are many occasions, though, when the rook is unable to attain its full power, or where a well-placed knight or bishop may be exceptionally strong. The sacrifice of the exchange — a popular theme in Russian games — is a way of trying to exploit the special features of such a position; the player giving up his rook sees deeper than the superficial material valuation of five points against three.

The exchange sacrifice has a better chance of succeeding if the rook is given up not merely for the minor piece but also for one or more pawns. In that case, it may be called a sacrifice only as a courtesy title. Although the table of material values suggests that rook equals minor piece plus two pawns, it does depend on how good the pawns are, and on other factors. Roughly speaking, bishop and one pawn is not far short of a rook, and bishop and two pawns will often get the better of a rook. Knight and two pawns are about equal to a rook.

Masters naturally rely mostly on calculation and the feel of the position when judging whether it is worth sacrificing the exchange, but certain other rules of thumb, derived from master experience, may help you to decide whether a particular sacrifice is sound. So here are a few:

(a) To exploit the advantage of the exchange, your opponent will need to get either an attack or a passed pawn.

(b) With a pawn for the exchange, normal play may well lead to a draw.

(c) A full exchange up, your opponent may return the exchange to win a pawn and so decide the game. (Rules b and c stem from Capablanca.)

(d) If the opponent has no bishop, two bishops can sometimes equal rook and knight.

(e) If pawns are only on one side of the board, there is less danger of losing in the endgame.

(f) Sacrifices that weaken the opponent's pawn structure, or which lead to a strong initiative, give winning chances.

The exchange sacrifice can therefore have a dual role. On the one hand, it can be a way of disrupting the opponent's position and playing for a win. In difficult positions, though, the exchange sacrifice may be the best way of playing for a draw.

## POSITIONAL EXCHANGE SACRIFICES

Sometimes an exchange sacrifice is the correct way of handling a position, even though no attack results. Or the sacrifice may be justified by tactical means in some variations, and on positional grounds in others — according to how the opponent plays. Diagram 13.1 shows a position reached by former World Champion Botvinnik (Black).

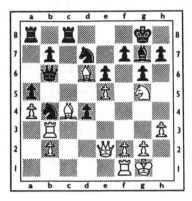

13.1 Black to move

White has given up a pawn, going for an attack based on threats of Rf3 or Nxe6. Botvinnik found a way to nip this in the bud and demonstrate the fundamental weakness of White's position (e.g. the pawn at e5).

He played 1 . . . Rxc4! 2 Qxc4 Nxe5, expecting 3 Qc5 when 3 . . . Qxc5 4 Bxc5 Nec6 would leave him with two pawns (one of them passed) and a knight for his rook, and no serious weaknesses — therefore with fair chances of Black winning.

White preferred to try his luck in the middle-game, but after 3 Bxe5 Bxe5 4 Rf3 Rf8 5 Rd1 Bg7 6 Ne4 e5 Black's position was more solid than ever and his central pawns were beginning to present a

real threat to White. Botvinnik's opponent now panicked with 7 g4? and soon lost.

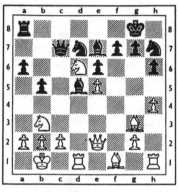

13.2 White to move

Diagram 13.2 was reached by Karpov on his way to the World Championship. The bishop on d5 is the pride of Black's position. White (Karpov) gave up a rook for this bishop and thus obtained the square f5 and various targets for attack.

Play went 1 Rxd5! exd5 2 Nf5 Qd8 3 Qg4 g6 4 Nxh6+ Kg7 and now the surest way to win would be 5 Nd4! (5 Nf5+, as played, won in the end) 5 . . . Kxh6 6 Nf5+ gxf5 7 Bf4+ Ng5 8 Qxf5 Kg7 9 hxg5 Rh8 10 Rh6 with mating ideas based on Bd3 followed by e6 and/or g6.

One logical kind of exchange sacrifice is that of an inactive rook for the opponent's fianchettoed KB. In this way, weaknesses around the enemy king are exposed, now that there is no bishop to guard them. The subsequent attack may build up slowly, but be none the less sure for that.

Diagram 13.3 can arise after **1 d4 Nf6 2 c4 g6 3 Nf3 Bg7 4 g3 d6 5 Bg2 c5 6 d5 0-0 7 Nc3 e6 8 dxe6** (this and the following exchange-winning manœuvre is extremely risky) **8 ... Bxe6 9 Ng5 Bxc4 10 Bxb7 Nbd7 11 Bxa8? Qxa8 12 0-0 d5.**

13.3 Position after 12 ... d5

It is impossible to give an exhaustive analysis of such a position. However the following plausible continuation shows how the attack on the white squares may develop: **13 b3 Ba6 14 Bb2 d4 15 Na4 Qd5 16 Nf3 Re8 17 Re1 Bb7 18 Rc1 g5** (to drive the knight away and then mate by ... Qh1 or ... Qg2) **19 h3 h5 20 Kh2 Ng4+** (20 ... g4 21 hxg4 hxg4 22 Nh4 is incon-

clusive) **21 Kg1 Nde5 22 hxg4** (22 e4 dxe3 23 Qxd5 exf2+) **22 ... Nxf3+ 23 exf3 Rxe1+ 24 Qxe1 Qxf3 25 Qe8+ Kh7 26 Kf1 d3! 27 Ke1 Be4! 28 Nc3 Bxc3+ 29 Bxc3 Qe2 mate.**

## THE SICILIAN SACRIFICE

In the Sicilian Defence, Black's rook often comes early on to c8, where it puts pressure down the half-open c-file. White must always be on the look-out for positional exchange sacrifices by Black once that happens. Here are two of the most typical Sicilian exchange sacrifices.

13.4 Position after 12 f4 ...

Diagram 13.4 could arise by the sequence **1 e4 c5 2 Nf3 d6 3 d4 cxd4 4 Nxd4 Nf6 5 Nc3 a6 6 Be2 e5 7 Nb3 Be7 8 0-0 0-0 9 h3 Be6 10 Be3 Nbd7 11 Kh1? Rc8 12 f4?** Black is now able to wreck White's position by **12 ... Rxc3 13 bxc3 Nxe4.**

Black threatens to regain the exchange by a knight fork on g3, and 14 Qe1 is no defence because of

14 . . . Bh4. So White tries **14 Rf3**, after which Black could play 14 . . . Nxc3.

Even better after 14 Rf3 is **14 . . . f5!**, since that weak c-pawn won't run away, and Black increases his hold on the centre. White can then try to hold his pawn by 15 c4, but only at the cost of progressive deterioration of his position: 15 . . . Qc7 (threatening 16 . . . Nxc3 17 . . . Nxe2 etc.) 16 Bf1 Bf6 etc. Black's 12 . . . Rxc3! undermined White's centre and so also the cohesion of his men.

The move . . . Rxc3 can be just as potent when White has castled on the Q-side. The Dragon Variation is especially fertile in possibilities for the Sicilian exchange sacrifice. Whenever White's attack falters or comes too slowly, as in the following example, the exchange sacrifice on c3 is likely to be playable.

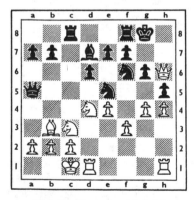

13.5 Position after 15 Qxh6

Diagram 13.5 arises after **1 e4 c5 2 Nf3 d6 3 d4 cxd4 4 Nxd4 Nf6 5 Nc3 g6 6 Be3 Bg7 7 f3 Nc6 8 Qd2 0-0 9 Bc4 Bd7 10 0-0-0 Rc8**

**11 Bb3 Ne5 12 g4 Qa5 13 h4 h5 14 Bh6 Bxh6 15 Qxh6**. Black now cuts open the dark squares around the white king by **15 . . . Rxc3! 16 bxc3 Qxc3** (threatening 17 . . . Qa1+ 18 Kd2 Qxd4+). White's attack on the g- and h-files, which could be very dangerous if Black had no counter-play, is now jeopardized and the advanced white pawns are all vulnerable (e.g. 17 Ne2 Qxf3).

A possible continuation is **17 Kb1 Rc8 18 gxh5 Nxh5 19 f4 Nc4 20 Bxc4 Rxc4 21 Rd3 Qb4+ 22 Rb3 Qd2 23 Rd3 Qg2 24 Rhd1 Bg4 25 R1d2 Qxe4 26 f5 Nf4 27 fxg6 fxg6 28 Rg3** (desperation) **28 . . . Qe1+ 29 Kb2 Qxd2 30 Rxg4 Nd3+ 31 Kb1 Qd1+ 32 Qc1 Qxc1 mate**.

Of course White has better lines against the Dragon, but even then . . . Rxc3 is often the idea on which Black bases his counter-play. If he can play . . . Rxc3 without his KB being exchanged, so much the better. He can then hope for an attack in which the bishop's pressure along the whole length of the a1–h8 diagonal will make life very difficult for White. More often, however, it is the exchange of bishops, decoying the white queen from the defence of c3, that is the signal for the sacrifice to be played.

## EXCHANGE ENDINGS

Endgame positions where one player is the exchange ahead can be very tricky, especially where there is one pawn for the exchange. When sacrificing or winning the exchange it is usually necessary to give some thought to the types of ending that will arise, because it is on a fairly open board that a rook is most likely to show its superiority over a knight or bishop. Diagram 13.6 shows a position where queens have just been exchanged, Black re-capturing with his f-pawn on e6 — not with the knight because of Rc6.

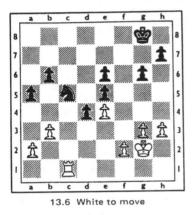

13.6 White to move

As things stand, Black has a good protected passed pawn for his ex-change and White's rook has no easy way into the position. If the black king were already at f6, in-stead of g8, a draw would be probable.

White cannot afford the time to guard his e-pawn. He played instead 1 f4!! in order to gain control of e5, so isolating the passed pawn, and to obtain an entry for his rook. The game continued 1 . . . Nxe4 (if 1 . . . exf4 2 gxf4 Nxe4 then 3 Re1) 2 Rc8+! Kf7 3 fxe5 Nc3 4 Rc7+ (forcing the king to the back row) 4 . . . Kg8 5 Rc4 (5 a4! is still better)

5 . . . Nxa2 6 Rxd4 Nc1 7 b4 axb4 8 Rxb4 Nd3 9 Rb5.

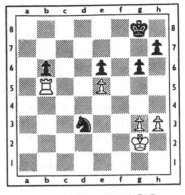

13.7 Position after 9 Rb5

White has simplified the game to increase the scope of his rook, but he may need the e-pawn to force a win. If Black had a bishop instead of the knight, his drawing chances would be much greater. Diagram 13.8, for example, would be very hard to win. But a knight does not defend the pawn which protects it, nor can it 'lose' a move.

13.8

So White won easily from 13.7:
9 . . . g5 10 Kf3 Nc5 11 Rxb6 Nd7
12 Rb5 h5 (or 12 . . . Nf8 13 Kg4)
13 h4 gxh4 14 gxh4 Kf7 15 Rb7
Ke8 16 Kf4 followed by winning
the h-pawn.

As a rule, a rook wins more easily
against a knight than against a bishop.
The presence of an extra pair of
rooks, which may be the saving
detail for the knight, may however
be just what is necessary to give
winning chances against a bishop
because of the possibility of creating
mating threats.

13.10 Black to move

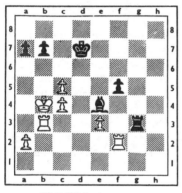

13.9 White to move

In 13.9, despite White's extra
exchange and pawn, there is no
obvious winning plan. White's pawns
are all weak and the black bishop is
a strong piece. Only by finding a
way through for his king can White
hope to make progress. Play went
1 Rh2! Kc7 (to keep b7 protected
against a possible counter-sacrifice)
2 Rh7+ Kc6 3 Ra3. Now White
threatens Rxa7 (sacrificing the e-
pawn), Raxb7 Rhc7 mate.

Black should now play 3 . . . a6
4 Rh6+ Kc7 5 Rf6 Rf3 (or 5 . . .
Kd7), waiting. White's only winning
chance then lies in playing c5–c6
at a time when the pawn recapture
would lose the a-pawn and the
bishop recapture the f-pawn. Even if
that can be forced, White would still
have technical difficulties to over-
come.

Black lost quickly because he
underestimated the danger to his
king, and he played 3 . . . a5+? and
only after 4 Rxa5 saw the line
4 . . . Rxe3? 5 Rb5 f4 6 Rb6 mate.
So he tried 4 . . . Rg2 5 Rb5 Rb2+
6 Kc3 Rxa2 (6 . . . Rxb5 would also
lose) 7 Kd4 (a new mate threat)
7 . . . Rd2+ 8 Ke5 (objective accomplished) 8 . . . Rd7 9 Rxd7
Kxd7. See diagram 13.11.

White now wins, following the
third rule of thumb: return the exchange to create a passed pawn:
10 Rb6 Kc7 11 Rf6 Kd7 12 Rxf5
Bxf5 13 Kxf5 Kc6 14 e4 Kxc5

13.11 Position after 9 . . . Kxd7

15 e5 Kxc4 16 e6 and White's new queen easily stops the b-pawn.

However there are also occasions where the minor piece wins the ending: this usually requires two passed pawns. In the following example White was steadily outplayed because he tried for a win when he should have been looking for a safe way to draw.

13.12 Black to move

If White held on to his pawn at g4, he would have only one passed pawn to contend with. But he was obsessed with the idea of trying to create a passed pawn of his own, so after 1 . . . Nf6 play continued 2 Na5?! Nxg4 3 Nxb7 Bf4+ 4 Kb1 (not 4 Kd1? Nf2+) 4 . . . Ne5 5 Nd8 Be3 6 Rh3 Bb6 7 Ne6 Kf7 8 Nf4 e6 (avoiding 8 . . . g5 9 Nd5) 9 Kc1 g5 10 Nd3 Nxd3+ 11 Rxd3? The last chance was 11 cxd3, making it harder for Black to create a passed pawn on the e-file.

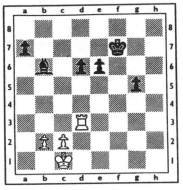

13.13 Position after 11 Rxd3?

White is now in trouble because it is hard to blockade two passed pawns when his king is so far away. The game went on 11 . . . d5 12 Kd2 Kf6 13 Ke2 g4 14 Kf1 Kf5 15 Kg2 Kf4 16 Rd1 (useful moves are hard to find) 16 . . . d4 17 Rf1+ (17 Rd3 e5 etc.) 17 . . . Ke3 18 Kg3 Kd2 19 Rf2+ Kc1 20 b3 d3! 21 cxd3 Bxf2+ 22 Kxf2 Kd2 23 d4 Kd3 easily winning the pawn ending.

## PUZZLES

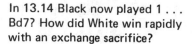

13.14 Black to move

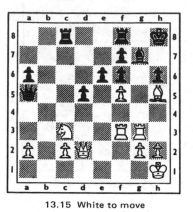

13.15 White to move

In 13.14 Black now played 1 . . . Bd7? How did White win rapidly with an exchange sacrifice?

Diagram 13.15 also features an exchange sacrifice leading to mate. The main variation is six moves long.

# IV. Defence

## UNIT 14   BE PREPARED!

### GOOD DEFENCE IS VITAL

Most players find defence much harder than attack. Therefore attacks often succeed even when they are not fully correct. It is particularly galling after you have lost a game, to be shown how you could have refuted your opponent's play.

The lesson is that nobody can afford to neglect the study of defensive technique. A good defender will draw, or even succeed in winning, games which the average player would lose. There will be several examples of this further on in the chapter, but here is one to be thinking about.

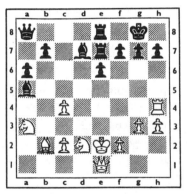

14.1  White to move

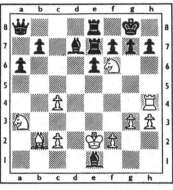

14.2  Position after 2 Nf6+!

White is the exchange and a pawn down, so goes for a last desperate throw: 1 Ne4!, putting his queen *en prise*. How would you play as Black?

In fact Black played 1 . . . Bxe1? and lost after 2 Nf6+! There is no way to avoid checkmate. See diagram 14.2.

Evidently 2 . . . Kh8  3 Rxh7 is mate, and 2 . . . Kf8  3 Rxh7 gxf6 4 Bxf6 is followed by the inevitable

5 Rh8 mate.

But 2 . . . gxf6 is also hopeless against correct attacking play: 3 Rg4+ Kf8 (3 . . . Kh8? 4 Bxf6 mate)  4 Bc1! and Black cannot improve upon 4 . . . Bd2  5 Bxd2 Rc8 6 Bh6+ Ke8  7 Rg8 mate.

But let us take another look at that position after 1 Ne4. Couldn't Black have done something else?

14.3 Position after 1 Ne4

Passive moves like 1 . . . b6 to protect the bishop at a5, would allow the same brilliant finish. Black needs a move that will give his king some air.

The correct move is 1 . . . f5! because now 2 Nf6+? gxf6 3 Rg4+?? is simply met by 3 . . . fxg4. Against other moves Black will be able to take either the knight or the queen. White's best follow-up would be 2 Qxa5 fxe4 3 Qh5 h6 4 Qg6 but Black now has the square g7 defended by a rook, and retains his material advantage. Best play then seems to be 4 . . . e5 5 Rxh6 Bf5! 6 Qg5 (or 6 Qxf5 gxh6 7 Qg6+ Rg7 8 Qxh6 Qc8) 6 . . . Qc8 7 g4 Bh7 and White has insufficient compensation for the exchange. All that concerns us at this point is that 1 . . . f5! is undeniably a better defensive move than 1 . . . Bxe1?

Why did Black choose the wrong move? The explanation probably lies in some combination of the following factors:

(a) Over-confidence. Black had been out-playing his opponent, and may have felt that nothing White could do would be dangerous.

(b) Greed. He could not resist being a whole queen ahead.

(c) Time-trouble. He had no time to calculate the variations properly, or to spot White's chief threat. Admittedly, 4 Bc1 in the main variation is not an easy move to see in advance.

(d) Defeatism. Conceivably, he may have seen the mating attack coming, and just could not muster his mental reserves to find a better defence.

You can probably call to mind games of your own, which you lost because of one or other of these factors. Note that psychology, in defence, is as important (or nearly so) as the technical factors like spotting the threat. The point is that if your temperament lets you down, then your emotions (excitement, fear, or whatever) will not allow your rational faculties to operate properly and whether you play the best move will become a matter of chance.

## PROPHYLAXIS

Because defence is such a strain, and because it often promises no more
than a draw, most players prefer to avoid the necessity of defending. This is
all very well if you have White, or are up against a considerably weaker
opponent. Then you can probably seize the initiative early on and keep it
throughout the game. But sometimes these favourable conditions do not
obtain, and you are faced with an attack. This happens to us all sometimes.

Many great players — like Capablanca, Karpov, and Petrosian — are
almost invincible. The secret of losing so few games (even against other
grandmasters) is that they take very few risks and can spot danger well in
advance, and be prepared to meet it.

When your king is under direct attack, it is vital to spot your opponent's
main threats and find the most economical ways of meeting them. But
how much better it would be if you could prevent the threats from material-
izing in the first place! If you hate quiet games, in which all the drama is
below the surface and the brilliant sacrifices are in the variations which
never occurred on the board, then this Unit is not for you. But you will
have to be prepared to lose lots of games you might have drawn . . .

The first rule of chess prophylaxis is to avoid weaknesses on principle.
This applies with particular force to weaknesses in the pawn structure next
to your king, as we saw in Unit 5. If there is a hole in your roof, you
must expect the rain to come in.

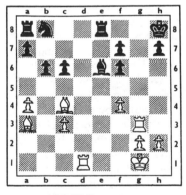

14.4 White to move

In this position, although White
is a pawn down and queens have
been exchanged, Black is completely lost. The reason for this is
that his pawn which should be at
g7, keeping his king covered, is instead standing uselessly at f6. This
means that the g-file has become
open, and White has sensibly
posted a rook to take advantage
of that.

White now wins by 1 Be7! (Note
that this threatens mate, whereas if
Black's pawn were at g7 the bishop
move would be meaningless.)

Black cannot play 1 . . . Rxe7
because 2 Rd8+ leads to mate,
while 1 . . . Nd7 (to guard f6) fails
to 2 Rxd7! Black actually played
1 . . . h5 and resigned after 2 Bxf6+
because of 2 . . . Kh7 3 Bd3+
followed by mate in two.

Where does prophylaxis come
in here? To answer that question,
think back to what must have

happened for the black g-pawn to reach f6: it must have captured something. Rather than allow this to happen, Black should have avoided the exchange on that square altogether, or arranged to recapture with a piece. If Black had only a choice between this evil and another, then one must go back further to find the original source of his difficulties, which was in fact his ninth move when he exchanged bishop for knight, allowing White to dominate the black squares subsequently. Seemingly innocuous decisions early in a game, like making an exchange or advancing a pawn, can have catastrophic consequences.

Sometimes your opponent will threaten to capture one of your pawns, and it will be tempting to meet the threat by advancing the pawn. However, it will usually be better to defend the pawn with a piece, because any pawn advance leaves potential weaknesses in its wake.

14.5 Black to move

In this position, White is not really threatening anything serious, but after a bad 'defensive move' Black collapsed. Black was worried about the mating idea Qg4 and Qxg7 mate, but this could be comfortably parried by either 1 . . . Bf6 2 Qg4 Kh8 3 Bg5 Qd8 or by 1 . . . Re8 2 Qg4 Bf8 3 Bh6? g6! 4 Bxf8 Kxf8: Black only moves the pawn when it really kills the attack.

Black panicked and played 1 . . . f6, with the idea of guarding g7 along the rank, but this move weakens the white squares (in particular e6). After the reply 2 Qg4, Black suddenly saw that both 2 . . . Rf7 and 2 . . . g6 fail to 3 Nh6+ and 4 Qxe6.

So after 1 . . . f6? 2 Qg4 Black had to play 2 . . . Bxf5 and he soon lost: 3 exf5! Rfd8 4 Bd5+ Kh8 5 Qh5 Bf8 (5 . . . Nb4 was the last chance) 6 Re4 Nb4 7 Qxh7+! Kxh7 8 Rh5 mate.

Unnecessary pawn advances often help the attack by weakening squares and opening lines. For example, when White plays g4 against the Sicilian, with the idea of driving the knight from f6 by a subsequent g5-g5, Black sometimes replies . . . h6. This is often a mistake, as after h2-h4 the advance g5 cannot be prevented, and either the g-file or h-file is likely to be opened in White's favour. The defender normally wants to keep lines closed.

## EXCHANGES

It is often said that the defender should seek exchanges, on the principle that the disadvantage of a cramped game is less when there are fewer pieces treading on each other's toes. There is also the point that mating attacks often require a lot of sacrificial cannon-fodder, to blast a way through the defender's pawn wall, so that any diminution in the attacking force means that the attacker will have to play more precisely. The exchange of queens is particularly important because the queen is the most powerful piece, and it is her mobility and her ability to cover simultaneously nearly all the squares around the victim which makes most mating attacks feasible.

Some attacks can indeed be broken by the exchange of queens, or of some other vital piece. This is particularly true when the attacker has sacrificed material, and is committed to pursuing his attack at all costs.

Here White probably expected 1 ... Qe6 2 Rxd4, regaining his piece with an extra pawn. But instead Black played the defensive combination 1 ... Qxf4! 2 Qxf4 Rg1+! 3 Kxg1 Ne2+ 4 Kf2 Nxf4 and won the ending. Also, 1 ... Qg1+ forces the same ending.

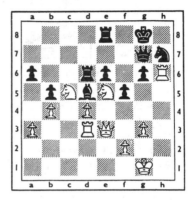

14.7 Black to move

Here is a more difficult example. You could be forgiven for thinking it's all up with Black, since 1 ... Nf8 fails to 2 Qg5. But grandmaster Grünfeld, Black, found an ingenious way to force exhanges: Can you see it?

He played 1 ... f4! 2 Qxf4 g5! 3 Qf7+ (White has no choice, because his rook is unguarded) 3 ... Qxf7 4 Nxf7 Kxf7 5 Rxh7+ Kg6 6 Ra7 g4 reaching a position (see 14.8) which he was able to draw. Although Black is now a pawn down, his bishop is better than White's knight and he can bring a rook into action down the h-file.

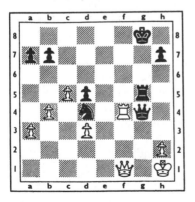

14.6 Black to move

*Be prepared!*

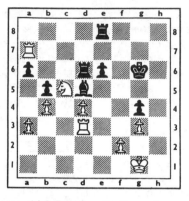

14.8 Position after 6 . . . g4

Exchanges do not always favour the defender, though. Remember 7.1? The exchange of your fianchettoed king's bishop will probably favour your opponent. Similarly, exchanges that give up the two bishops (or, in a blocked position, your well-placed knight) are suspect. You should try to avoid exchanging rooks when this will leave your opponent in permanent possession of an open file, or with a queen invading your position. Ideally, you want to exchange your poorest pieces for the most advanced and threatening of his.

You must also bear in mind which are the weakest points in your position, which will need pieces to defend them, and not exchange those key pieces. Also, be on the look-out for sacrifices your opponent may play in order to disrupt your defences.

Even queen exchanges must be judged carefully. Sometimes it is only your queen that holds the position together. Or the endgame without queens may be hopeless, so that keeping the ladies on is your best swindling chance.

A final point to note about exchanging is that it often makes a difference whether it is you or your opponent who makes the first capture. Making the exchange yourself can sometimes lose time and cause your opponent's initiative to develop, by allowing him to recapture with a piece that was previously out of the attacking zone. It is almost impossible to lay down general rules about this. You have to rely on your calculation of variations and upon your general judgement.

## SET UP COUNTER-PLAY

If your position offers no active prospects, and all you can do is wait and hope to parry your opponent's threats, then you stand badly. If he has nothing to fear from you, he can build up his attack massively at his leisure, manœuvre and feint to unsettle your nerves and keep you guessing. Finally, he can strike at the place and time that suits him. To avoid this happening to you, you need to have counter-play.

Counter-play may just be the chance to create a diversion on another part of the board, so that your opponent does not have things entirely his own way. If you have played well, it may be a big counter-attack or break-through in the centre which you have up your sleeve to play as soon as the time is ripe.

Positions often arise where you cannot do much as long as the opponent sits tight in the centre. Then he takes the decision to attack, and starts to switch forces over towards the king-side, leaving some points in the centre or on the queen-side open to attack. He hopes that you will not be able to make enough of them before he breaks through, or that you will be so scared of his attack that you will forget to strike a blow on your own account.

It is obviously essential to spot his chief threats — to mate, win material, or go into a won ending — but apart from avoiding major disasters there is usually nothing more important to a defender than setting up counter-play. Here is an example of counter-play succeeding just when it seemed that the attack must triumph. White starts by getting a bad opening: **1 e4 c5  2 Nf3 Nc6 3 Nc3 g6  4 g3 Bg7  5 Bg2 d6  6 d3 e5  7 Bd2 Nge7  8 Qc1 h6!?  9 0-0 Be6  10 a3 Qd7  11 Rb1 Bh3  12 b4** See diagram 14.9.

White's position is passive and disjointed. He cannot avoid the exchange of his KB, which must leave him with weaknesses. However, he has taken steps to obtain counterplay on the Q-side, and is making it difficult for Black to castle (because the h-pawn would be *en prise*). Black's next move probably helps White: **12 ... cxb4  13 axb4 h5**

14.9 Position after 12 b4

**14 Ne2! f6** (to control g5) **15 b5 Nd8  16 Qa3 h4**. See diagram 14.10.

Black's attack is taking shape. He has kept White guessing about when he will exchange bishops, and the advance of the h-pawn is calculated to open the h-file and soften up the white king position. White does not consider accepting the offer of the h-pawn (tantamount

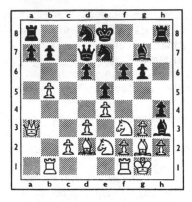

14.10 Position after 16 . . . h4

to suicide in such positions) but instead chooses a move that increases his pressure on the centre: **17 Bb4**. The game could go either way if Black now played the move 17 . . . Nf7, defending the pawn, but instead he went for an all-out attack.

After 17 Bb4 he played **17 . . . Qg4**, seeing that 18 Bxd6 would lose to 18 . . . Bxg2 19 Kxg2 h3+ 20 Kg1 Qxf3. White has to guard the knight, so he played **18 d4! Bxg2 19 Kxg2 Qxe4**, and what now?

14.11 Position after 19 . . . Qxe4

Black has won a pawn, and threatens to take the knight on e2. However, the insecure sides of his position — uncastled king, pawn on d6 — will now catch up with him, for White shows that his eighteenth move was not just defensive, but also inaugurated a counter-attack. White played **20 dxe5!**, a move which has the nice point that 20 . . . Qxe2 21 exd6 Nf5 22 Rfe1 wins the black queen by the pin on the e-file, which not so long ago had been clogged up with pieces! Black met 20 dxe5 by **20 . . . fxe5** but after **21 Neg1! hxg3 22 hxg3 Nf5 23 Rfe1 Qg4 24 Bxd6 Nf7 25 Nxe5** his position had totally collapsed.

White won this game because he combined economical defence of his king with the preparation of counter-play on the Q-side and in the centre. Black lost it because he played the attack with too much optimism and not enough concrete calculation of the risks he was taking.

This game also illustrates the point that although the opening is important, there is no guarantee that an opening advantage will lead to a win. Good, active defence can often make up for indifferent handling of the early moves, while poor middle-game play is usually fatal. Strong players have to be beaten in every phase of the game — opening, middle-game, and ending — before the full point can be scored. In open tournaments it is not unusual to see an outsider obtain a superb position against a master — but how often does the amateur go on to lose!

## PUZZLES

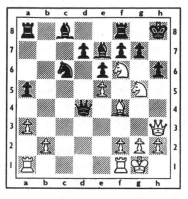

14.12 White to move

14.13 White to move

In diagram 14.12, White's attack looks very dangerous. 1 Nge4!, threatening 2 Bxh6, should have been played. Instead White played 1 Nxe6?! How did Black defend?

In diagram 14.13, Black has just played . . . a3. His attack looks fierce, but note that the knight is pinned, and the bishop is hemmed in by its own pawns. So how does White defend?

# UNIT 15   UNSOUND ATTACKS

*HEROIC DEFENCE*

A small minority of players actually prefer defending to attacking. In this group we find the nineteenth century World Champion, Steinitz, and world title candidate, Korchnoi. They will accept pawn sacrifices that most players would not consider taking, in the belief that they can repulse the attack that inevitably follows. They will play 'undignified' moves, such as retreating knights to the back rank or go for bold walks with their kings, if they believe that is the way to prove that their position is fundamentally sound and the attack incorrect. Indeed, they will often choose moves, especially in the opening, that are calculated to provoke risky attacks.

'The king is a strong piece, which can look after itself' was a favourite dictum of Steinitz's. Many an attack which, without careful calculation, looks as if it must end in checkmate will after all yield only perpetual check or obscure complications — if the defender is a genius who knows what he is doing. Even Steinitz and Korchnoi were sometimes defeated after taking their views to absurd lengths. On the other hand, 'heroic defence' (as this outlook has been called) must have its place in the repertoire of master tactics. Sometimes, there is no other way of handling a position.

Here is an example of Steinitz (White) in action: **1 e4 e5  2 Nc3 Bc5  3 f4 d6  4 Nf3 Nf6  5 fxe5 dxe5  6 Nxe5** (Steinitz accepted virtually any gambit) **6 . . . Qd4 7 Nd3 Bb6  8 Qf3 Nc6  9 Be2 Bg4 10 Qf4 Bxe2  11 Kxe2.**

15.1 Position after 11 Kxe2

Steinitz even gives up the right to castle, because he is confident that his position is sound. If 11 Nxe2 Qxe4 Black regains his pawn and it is still not easy for White to castle.

Black expected to get a strong attack to compensate for the pawn, but the World Champion defended very coolly: **11 . . . 0-0-0  12 Ne1!** (to unravel the Q-side) **12 . . . Nb4** (to meet 13 d3 by 13 . . . Nxc2! etc.) **13 a3 Rhe8!?  14 axb4 Nxe4**. See diagram 15.2.

Steinitz is a piece up now, but his king looks dangerously exposed. Yet Black is never able to build up threats, because Steinitz is careful to avoid weakening his position any further: **15 Qf5+!** (a safer square for her) **15 . . . Kb8  16 Nxe4 Rxe4+  17 Kd1 Rf4  18 Qh3 Re8  19 c3 Qc4 20 Kc2 Rf2  21 Nd3 Rfe2** (if 21 . . .

15.2 Position after 14 . . . Nxe4

Qe4, 22 Re1 simplifies) **22 b3 Qc6
23 Qf3 Qg6 24 Rf1!**

15.3 Position after 24 Rf1!

A piece up, White is not concerned about his g-pawn. He gives
priority to unpinning the knight.

The game ended **24 . . . R8e3
25 Qf5** (the point) **25 . . . Qc6
26 b5 Qd6 27 Nf4! Re5 28 Qxf7
R2e4 29 d3 Re2+ 30 Nxe2 Rxe2+
31 Bd2** and **Black resigned**, being a
rook down and with no defence
against Qf8+.

## DON'T BE PSYCHED!

If your opponent plays a combination that you had not foreseen, do
not assume that he knows what he
is doing, and that the sacrifice is
sound! Other people make mistakes,
too, and you may be the lucky
beneficiary. However, you have to
analyse carefully the consequences
both of accepting and declining, in
order to seek out whatever flaw
there may be.

15.4 White to move

In this position, White played the
unexpected 1 Nb5?!; if the knight
is not taken, it will go on to great
things at d6. Black's first reaction
was despair, since there seemed no
way to hold the piece after 1 . . .
cxb5 2 cxb5, whereupon the white
rooks would become very active.
The confident demeanour of the
opponent and the looks of the spectators seemed to say 'You're losing'.
However, after ten minutes, Black
cooled down and saw that in fact it
was a winning position for him.

After 1 . . . cxb5 2 cxb5 Nc5

3 Qc4+ Be6! (the only move) White cannot play 4 Qxc5 because 4 . . . Rxd1 is check, while 4 Rxd8 Bxc4 loses the white queen for insufficient compensation.

15.5 Position after 3 . . . Be6

White played 4 Bxe5, but the ending was lost for him after the simplifying continuation 4 . . . Rxd1+ 5 Rxd1 Bxc4 6 Bxc7 Bxb5 7 Bxa5 Nce4. Black won in due course.

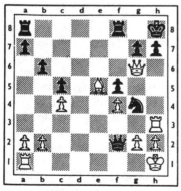

15.6 Black to move

In this position, White has just played his queen to g6. In view of the threatened mates at g7 and h7,

he probably thought his opponent would resign.

Black, however, replied with a coup de grace of his own: 1 . . . Qe1+!! 2 Rxe1 Nf2+ 3 Kg1 Nxh3+ 4 gxh3 hxg6 reaching an ending the exchange ahead, and winning. Would you have seen that elegant refutation?

## DEFENSIVE COMBINATIONS

Opportunism of this kind saves a lot of points and half-points. Sometimes the chance for a defensive combination arises only as the result of an error by the attacker. On other occasions, the possibility of a coup is the basis for a sound defence. Seeing the resource far enough in advance to make use of it is crucial.

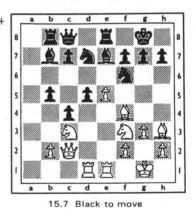

15.7 Black to move

Here Black seems to be in trouble with his knights. 1 . . . Ne4 would fail to 2 Nxe4 dxe4 3 Bxd7, and 1 . . . Nh5 could be met either by 2 Nxd5 or 2 e6.

Notice that the white KN and KB are unprotected. Black must

have seen this some way ahead.

He answered White's last move (1 e5) by 1 . . . Nxe5! 2 Rxe5 Qxh3 and eventually won, as White's attack was not worth the two pawns sacrificed.

Why didn't White reply 2 Bxc8? In that case, after 2 . . . Nxf3+ 3 Kf1 Nxe1 (threatens the queen) 4 Rxe1 Bxc8 Black would have rook, bishop, and three pawns for his queen — more than enough.

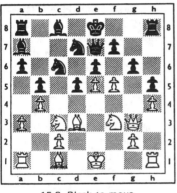

15.8 Black to move

In this example from a grand-master game, White has just played f5, which was clearly intended to break up the pawn defences around the black king. 1 . . . exf5? would soon lose after 2 Nxd5, while 1 . . . gxf5 2 Bxf5 would also hold promise for White (2 . . . exf5? 3 Nxd5 Qd8 4 Bg5).

At first sight, the Q-side pieces stand irrelevantly on the sidelines, yet by moving one of them Keres (Black) was able to demonstrate that the white attack was premature. He played 1 . . . Bb8!! 2 fxg6 N(d7)xe5 3 gxf7+ Qxf7 4 Ng5

Qf6 and suddenly it was clear that Black had an active game and White only weaknesses — a clear vindication of the principle that the answer to a wing attack is a counter-blow in the centre. White was in fact so taken aback at this reversal that he lost a piece in only two more moves: 5 Rf1? (5 Rb2 is better) 5 . . . Ng4! 6 Qf3 Qxc3+.

15.9 White to move

Sometimes it only takes a little trick to turn the tables. In 15.9 White, who has attacking chances on the K-side, threw it all away by 1 Qe6? Black hit back with 1 . . . Ne5! and after 2 Qxd6 Nxf3+ 3 gxf3 exd6 was bound to win a pawn.

### ANOTHER TRIUMPH FOR WOMEN'S LIB

It was time for Mary Mashem to play Harry Hacker in the Midlington club championship. As she had Black, she was a bit worried. She knew that, whatever defence she adopted, Harry would play a gambit and go for a berserk attack. From time to time Harry's attacks come off, so against his 1 e4 it was out of the question to play the Sicilian, or the Pirc or 1 . . . e5. The Caro-Kann (1 . . . c6) would be unlikely to give winning chances, so Mary decided on her reliable stand-by, the French Defence.

So the game began **1 e4 e6 2 d4 d5.** Mary was expecting the Milner-Barry Gambit now, but to her surprise Harry rejected 3 e5 and instead played 3 Nd2. She wondered who had told him about that move.

The next few moves were played quite quickly: **3 . . . Nf6 4 e5 Nfd7 5 f4 c5 6 c3 Nc6 7 Ndf3 cxd4 8 cxd4 h5 9 Bd3 Nb6 10 Ne2 Bd7 11 0-0 a5 12 a3 a4 13 Qe1 g6.**

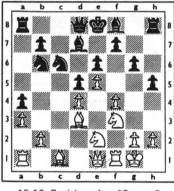

15.10 Position after 13 . . . g6

Both players felt quite happy at this stage. Mary knew she was following analysis by grandmaster Uhlmann, a world authority on the French. Although her development looked backward, the position was too blocked for this to be dangerous. Harry would have to sacrifice some-

thing to get at her king, and this would give her winning chances, too, especially because she knew of old that she could calculate tactical variations better than Harry. That was why she had decided from the start to rely on provocative defence.

Harry has never heard of Uhlmann, but he can spot sacrificial ideas. He thought a while about opening lines by 14 f5, but it did not look clear-cut; no, the square to sacrifice on would be g6!

So he played **14 Qg3 Ne7 15 Nh4** and after **15 . . . Nc4** reached out his hand to play 16 Nxg6. That would send her king on the run! At the last minute, fortunately, before he could touch the knight, he saw the sneaky reply 16 . . . Rg8! He withdrew his hand and started thinking. Finally he decided that if he fiddled about a bit on the Q-side, he would be able to discourage Q-side castling and a chance would come later to sacrifice on g6, when she had forgotten about defending it.

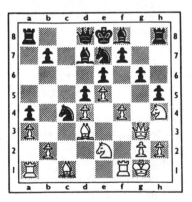

15.11 Position after 15 . . . Nc4

So play went on **16 Rb1 Qb6 17 Qf2 Nc6 18 Bc2** (Harry later regretted that he did not play 18 Kh1 here) **18 ... N(c6)-a5**, and Harry saw his chance. He played **19 Nxg6 fxg6 20 Bxg6+ Kd8 21 f5**. 'If she doesn't take that' he said to himself 'then it becomes a strong passed pawn at f6. If she does take it, then I play the bishop check. When her bishop goes in the way, I take it and she takes back; then Qh4+ and she has to go to f8. Mate can't be far off.'

15.12 Position after 21 f5

Mary was pleased that her psychological plan was succeeding. Harry was committed to an almost endless series of dubious sacrifices. He must have missed her next move, she realized. After one more check of the variations, she played **21 ... Nxe5!**

'That's the second thing I've overlooked today' Harry thought; 'I just didn't see that if the knight's taken, then ... Bc5 wins my queen. Never mind, my next two moves are

obvious enough, and I've never yet lost to a woman.'

Harry played **22 Bg5+ Kc8** (not 22 ... Kc7 23 Bf4) **23 Bf6 Ng4** (not 23 ... Nxg6 24 fxg6!) **24 Qh4**. 'I've still got pretty good chances' he thought. 'But I wish she wasn't defending quite so well.'

15.13 Position after 24 Qh4

Mary's natural inclination was to swap off, now that she was ahead on material. She looked at 24 ... Nxf6 25 Qxf6, but after 25 ... Rg8 26 Qf7 she would certainly not be winning. So the rook must move right away — and not to h6, because Bg5 might lead to a draw by repetition.

So Mary played **24 ... Rg8 25 Bf7 exf5!** Now if 26 Bxg8 Qxf6 the simplifications would leave her with two bishops against a rook. Harry would prefer to go down fighting, she knew. Probably he had not foreseen 25 ... exf5, and indeed all her other possible moves would probably have allowed Harry to force a win.

Harry tried not to show how

worried he really was; he knew he had lost control of the position now. For the first time, he realized he might lose. But he soon shook himself out of that mood: 'Remember the Dunkirk spirit, lad. Plenty of pieces left to fight with, yet!' So **26 Rbc1+ Nc4** ('Pity she didn't block her queen with Nc6, or allow a bishop check') **27 Bg5.** (Mary had worried more about 27 Bxd5, although after 27 . . . Nxf6 she reckoned she would win.)

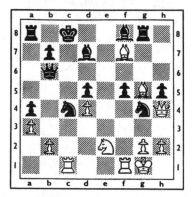

15.14 Position after 27 Bg5

Now, Mary decided, it was time to give back some material and get her king to safety: **27 . . . Rxg5 28 Qxg5 Kb8.** Harry groaned; one last desperate throw, then! He played **29 Nc3.**

Mary was surprised at first. Then she recognized a typical Harry Hacker ploy. He was trying to lure her into 29 . . . Qxd4+ 30 Kh1 Nf2+ 31 Rxf2! Qxf2 31 Qd8+ which indeed looked like a good swindle, probably worth a draw. He must be naive to think she would fall for that.

She played **29 . . . Bh6! 30 Qe7 Qxd4+ 31 Kh1 Qe5,** threatening mate on h2. When Harry worked out that he could only avoid this by exchanging queens (32 Qd8+ Ka7 loses the queen) he counted up the pieces for the first time. A rook up, good; bishop, knight and pawn down, and lots of things *en prise*, not so good. He knocked over his king. 'I was unlucky, wasn't I, Mary?'

'You should calculate *before* you sacrifice, Harry!'

## MORAL

There is a natural tendency to assume that the player who is attacking has a decisive initiative. He creates strong threats, forces his opponent's moves, or makes dramatic sacrifices.

But by no means all attacks are sound. Correct attacks are based on positional advantages obtained before the attack commences — e.g. a lead in development, more space, or control of key squares or open lines. Attacks launched before this preparation has been made will founder against good defence.

Experts know Steinitz's principle, that one should not attack before the balance of the position has been disturbed in one's favour (by errors made by the opponent). However, this is easier said than done. How can one tell when the balance has been disturbed, or whether the envisaged attack will disturb it in the opponent's favour? Accurate calculation of variations should give a guide, but there is no real substitute for the 'feel for the position'. Great players like Capablanca and Morphy seem to have had this from birth, while the rest of us must learn it as best we can by experience and study. For most players, there is nothing better than playing a lot of chess (e.g. five-minute chess) to gradually instil a feeling for what is possible (and what is not) in various types of position.

Incorrect attacks do often succeed. Some are less unsound than others, and an ingenious tactician can create new complications that may turn even the most lost of positions if the defender becomes confused and falters. The early career of Tal shows that even masters can lose their way in a maze of tactics — though usually only when time-trouble prevents them exerting their full powers. It is noteworthy that the very fine defender Korchnoi has a very large career plus score from his games with Tal. Tal's play grew sounder after he lost the World Championship, but he has still only beaten Korchnoi once.

## PUZZLES

In double-edged positions like 15.15, the attacker must often choose between several enticing possibilities. Sometimes many sacrifices are in the air, and it is vital to play the right ones, and to play them in the right order.

defences are against tries like 1 Bxh6? and 1 Nf6?

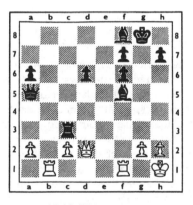

15.16 White to move

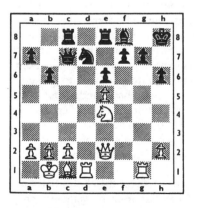

15.15 White to move

Can you see how White wins by force from 15.15, and what the

White played to reach diagram 15.16, because he thought his pin on the black rook could now be exploited by 1 Rxf5 (1 . . . Qxf5 2 Qxc3). But what actually happened after White took the bishop?

# UNIT 16   DIFFICULT POSITIONS

*HANGING ON*

Sometimes one gets into difficult positions, where one's pieces are cramped or discoordinated. The opponent's attack is imminent or already under way. Yet the position does not seem so bad that desperate measures are called for. Perhaps it is possible to hang on by straightforward good defensive play, maybe aided by setting a trap or two.

Before looking at some examples, let us look at some of the basic principles of handling this kind of situation where you are under pressure. Most of these were explicitly formulated by one or another of the great masters of the past.

(a) Avoid further weaknesses in the pawn structure, if possible.

(b) The defence should make the minimum concessions (in material or position) required to meet direct threats.

(c) Cramped positions should be freed, slowly.

(d) Give back surplus material to break the attack or launch counterplay.

(e) Seek appropriate exchanges (see Unit 14).

(f) Do not spurn the chance to force a draw.

(g) Set traps only if they fit naturally into your general plan.

*CONCESSIONS*

In the previous unit, we dealt with attacks where the defender was justified in thinking his position was ultimately sound, and so he acted accordingly. But when you are under pressure and your position is far from ideal, you have to accept that you have already made a mistake somewhere and try to assess the damage. Your opponent's threats may soon force you to weaken your pawn structure, or to send your king on a route march, or to give up a pawn or the exchange, or to allow transition into a nasty endgame.

When you have the worse position, you cannot hope to avoid concessions altogether if your opponent plays well. Your object must be to fight the best rearguard action you can, until through impatience or lack of experience he starts to make mistakes. Dogged defence often does wear down the attacker in the end.

Sometimes the defender is able to offer the attacker the choice between continuing his attack, without certainty of success, or exchanging into an endgame with some advantage. Many masters will abandon their attack (since nearly all attacks involve risk) for the security of the endgame, even though the defender may then be able to survive if he plays accurately.

At club level, most players are prone to the opposite error. They will often reject the chance of a clearly favourable ending because they think endings are boring, or because they know their technique is poor. Instead they press on with an attack which, having passed the flood, is less and less easy to justify.

The skill of the defender in such cases involves psychology, preferably based on good knowledge of the opponent. Will this man prefer to play the ending or the attack? It also helps to know if he prefers to be material up or material down.

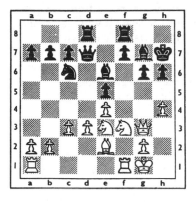

16.1 Black to move

Black is struggling to keep the wolf from the door, despite having several apparently well-placed pieces. The problem is that White's centre is quite firm, thanks to the bishop at e2, and he has definite chances of breaking through on the K-side where his queen and knights harass the black king.

White has just played 1 h4, and Black replied 1 ... Rg8, to discourage the further advance of the h-pawn. Then came 2 Qh2 (threatening 3 Ng5+ Kh8 4 Nxe6) 2 ... Rh8 (now the knight could be captured) 3 h5 Qe7! Note that Black avoids the move 3 ... g5, although it stops the immediate threats, because of

the very real danger that White would eventually occupy f5 with his pieces. Instead Black makes piece moves, which are less committal than pawn moves, even if they appear to achieve less from a positive point of view. In fact 3 ... Qe7 is a very important move, because it creates a chance of counterplay with an eventual ... Qc5 pinning the white Ne3.

After 3 ... Qe7 White played 4 Qg3 Rhg8 5 hxg6+ fxg6 6 b4, bringing the game to crisis point. The main threat appears to be b5, followed by (if the knight moves) Nxe5, or if ... a6 then a4 opening avenues of attack on the Q-side.

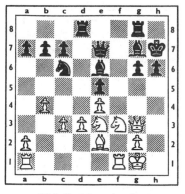

16.2 Position after 6 b4

The e-pawn cannot be guarded by . . . Bf7 because Ng4 is a strong reply, while . . . Bc8 (met by Nd5) is also exceedingly unpalatable. But evidently Black must make some concession. What should he play?

Black played 6 . . . Bh8!, at first sight a meaningless move, but actually very subtly played: . . . Bf6 would not work because of the reply Ng4. But . . . Bh8 sets an ambush: White is induced to think that Black's defences have cracked, and so he goes for the 'quick kill' instead of playing 7 Ng4, which is still the best move and would continue to set serious problems.

After 6 . . . Bh8 White went 7 b5, and in reply to the obvious 7 . . . Qc5 he confidently played 8 Ng5+ hxg5 9 bxc6 (see diagram 16.3). Doubtless he now expected 9 . . . Qxc6 10 Qh2+! Kg7 11 Qxe5+ when it would be all over. The point of Black's defence, however, is that he 'sacrifices' his pawn structure in order to get active piece-play based on pinning the white knight.

16.3 Position after 9 bxc6

Black played 9 . . . bxc6! and after 10 Qxg5?! (White was afraid of remaining a pawn down) the ambush bishop leaped from its cover: 10 . . . Bg7! 11 Qh4+ Bh6 12 Rf3 Rdf8 13 Raf1 Kg7 and White was now definitely the one struggling to save the game.

The main lesson of this example is that you must always calculate the variations arising from your opponent's threats. If you see deeper, and find a way to allow your opponent's threats and turn them to advantage, then you win a psychological battle and often the chessboard battle too.

## PLAYING FOR A DRAW

The majority of players probably prefer to play for a win at all costs, a laudable sporting attitude. However, there are times when your position (and the strength of the opponent) is such that a win is out of the question, and you should seek a draw. This is especially true if you are playing for a team — except where the state of the match means that a draw is no use.

Therefore it is worth paying some attention to ways in which you may be able to bring about a drawn result from a difficult position. If your opponent knows he stands well, he is unlikely to offer you a draw, or accept the offer if you make it (though see the Epilogue for the psychology of draw-offering!). But there are methods, besides forcing exchanges into a theoretically drawn endgame, by which you can force him to share the point in the end.

The most dramatic (and least likely) of these is stalemate. This is normally only a possibility for the endgame, but both the following examples actually occurred in master chess. Who says stalemate only occurs in dreams?

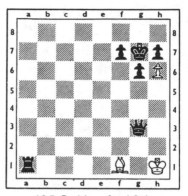

16.5 Position after h6+!

16.4 White to move

White was the exchange and a pawn down; all seemed lost. He played 1 Qa8 and Black replied 1 . . . Rxg3 2 Rxg3 Qxg3? (2 . . . Rxf1+ would probably still win). White now uncorked the amazing resource 3 Qa1+!! Rxa1 4 h6+!, bringing about diagram 16.5. Whether Black takes the pawn or retreats his king, White is stalemated!

In 16.6 White appears to face a difficult defence after 1 Qe1 Nb2+ etc., but he found a way to make a draw certain. He played 1 Qxb7+!! Kxb7 2 Rg7+ Kc8 3 Rc7+ and if Black, now or ever, takes the rook with the king then White is stalemated. Otherwise White gives per-

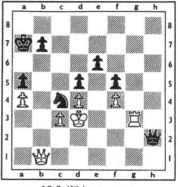

16.6 White to move

petual check with the rook, viz. 3 . . . Kd8 4 Rd7+ Ke8 5 Re7+ Kf8 6 Rf7+ Kg8 7 Rg7+ Kh8 and now, not 8 Rh7+?? Qxh7!, but 8 Rg8+! Kh7 9 Rh8+!

These kinds of finish are exceptional. Draws are more likely to arise by perpetual check, as the result of an attack that is not strong enough to force checkmate, or by repetition of position (which often involves checks, too) from which the apparently better-placed player cannot deviate, because of a tactical resource conjured up by the de-

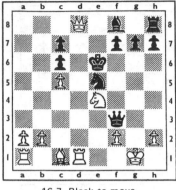

16.7 Black to move

Here both players are attacking their opponent's kings. After 1 e7, though, Black seems to be in trouble. He played 1 . . . Bxf4 2 exd8=Q+ Rxd8 3 Re7 Qh1+ 4 Kf2, putting his queen *en prise* while he is threatened with mate on b7.

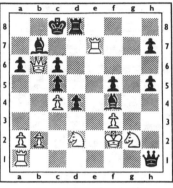

16.9 Position after 4 Kf2

fender. In 16.7, Black played 1 . . . Be7!

Now if 2 Qxh8 Black, although a rook down, would have at least a draw by perpetual check: 2 . . . Qxd1+ 3 Kg2 Qf3+ etc.

So White played 2 Qd4 (threatening 3 Ng5+) but after 2 . . . Qg4+ 3 Kf1 (3 Ng3? Nf3+ and 4 . . . Nxd4) 3 . . . Qh3+ 4 Kg1 the game was drawn by repetition. Lasker, who was White, dared not risk the attack arising from 4 Ke2?! Qf3+ 5 Ke1 Rd8 etc.

With one bound our hero was free: 4 . . . Be3+! White had to play 5 Nxe3 and after 5 . . . Qh4+! where can the white king go? The game ended 6 Kf1 Qh1+ 7 Kf2 Qh4+ etc. with a draw. The king can't go to the e-file because after . . . Qxe7, the knight on e3 would be pinned, while going to the g-file would expose him to rook checks. But after Kf1, . . . Qxe7 would not be sufficient for Black, as he would remain a piece down.

## COUNTER-SACRIFICES

We have already seen something of the importance of counterplay in repelling strong attacks. Sometimes the only way to get counterplay is by means of a sacrifice. In diagram

16.8 White to move

16.10, for example, White is preparing a mating attack based on the advance f4-f5. White's light-squared bishop will play a major role in creating threats, for example against the square h7.

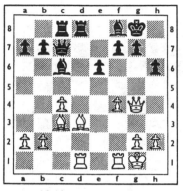

16.10 Black to move

Black did not wait for these grisly events to transpire. He sacrificed the exchange for a pawn, at the same time ensuring that White's attack would be considerably slowed up: 1 . . . Rxd3! 2 Rxd3 Be4 3 Rd2 Qxc4 4 Rfd1 Bd5 and Black got a draw in the end. Note that 3 Rd4 Bc5 4 Kh1 would have been met by 4 . . . Bxd4 5 Bxd4 f5 protecting the g-pawn.

Fobbing the attacker off with a pawn is often the key to a successful defence. It is important, though, that either the attack should dry up or a counter-attack develop. The following imaginative defence by Alekhine is worth careful study. See diagram 16.11.

Black's queen cannot defend both the b-pawn and the Rf8. 1 . . . b6 does not help, as White keeps

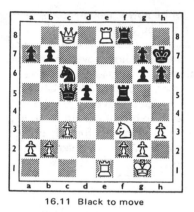

16.11 Black to move

the initiative and the better endgame chances. Alekhine sacrificed his weak isolated d-pawn by 1 . . . d4! 2 cxd4 Qd6! White gains little by 3 Qxb7 now, because of 3 . . . Nxd4 4 Nxd4 Qxd4 threatening f2, whereas 1 . . . Qd6 2 Qxb7 d4 would have been hopeless because of 3 R8e6.

After 1 . . . d4 2 cxd4 Qd6 the game continued 3 Rxf8 Rxf8; see diagram 16.12. Once again, 4 Qxb7 would lead to a drawish position after 4 . . . Nxd4 5 Nxd4 Qxd4 6 Rf1 Re8.

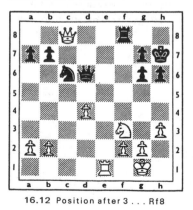

16.12 Position after 3 . . . Rf8

White now played instead 4 Qe6 and the reply was 4 . . . Qb4!, making use of another square gained by the clever first move. The double threat of . . . Nxd4 and . . . Qxb2 could only be parried by 5 Qb3, after which 5 . . . Qxb3 6 axb3 Rd8 7 Re4 Rd5 brought about an ending which Alekhine comfortably drew. Now it was White who had weak pawns.

were at h1, the position really would be lost for him, but thanks to the fact that he is off the back row, White has a forced draw commencing 1 Rf1!! d1=Q. Can you see the continuation? The solution is at the back of the book.

16.14 Black to move

## EXERCISES

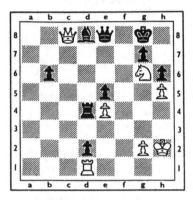

16.13 White to move

So, do not despair. In diagram 16.13, White is two pawns down, and his rook seems to be tied down by the black d-pawn. If the white king

You have to be alert for every tactical resource that could work in your favour. Here you might think that White is winning a piece, because his rook forks the black bishops. But a clever idea, four moves deep in the main variation, saves Black. Can you see it? The answer is in the back.

# UNIT 17   DESPERATION

*'HOPELESS' POSITIONS*

It has been said that the hardest thing in chess is to win a 'won' position. So defenders of hopeless positions should take heart. The law of averages suggests that from time to time you, too, will win a lost position. After all, sometimes it only takes one horrible blunder by your opponent.

17.1  White to move

White's passed pawn is so strongly supported by his pieces that almost any reasonable move wins for him here. For example, Black feared 1 g3 when he has nothing better than 1 . . . Rxa5 2 d6 Bxd6 3 Rbxd6 when moderately good technique will soon win for White.

But White played immediately **1 d6?? Rxe6! 2 d7** whereupon Black sprung his trap: **2 . . . Rd3!!** Because of the threats of back-rank mate, White loses his passed pawn, remaining a piece down.

It is almost impossible to lay down rules about how you should play in 'hopeless' positions. There are so many different kinds of them, and anyway so much depends on the opponent. Time-trouble, for one player or both, is an additional factor. Some players, realizing their situation is desperate, deliberately let themselves get into bad time-trouble. They feel they have nothing to lose by this (except the game which is 'lost' already), and the circumstance of time-trouble can only be in their favour. Their opponent may try to rush things, in the hope of winning on time, and so play inferior moves and spoil his position.

In positions where you have little or no counter-play, so that all the possible sacrifices are evidently pointless, all you can do is find the toughest defensive moves. The aim is to give the opponent a plausible choice on every move, so that he may stray from his intended plan, and try to reach an ending where his technique may not be as good as his middle-game play. But if the game is to be adjudicated early, there is little you can do, because all he need do is sit tight.

Sometimes, though, you would have fairly active chances, if only your opponent did not have the initiative and a winning line that would get home first. In that case, it is a good idea to keep your threat 'on', defending as best you can with your other pieces. Then if your opponent makes an error, such as taking an unnecessary check or grabbing too much material, you may get a chance to put in your blow. Even if the counter-play does not lead to anything concrete such as a perpetual check, it is usually worth having a go rather than just be beaten without a fight.

Often your only chance of a swindle will rest in your opponent mis-handling his attack in a particular way, such as playing two moves in the wrong order. If possible, you must try to steer your opponent into variations where such swindling chances exist. Most players will see 'brilliant' finishes, if they are not too deep, but they may go wrong when they think they are well on top and it hardly seems to matter what they play.

### REVERSAL OF FORTUNE

Johnny Brain suffered a very painful defeat at the hands of Tom Smith in the Midlington club championship. To this day, he doesn't really understand how he managed to lose from such a beautiful position — even though he plays through the game as often as he can bear to. 'It's the ones you lose, that you learn from' the Champ told him after the game, and he could see why.

Tom went pawn-grabbing in the opening and Johnny quickly established a strong position: **1 d4 Nf6 2 c4 e6 3 Nc3 Bb4 4 a3 Bxc3+ 5 bxc3 c5 6 f3 d5 7 cxd5 Nxd5 8 dxc5 f5 9 e4 fxe4 10 Qc2 exf3? 11 Nxf3 Qa5 12 Bd3 Nc6? 13 0-0 Qxc5+ 14 Kh1**

**17.2 Position after 14 Kh1**

Tom realized his position was hopeless unless he could castle Q-side; so he played **14 . . . Bd7**. Johnny replied **15 Ng5!** so that 15 . . . 0-0-0 would lose the exchange to 16 Nf7.

Which were the most important threats? After a while Tom decided the h-pawn was not important. It could not really be defended anyway, since 15 . . . Nf6 would fail to 16 Bg6+! when, if the bishop were taken, White's queen would go marauding.

Tom chose **15 . . . Ne5 16 Ne4 Qc7**, trying to protect d6 and set up threats of his own against h2. But Johnny found **17 Bg5!**, ruling out castling again. See diagram 17.3.

Tom's **17 . . . Ng4** swindle would not work now, because of 18 Nd6+! Qxd6 19 Bg6+! hxg6

17.3 Position after 17 Bg5!

20 Qxg6 mate. The knight had to stay at e5, so the next best thing was to challenge the f-file.

After **17 . . . Rf8** Johnny increased his grip by **18 c4 Ne7 19 c5 Bc6 20 Nd6+ Kd7**. Black's queen was now out of things and the king was on the run.

17.4 Position after 20 . . . Kd7

Tom felt very unhappy, although he was pretty sure he could not have done any better since his weak twelfth move. He had one chance left. If Johnny now played

**21 Bxe7! Kxe7** (21 . . . Nxd3 22 Bxf8) **22 Qc3** White would win a piece, but maybe the lad, who was looking excited at the prospect of a quick win, would play the queen move first.

That's how it turned out. Johnny quickly saw that the knight on e5, which guarded the way to g7, was no longer guarded, and that Qc3 would therefore be embarrassing for Black. He didn't stop to think whether he had a better move.

After **21 Qc3**, which Johnny played, Tom of course went **21 . . . Nxd3** but after **22 Bxe7** there came **22 . . . Bxg2+!** (Johnny had only seen 22 . . . Nf2+ 23 Kg1!). Tom knew he was still losing really, but he had surprised the boy and now he could make a fight of it.

Johnny took the bishop **(23 Kxg2)** and after **23 . . . Nf4+**, in view of the dangerous knight forks, he continued **24 Rxf4 Rxf4.** Here he made his second mistake.

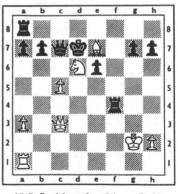

17.5 Position after 24 . . . Rxf4

He played **25 Rd1?**, but 25 Qd2 attacking the rook would have been much stronger. It is often the way that once an attacker starts to play second-best moves, the path to victory becomes harder and harder to find. After 25 Qd2 Johnny could have met 25 . . . Rg4+ by 26 Kh3 and 25 . . . Qc6+ by 26 Ne4+ and 27 Qxf4. But now that queen check is playable.

The game went **25 Rd1? Qc6+ 26 Kg3 Qa4 27 c6+?** (27 Rb1 should still have won) **27 . . . bxc6 28 Qxg7** (see 17.6). Johnny still thought he was winning, because 28 . . . Qxd1 allows 29 Bf8+ Kd8 30 Qe7 mate. But a horrible shock awaited him.

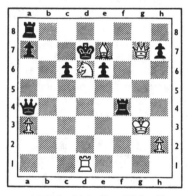

17.6  Position after 28 Qxg7

Tom's first reaction was that it must be the end for him now. But as a matter of course, he looked at all the checks he could give, to see if any of them concealed a resource. If only he could take that white rook with check! Suddenly he saw the solution: **28 . . . Rf3+!**

Johnny had no way out. The game continued **29 Kg2 Qc2+!**

**30 Kxf3 Qxd1+ 31 Ke3 Qc1+ 32 Kd3?**. Johnny was so disillusioned that he couldn't tell the difference between the moves. (32 Kf3 Qxa3+ 33 Kg2 Qa2+ 34 Kh3 Qb3+ 35 Kh3 c5 would probably win for Black in the end, but not so simply.)

Tom now exchanged off into a winning queen ending by **32 . . . Qb1+ 33 Ke3 Qg6 34 Qb2** (what else?) **34 . . . Kxe7 35 Qb7+ Kxd6** and duly won, thanks to his extra pawns and safer king. 'What did I do to deserve that?' asked Johnny.

## AVOID DEFEATISM

Another game in the same round of the Midlington club championship gave a good example of how *not* to conduct a defence. After twenty moves, the Bookworm (Black) was already in big trouble against the Champ. His pieces were all muddled up and now White was getting threats on the K-side.

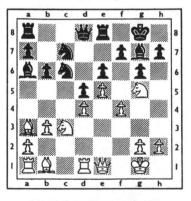

17.7  Black to move

The Bookworm was worried about the knight which had just

come to g5. He did not realize that White was just probing, hoping to induce a pawn move that would further weaken the black king's defences. So he played 1 . . . f6?! and got a horrible surprise when the reply was not pawn takes pawn, or a knight retreat, but instead 2 Nxh7!

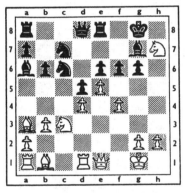

17.8 Position after 2 Nxh7!

He was filled with foreboding. The Champ's sacrifices were always sound. If 2 . . . Kxh7 3 Qh4+ and 4 Bxg6 would force mate, since f8 and e7 were controlled by that bishop on a3. And 3 . . . Bh6 was not much better after 4 exf6, followed by g4-g5 or Bc1 and f5.

After a lot of head-scratching Black played 2 . . . f5, a move which everyone castigated as 'defeatist' after the game. 'What good did that do you?' Harry said. 'You just gave the Champ a pawn, and after 3 Ng5 he still had his attack on the h-file.' For once Harry was right.

'Since you had played 1 . . . f6' Mary put in, 'you might as well have continued consistently by 2 . . .

fxe5. That would have made much more of a fight of it, because you threaten to undermine White's centre.'

'But he just goes 2 . . . fxe5 3 Ng5 exf4 4 Qh4' protested the Bookworm.

'3 . . . Bf6 is better' said the Champ quietly. 'Of course White should still win, but they are right; 2 . . . fxe5 was best.'

## TRAPS

If you really are sure that your position is inevitably lost if you continue 'normally', then it is worth looking to see whether you can set a trap of some kind. This may involve playing a 'silly' sacrifice, which if accepted in the wrong way gives you an escape route, or at least lets the opponent in for more hard work just when he thought he could go home early.

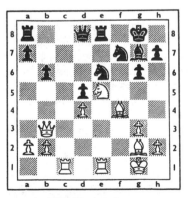

17.9 Black to move

Black reckoned there was only one way his position could go from here — down. In the long run the d-pawn is indefensible and all his pieces are passive while White's are active. So he resolved to try a final fling: 1 . . . Nxd4!?

Queen retreats and even 2 Nxf7 Nxb3 3 Nxd8 Rxe1+! do not lead to anything clear for White. Unfortunately, he was not bluffed and played simply 2 Qxd5 Qxd5 3 Bxd5. Black now tried the move he had prepared, 3 . . . Bxe5.

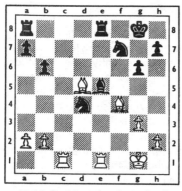

17.10 Position after 3 . . . Bxe5

Would White become confused, with so many captures to choose between? Black prayed for 4 Bxa8? Rxa8 5 Bxe5 Nxe5 when the knight fork on f3 becomes a reality.

No. White just played 4 Bxe5. What now?

4 . . . Rad8 was hopeless because 5 Bxd4 Rxe1+ 6 Rxe1 Rxd5 7 Re8 is checkmate!

So Black played 4 . . . Rxe5, hoping for 5 Bxa8? Ne2+ regaining the exchange. However, White saw this too and after 5 Rxe5 Rd8 6 Bxf7+ he had a winning ending, being the exchange ahead.

## FACE IT OUT

What do you do when you suddenly see that your opponent has a strong move which you did not see in time? In many cases, there is a good chance that he will not see it either; even if he does play it, it may not be immediately decisive. Changing course at the last minute is often the worst possible thing you could do.

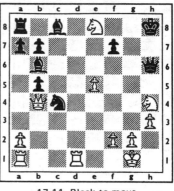

17.11 Black to move

Here White is the exchange and a pawn ahead. Black now played 1 . . . Be6, so that if the knight from e8 retreats, then the black rook prevents Qf8+, the black queen can take the knight at h4. Material would then be roughly equal, but all winning chances would lie with Black.

White intended to meet this with 2 Qe7, protecting both knights and pursuing his attack. Suddenly, he saw that Black had a strong counterattack.

2 Qe7 can be met by 2 . . . Bxf2+! See diagram 17.12.

The bishop cannot be taken: 3 Kxf2 Qe3+ 4 Kf1 Nd2+! 5 Rxd2

17.12 Position after 2 . . . Bxf2+!

17.13 White to move

Bc4+ 6 Re2 Bxe2+ 7 Ke1 Bd3+ etc.
White was filled with despair and
began to rue errors made earlier. He
looked at lines arising from 2 Nf6,
but there was no constructive move
that did not allow Black's combination. A continuation like 2 Nf6
Qxh4 would break the golden rule
of complicated positions that you
should ensure that there is *something*
going for you.

Finally, White with a straight face
played 2 Qe7. If 2 . . . Bxf2+ he
would calmly play 3 Kh1 Bxh4
4 Nf6 and hope for the best, though
he felt he was losing.

As it turned out, Black played
2 . . . Kh7?? and soon lost. He never
realized, until White told him after
the game, that he had missed a
chance to win. He thought he was
losing all along, and White's calm
demeanour had helped to convince
him.

## QUESTIONS

Diagram 17.13 occurred in a grandmaster tournament; Black has had a

winning position for some time.
Play now went 1 Qg5 Bxf3 2 f5
(protecting d2) and White's desperate
throw paid off when his opponent
replied 2 . . . exf5?? What happened
now, and how should Black have
played?

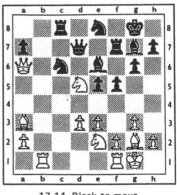

17.14 Black to move

In diagram 17.14, Black has
defended carelessly, and allowed
the combination 1 Nc3xd5! (1 . . .
Bxd5? 2 Bxd5 Qxd5 3 Qxc8).
How should he play now to cut his
losses and keep chances?

# V. Positional play

## UNIT 18  PLANNING

### CHOICE OF OPENINGS

So far we have concentrated on the cut-and-thrust of tactical play, because so many club games (and not only club games) are lost through threats underestimated and resources overlooked. The stronger the opposition you meet, though, the less you can count on such errors and the more you need to work to a plan based on the characteristics of the position. This planning should begin at move one.

It matters a great deal what opening you play, because each opening leads to its own characteristic type of middle-game position and, to obtain optimum results, you want to reach the kind of middle-games that you understand and enjoy. If you like blocked positions, the French Defence (1 e4 e6) and the English Opening (1 c4) should suit you. Players who like early attacks and sharp play before the completion of development prefer 1 e4 followed by one of the old gambits like the Evans or the Muzio (see 12.4). The popular opening move 1 d4, on the other hand, usually leads to a slow struggle for key points in the centre, leading either to an attack or to an endgame in which the players try to exploit any weaknesses they have induced in their opponent's position.

There are many good openings and defences, so the choice between them is largely a matter of style. If you have been doing badly with one or two of the openings in your repertoire, it is probably time to get hold of a book on openings and find something that suits you better. For example, you may play the Sicilian Defence with Black, but you keep on losing to White's attack before you can clear up the centre or get your blows in on the Q-side. In that case, you probably should switch to a defence in which it is harder for White to build up an attack — say the French Defence or the Petroff (1 e4 e5  2 Nf3 Nf6). On the other hand, if you feel you are drawing too many games, you might do better to find openings in which there are not too many early exchanges, and in which asymmetrical pawn structures naturally arise — such as the Dutch Defence (1 d4 f5) or the Modern Benoni (1 d4 Nf6  2 c4 c5  3 d5 e6) or the Alekhine (1 e4 Nf6).

If you take a chess magazine, or talk to strong players, you can easily find out which openings masters chiefly play, and consider to be sound. Some openings which you will find in the books, though, are almost never to be seen in master play. This is occasionally due to changes in fashion, but in many cases there is a more substantial reason for their neglect. If you are a gambler, you may welcome such openings for their surprise value, but you have only yourself to blame if you lose with them.

Many of the gambits, for example, are considered unsound because there is a defence which will leave you material down without compensation, or just cause you to lose the initiative. That is why you will rarely see the Danish Gambit (1 e4 e5  2 d4 exd4  3 c3), the Blackmar Gambit (1 d4 d5  2 e4) or the Albin Counter-Gambit (1 d4 d5   2 c4 e5). Various other openings are not practised because of inherent positional defects. These include openings where the queen comes out too early (e.g. Greco's defence 1 e4 e5  2 Nf3 Qf6), where the pawn structure is badly weakened (1 g4), where the natural development of the pieces is impeded (1 c3 or 1 e4 e5  2 Ne2) or where insufficient attention is paid to controlling the centre (1 d4 b5 or 1 e4 Nc6). If you play any of these, you impose a handicap upon yourself from the start.

Let us assume that you have decided a repertoire of sound openings — for both White and Black. This probably means you have about six lines you use fairly often — your chosen defences against 1 e4 and 1 d4, your main choice with White (the Ruy López, Exchange Variation, let's say), and lines to play against the Petroff, the Sicilian, and the French. If you avoid the most popular lines — by playing, for example, 2 c3 against the Sicilian instead of 2 Nf3 and 3 d4 — you can cut down drastically on the amount of advance preparation you need, without having to play inferior moves, and you will upset some of your opponents if they have learned only the main lines.

## FROM OPENING TO MIDDLE-GAME

Now that you have decided on your openings, you should stick with them, for a season at least, and get to know them well. You will gradually see this perseverance pay off, even if you suffer an early setback or two while you are still learning an opening and the types of middle-game and ending that follow from it. Eventually, if you have made a sound choice, you may find new moves of your own, as good as the ones in the books.

This is not an openings treatise; so I shall avoid giving a lot of detail. But, so you can see how preparation helps, let us have a look how Mary Mashem set about learning to play the Exchange Variation of the López, **1 e4 e5  2 Nf3 Nc6  3 Bb5 a6  4 Bxc6 dxc6  5 0-0.**

Mary chose the Exchange Variation because it enables White to avoid complicated middle-games, and often leads to endgames within fifteen or twenty moves. Most of the opponents she meets do not like endings, while she enjoys them, so this was a good choice for her.

18.1 Exchange López

The most obvious characteristics by which the middle-games from various openings can be distinguished from one another are: the side on which the kings castle, the pieces which are exchanged early on, and the pawn structure — particularly whether the centre is blocked or fluid, and whether there are any isolated, doubled, or backward pawns.

Positions arising from the Exchange López can be recognized by the fluid centre, the doubled black c-pawn (following the exchange of bishop for knight), and Black's uncertainty about what to do with his king. One of the advantages of this opening from Mary's point of view is that she knows that if she can get a position like 18.2 or 18.3 she is doing well, whereas Black has more difficulty in finding a plan. That is because these characteristic and relatively permanent features of the variation favour White, whereas Black's countervailing advantage (the possession of the two bishops) is much less tangible here.

18.2 Exchange López

18.3 Exchange López

Mary looked up a book which discussed the Exchange Variation and then she found a couple of master games in a chess magazine. She played all these through on her set, paying attention to the notes given, and then fixed in her mind these two positions. Whenever she plays the Exchange Variation now, as soon as Black (at move five or six) reveals his line of defence, she has a good think and decides which of these two is more relevant, and then tries to steer the game in that direction. More often than not she succeeds, because her opponents often don't think about the middle-game until it is too late. By starting her planning at move six or seven, while there are still alternative ways of developing most of the pieces, Mary avoids this kind of short-sightedness.

Diagram 18.2 is reached by the sequence **1 e4 e5  2 Nf3 Nc6  3 Bb5 a6 4 Bxc6 dxc6  5 0-0 f6  6 d4 Bg4  7 c3 exd4  8 cxd4 Qd7  9 h3 Bh5 10 Ne5! Bxd1  11 Nxd7 Kxd7  12 Rxd1 Re8  13 Nc3.** It is good for White, because in the ending she should be able to advance her K-side pawns and create a strong passed pawn on the e-file or f-file. Black, because of his doubled pawn, has much less chance of getting a Q-side passed pawn to compensate for this. White will therefore try to exchange at least one pair of rooks, advance her K-side pawns, and centralize her king, while Black has no active plan.

Similarly 18.3 favours White, although here there are also chances of deciding the issue in the middle-game. This position came about by **6 . . . exd4** (instead of 6 . . . Bg4) **7 Nxd4 c5  8 Nb3 Qxd1  9 Rxd1 Bd6 10 Na5! b5  11 c4! Ne7  12 Be3.** White has chances of breaking through with her minor pieces on the Q-side, in addition to her endgame prospects on the K-side.

## MIDDLE-GAME STRATEGY

Planning that begins in the opening is the ideal, but it is not always possible. Sooner or later your opponent plays an unforeseen move. It may be good or it may not, but you have to revise your ideas to fit the changed situation. Or you may have just drifted along from move to move, until suddenly the moves are no longer easy to find.

If this happens to you, the first step is to try to form an assessment of the position, and decide if you can whether the game offers equal chances, or favours you, or your opponent. Count the material, see who has the safer king, the better development, who controls the centre and the open files or diagonals. See where one player or other may create an outpost for a knight, or a strong passed pawn. Make special note of doubled, isolated, or backward pawns and try to work out who would win the ending if there were no pieces left, except a pair of knights, or a pair of bishops, or a pair of rooks.

This kind of stock-taking will give you a fair idea of how you stand, and should already suggest some ideas for plans.

Before deciding what to do, though, you should also try to spot any tactical threats or combinations that may be in the air for you or your adversary, because it is no good forming a beautiful ten-move deep strategy if it loses a piece on move three. Equally, if you have tactical chances, the task before you is to find a way of integrating these into a strategy for taking advantage of the permanent features of the position, such as a weak pawn of the opponent's.

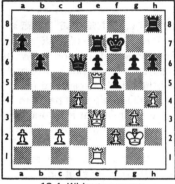

18.4 White to move

18.5 White to move

and the vulnerability of Black's remaining pawns.

Diagram 18.4 is a fairly simple example, to show how attention to the chief features of the position can quickly lead to victory. It's no secret that White has heavy pressure against the backward pawn at e6, and White could consider slow manoeuvring plans to increase his positional advantage — for example c2-c4, followed by Rc1 and c4-c5 or d4-d5. But if you notice that the queen at d6 is unguarded, a more straightforward solution should become clear to you.

White plays 1 d5, forcing Black to surrender the e-pawn. For if 1 . . . Rhe8 2 Qxh6 exd5 3 Rxf5+! Now 3 . . . exf5 4 Qxd6 Rxe1 5 Qxd5+ should be an easy win for White, thanks to his passed h-pawn

18.5 is a more complicated example at first sight. White has prevented K-side castling (thanks to opening errors by Black) and now in reply to d4-d5 Black played . . . Nc6-a5 rather than a move like . . . Nb8 which would have been safer although it would have impeded castling. White's problem is to find a way to win before Black can castle and extricate his badly placed pieces. You will notice that his pawn on c4 is *en prise*.

White actually played here 1 b4!? and only won after great complications and forty-six more moves. However, he could have won material almost effortlessly by a neat manœuvre. White saw the potential pin on the e-file, and the insecurity of the knight at a5, but did not see that it was possible to guard the c4 pawn without loss of time.

1 Nd2! was the correct move, for it carries the double threat of 2 Bxg4 or (if the bishop moves) 2 b4. After the forced reply 1 . . . Bxe2 White plays 2 Qxe2 c5 (else White plays b2-b4) 3 Bg7 Rg8 4 Bf6 Nc8 reaching diagram 18.6.

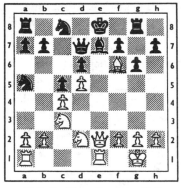

18.6 Position after 4 . . . Nc8

At first sight, Black is hanging on, but in fact a further manœuvre by the knight exploits the weakness of the dark squares to win at least the exchange. White plays 5 Bxe7! Nxe7 (not 5 . . . Qxe7 6 Qg4 winning the queen) 6 Ne4. The threatened 'family fork' by Nf6 is very strong, and it is probable that Black has no better move than 6 . . . Kf8.

It is clear from this that if White had approached diagram 18.5 in a logical way, he would have saved himself a lot of hard work, and denied his opponent any chance of saving the game. This is also a case where the rule applies: when you have found a good move, try to think of an even better one!

# UNIT 19    MORE ABOUT PAWNS

*PAWN MAJORITIES*

The fundamentals of pawn play were explained in Unit 4. It is now time
to consider more complicated cases where the handling of pawns is all-
important.

Before masters decide on any line of play, they give a lot of thought to
what the consequences will be upon the pawn structure. For example, a
series of exchanges (of pawns and/or pieces) will often lead to a situation
where one side has more pawns than his opponent on the Q-side, while on
the K-side the situation is reversed. It is therefore necessary to have some
way of judging, preferably in advance, which of the two pawn majorities
will be more significant.

Pawn majorities confer an advantage in space in many cases, but the
most important thing about them is that if they can be advanced they will
usually lead to the formation of passed pawns. Passed pawns, as we saw in
Unit 4, are pawns that are no longer obstructed by enemy pawns; they
will run on to queen unless a piece is deployed to hold them up.

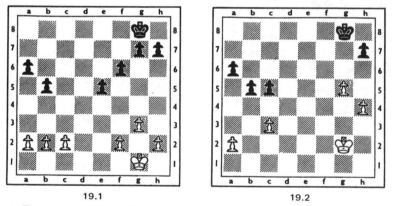

19.1                                    19.2

These two diagrams illustrate various kinds of pawn majority (there may
be other pieces on the board in each case). White in 19.1 has an advantage
of three pawns to two on the Q-side, with good chances of creating a
passed pawn on the c-file by c3 (to prevent . . . b4), then b3 and c4.
Black's 3–2 Q-side majority in 19.2 may not yield a passed pawn so quickly,
because White's two pawns are split; it will take two exchanges of pawns
before the passer is established. Pawns which are isolated may be vulnerable
to piece attack, of course, but it is a paradox well known to masters that
they can be better at defending against a pawn majority.

In both cases, though, other things being equal, the player with the

Q-side majority has the advantage. This is because the kings are too far away to hold up a Q-side passed pawn, or at least will lose a lot of time doing so. Given time, Black in 19.1 and White in 19.2 can set up a passed pawn on the K-side, but it couldn't be promoted because the defending king is already on the spot to blockade it. This is why, in general, it is better to have the Q-side than the K-side majority. Of course if both sides castle Q-side, then it is the K-side majority you want, while in the case of opposite-side castling the distinction does not apply.

Another important factor that sometimes determines the value of a pawn majority is the number of pawns. In general, you can develop a passed pawn more quickly from a 2–1 majority than from one of 3–2, and from 3–2 more quickly than 4–3, though it does depend exactly where the pawns are placed.

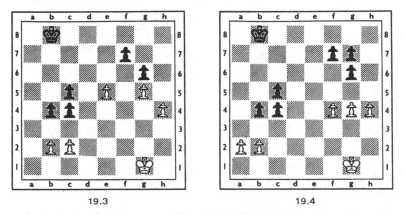

19.3                    19.4

Pawn majorities that contain doubled or isolated pawns are often no good for creating passed pawns. In 19.3 Black cannot make a passed pawn unless White blunders. After 1 ... b3 White should play 2 c3! and the extra black pawn at c5 is useless. But 2 cxb3 would be bad because of 2 ... cxb3, followed by ... c5-c4 then ... c4-c3, and after b2xc3 the black b-pawn goes on to queen. To make a passed pawn from a majority containing a doubled pawn, it is usually necessary to have pawns on one file where the opponent has no pawn, as in 19.4.

In 19.4, Black can create a passed pawn on the c-file by 1 ... c3 2 bxc3 bxc3, but note that the c5 pawn might as well not be there. Also, White gets a passed pawn on the a-file.

Doubled pawns are usually just as good as ordinary pawns when it comes to preventing the opponent from making a passer. The doubled black g-pawn in 19.4 prevents White from making a K-side passed pawn, just as it would if it were at h7 instead of g6.

Isolated pawns are a liability in pawn majorities because there is no pawn to recapture with when they advance. This means it is either not possible to make a passed pawn at all, or sacrifices are necessary to achieve it. In 19.3, White can get a passed pawn by 1 e6! fxe6 2 h5 gxh5 3 g6.

### PAWN PROMOTION

The finest hour of the pawn majority and the passed pawn is usually in the endgame, as we shall see in Unit 29. However, there are cases where the fight to promote a pawn becomes the dominant theme in a middle-game.

4 . . . a5  5 Qe4 Bf5  6 Qe5 Be6 7 Rc7 Bc8  8 d6! Black's tricks have come to an end and the passed pawn is able to take another step forward.

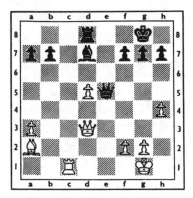

19.5 White to move

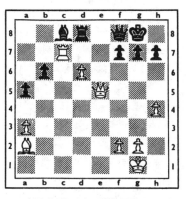

19.6 Position after 8 d6!

Black is defenceless. If 8 . . . Bd7 9 Qe7!, threatening both 10 Rxd7 and 10 Bxf7+ Qxf7 11 Qxd8+ etc.

White's d-pawn was forced through from 19.5, because Black did not have it adequately blockaded (a knight on d6 would have been much better than the bishop) and because White was able to create other threats. Not 1 d6? however because of 1 . . . Bf5 winning the pawn.

White played 1 Qc4! Qe8 (to meet 2 Qc7 by . . . Rc8) 2 Qb4 b6 3 Re1! (not 3 d6 Be6 nor 3 Rc7 Rc8 4 Rxa7? Rc1+ 5 Kh2 Qb8+) 3 . . . Qf8 4 Re7! (the new target is f7)

Black played 8 . . . Re8, but resigned after 9 Qxe8! The final point is 9 . . . Qxe8 10 Bxf7+ Qxf7 11 Rxc8+ Qf8 12 d7 and the pawn promotes.

Two passed pawns, especially if they are connected (on adjacent files) are rarer in the middle-game, but much more powerful than one. If they are far enough advanced, it can be worth sacrificing to force them through.

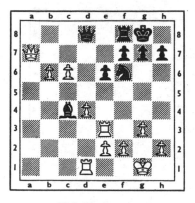

19.7 Black to move

Black played 1 . . . Nd5, calculating that if the attacked rook moves away then he would win the pawn at b6. This would leave him with bishop and knight against rook and two pawns, which should be about equal as the pawn at c5 would be too far advanced to defend easily.

White however replied 2 b7! Nxe3 3 fxe3 threatening Rc1, c7 etc. Black has an extra piece but it is no good as a blockader.

The game ended 3 . . . Qg5 4 d5! White thus defends e3 with his queen, so Black (now faced with three connected passed pawns) resigned.

3 . . . Qc7 would not have been any better, for White could still have replied 4 d5. If then 4 . . . Qxc6 5 b8=Q wins easily.

## CREATING PASSED PAWNS

Even if the passed pawn is not promoted until the endgame in most cases, the hardest part is often creat-ing it, in the middle-game. Sometimes advancing a pawn majority is not sufficient, or perhaps there is no obvious way to break a blockade of an existing passed pawn which therefore has to be sacrificed.

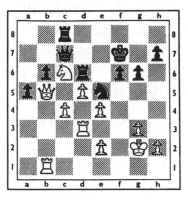

19.8 White to move

Here White's extra pawn (on e2) means little, and his passer at d5 isn't going anywhere (nor is the passed black a-pawn). After 1 Nxe5+ fxe5 the game would probably stagnate and be drawn.

So White played 1 Qxb6! and after 1 . . . Nxc6 did not recapture immediately (since 2 dxc6 Rxc6 leads to a certain draw). He played 2 c5!, an instructive intermediate move.

Then the game went on 2 . . . Rd7 3 dxc6 Rxd3 4 Qxc7+ Rxc7 5 exd3 Rxc6 6 Rc7+ Ke8 7 d4 reaching diagram 29.2 (the continuation is in chapter seven). White now has two connected passed pawns and so his centre cannot be undermined. He forced a neat win in a few more moves.

## THE BLOCKADE

The passed pawn's enemy is the blockader, particularly the blockading knight. See diagram 19.9.

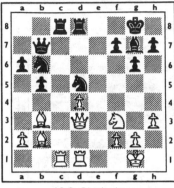

19.9 Blockade

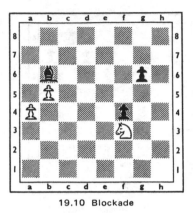

19.10 Blockade

The blockader sits on the square in front of the white d-pawn, so obstructing its advance and allowing Black to gradually bring up attackers to bear on d4. At the same time the blockading knight is shielded by the pawn from attack down the file. Meanwhile the knight puts pressure on important squares like b4, c3, e3, and f4. A blockading bishop is also quite a good piece as long as it has an open diagonal or two to exert influence on other parts of the board. Against connected passed pawns, the bishop may actually be a superior blockader. See diagram 19.10.

The black bishop is able to cope with both the a-pawn and the b-pawn. But White's knight has a blind spot — the square g4 (which a bishop would control). If Black can get his g-pawn across the attacked square

g5 (for example by playing first 1 ... Bd8) then White's blockade may be broken.

The only other piece that makes a reasonable blockader is the king, because it is a short-range piece anyway. The king also has the advantage that (unlike bishop or knight) it threatens to capture the pawn it is blockading. Rooks and queens are too important to do permanent duty as blockaders. The enemy passed pawn restricts their action in a forward direction; moreover the rook suffers from the same blind spot as the knight. So blockade passed pawns with these pieces only when there is no alternative.

Diagram 19.9 incidentally shows that blockading need not be just a defensive measure. In fact Black probably has a positional advantage. It is not only *passed* pawns that are usefully blockadable in this way — any mobile pawn should be kept under control. Give Black a pawn at e7 and White a pawn at c3 (or b3, with the bishop instead at b1) and the main features of the position are not changed all that much.

However, if a blockade is necessary it is best to set it up as near as possible to the centre of the board, so that the blockading piece can have some positive work to do. A blockading knight on d6 is also a useful piece, but on d7 or b6 its role becomes chiefly defensive, and if it were stuck on the a-file it would be a poor piece indeed.

For this reason, a passed (or at least, mobile) pawn on the wing (the Q-wing especially) can give much more trouble to the defender than one in the centre. A central passed pawn, or mobile central majority, is usually effective only when — as in 19.5 — threats can be generated in the vicinity of the king.

### PAWN CHAINS

When you have a series of pawns protecting each other on squares of one colour, as in 19.11 we speak of *pawn chains*. These often arise from openings like the Czech Benoni (1 d4 Nf6  2 c4 c5  3 d5 e5) and the King's Indian and French Defences. The special kinds of problems resulting from these blocked situations will be discussed in more detail in units 21 and 25.

### PAWNS AND SQUARES

In positions where pawns are relatively immobile, there is sometimes a danger of confusing a pawn with the square on which it has

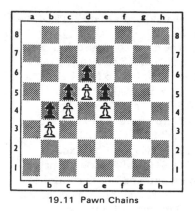

19.11  Pawn Chains

been standing for so long. You may think you have to defend a particular pawn, when it is really the square on which it stands that is strategically important. In that case it will not be enough to advance the pawn to the next square or exchange it. In 19.12 the fight is on to control the square e4.

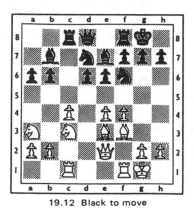

19.12  Black to move

Play through the following continuation from the diagram, and see if you can spot where White fails to realize the importance of keeping e4 under control. There are some comments at the back of the book.

. The game continued 1 . . . d5 2 cxd5 exd5 3 e5 Ne4 4 Bxe4 dxe4 5 Nc4 b5 6 Nd2 Qa5 7 Ncxe4 Qxa2 8 Bd4 Qd5 9 Qf2 f5 10 exf6 Rxc1 11 Rxc1 Nxf6 12 Nxf6+ Bxf6 13 Bxf6 Rxf6 14 Rc7 Rxf4 15 Qe2 h6 (but not 15 . . . Qd4+ 16 Kh1 Qxd2 17 Qe6+!) and Black won thanks to his extra pawn and control of the centre and the a8-h1 diagonal.

Remember also that every time a pawn advances, it leaves behind it two squares that it can never control again in the game. Before you relinquish control of those squares, make sure that your opponent has no way of occupying or attacking them that you cannot cope with easily. Ill-considered pawn advances cause a great many defeats. In a quiet position a pawn move may not appear to matter. But your opponent, if he is a strong player, will immediately look to see how this changes the situation, and what new squares may now be accessible to his pieces.

## PUZZLES

Combinations based on the promotion of passed pawns form the subject of the puzzles in this unit. In each case White is to play and win.

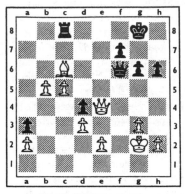

19.13 White to move

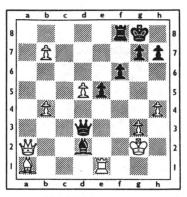

19.14 White to move

# UNIT 20  POSITIONAL JUDGEMENT

*TAKING STOCK*

In just about every game you play, a time will come where you want to pause and take stock of the position. Plans based on over-optimistic or faulty assessments are apt to go awry, while there are also occasions when players miss chances to go for a win because they do not appreciate that they hold the advantage. Therefore, whenever it is not absolutely obvious what you should play, you need, as the first stage in your planning procedure, to form as clear an assessment of the position as you can.

Any positional assessment must naturally take account of tactical factors. It is no good having a 'winning' endgame thanks to good pawns if your opponent's threat of mate in three forces you to give up a piece. In complicated positions, therefore, you have to begin by looking for threats (for both yourself and your opponent) and parries to those threats. But in the majority of middle-games, tactical threats alone will not decide the game, and positional judgement becomes very important.

Some players undeniably have a better instinct for positional play than others, but there are nevertheless several ways in which you can set about developing your positional judgement. One helpful method is to play through annotated master games, which you can find in chess magazines or newspaper columns; this is also a good way of keeping up with contemporary opening ideas and news of the chess world. Playing through your own games afterwards and inviting criticism from friends can be useful, at least if they are stronger players than you are. Neither of these methods, however, can be guaranteed to give you a balanced picture of positional ideas. A firm grounding in the basic rules is essential before you attempt to master more subtle ideas such as those of grandmasters like Karpov and Petrosian.

In the Middle-Game Strategy section of Unit 18 some of the basic parameters for positional judgement were listed. Let us have another look at the list and see where in the book they have been discussed in more detail.

(a) Material Advantage — *Unit 1*

(b) Safety of the King — *Units 7 and 8*

(c) Better Development — *Unit 5*

(d) Central Control — *Unit 6*

(e) Control of Open Lines — *Unit 5*

(f) Outposts — *Unit 5*

(g) Overall Pawn Structure — *Unit 4*

(h) Passed Pawns — *Unit 19*

(i) Pawn Majorities — *Unit 19*

(j) Weak Pawns — *Unit 4*

(k) Endgame Prospects — *Unit 27*

(l) Attacking Prospects — *Units 5–9*

## *RELATIVE VALUES*

When you ask yourself the question 'How do I stand?', answer it in terms of these twelve factors. Frequently there will be nothing to choose between your position and that of your opponent; e.g. in position 20.1, material is level, there are no passed pawns, nor pawn majorities, nor obvious pawn weaknesses, and each player controls an open file. In such cases your assessment will depend on the relative advantages of the two players in terms of central control, king safety, and so on.

The factors vary from one position to another, sometimes to the extent that a big advantage in one outweighs almost any number of small advantages in the others. A player who is a rook up, or has an unstoppable passed pawn, will win — one with a desperately unsafe king, or wretched pawns, will lose — unless there is exceptional compensation in the other positional factors. In most cases the relative values of the positional advantages held by White and Black will be subtler, requiring a more thorough assessment.

Here are three positions for assessment; in each case White is to move. Before reading any further, form your own judgement about them.

20.1 How does White stand?

In 20.1, White has pressure on the open c-file, counter-balanced by Black's on the open e-file. The material balance is slightly in White's favour, as he has 'the two bishops', but this is not yet crucial because the Be3 is only employed in a defensive role at present. White also has an outpost at c5, which he may be able to maintain for some time. If Black ever plays . . . b6 he will have to be careful about the consequent weakness at c6 which will enhance the value of the white queen's rook. The central pawn structure (mutual isolated d-pawns) often leads to a draw, but in this case White has a slight advantage which he might be able to increase, since it is his move. 1 Bf3 is one possibility, discouraging 1 . . . Ne4 because of 2 Bxe4 dxe4

3 d5 obtaining a mobile passed pawn and central control, and an initiative based on threats against the black b-pawn and e-pawn. Other moves to consider are 1 Bb5 and 1 h3.

20.2 How does White stand?

The position 20.2 displays a pawn structure typical of the classical Dragon Sicilian. White has a half-open d-file and more space in the centre, as well as vague attacking chances based on Qh4 and f4-f5. Black, however, threatens to win the b-pawn, and if White plays 1 Bc1 then the advance of the b-pawn will give Black a Q-side attack. White must also worry about his long-term weaknesses if he allows his opponent to obtain the two bishops. Were it not for one detail, Black would definitely stand better. The complicating factor is that White can, either now or in a move or two, play Nd5, threatening a fork on e7, and after the likely reply . . . Re8 he can drive away the outpost knight by b3. White must work out how to combine this with the possible e4-e5 thrust (so the Bf3 attacks the Ra8) in order to obtain chances in the centre. The next three or four moves should decide which player will obtain the initiative, which is crucial when both players have weaknesses. For example, White should not go in for 1 Bc1 b5 2 Nd5?! Re8 3 b3 Nb6 4 Nxb6 because after 4 . . . axb6 both his a- and c-pawns are *en prise*.
See diagram 20.3.

White is a pawn up in 20.3, giving him a Q-side pawn majority, and he also has an outpost at e5. However, Black has completed his development, whereas White not only has to find a square for his QR, but has not achieved good co-ordination of the pieces which he does have in play. The Na4 is vulnerable and the threat to the queen means White must either make a feeble move like Qc1 or allow a self-pin by Bd3. White's pawns at c2 and f4 are potential targets, and Black also has chances to obtain the two bishops.

20.3 How does White stand?

Tactical complications are almost inevitable, White is struggling to survive, despite his apparent advantages, because the open centre means that Black's active pieces have great freedom of action.

The twelve listed factors are often linked in typical ways. Lead in development is rarely decisive in a blocked position, but with an open centre or fluid pawn structure it means control of open lines and (if the enemy king is relatively unsafe) attacking chances. This complex of advantages is often compensated for to some extent by material imbalance.

A static pawn structure plus enemy pawn weaknesses usually means good endgame prospects. A fluid position with the advantage of the two bishops means the same, but can give attacking chances too. A blocked position with knight outposts, a Q-side majority with central control, or a static centre with doubled rooks on the only open file — these are all typical conjunctions that offer good winning chances.

## ACCUMULATION OF ADVANTAGES

One type of advantage that is particularly important in positional play is the weak enemy pawn — whether doubled, backward, isolated, or vulnerable for some other special reason. Sometimes this can be converted into a win simply by capturing the pawn and advancing the consequent pawn majority, finally queening the resultant passed pawn or winning a piece. More often than not, this simple procedure will not work, either because the pawn is adequately defended for the moment, or because taking the time to capture it will open a line for the opponent and allow him counter-play. Rather than cash in the chips too early, it is generally a good policy to look for new weaknesses, since the opponent will probably be unable to get rid of the first one.

The strategy of accumulating small advantages until you have enough to force a win has been the cornerstone of grandmaster chess ever since the days of Tarrasch, Rubinstein, and Capablanca. It is particularly important in static positions, where the relative permanence of the pawn structure means that an advantage once gained is not easily dissipated or compensated for by a tactical diversion.

Control of the centre is crucial in 'quiet' positional games. Centralization of the pieces means that the player is ready to act on either wing, often alternating attacks on a Q-side target (such as a backward pawn) and a K-side target (such as a somewhat vulnerable king). Good manœuvring can lead to one or other target finally yielding, or to a complete stranglehold on the enemy position. Most defenders will prefer to play a speculative sacrifice to break out of such a situation, but firm central control prevents desperation being effective.

## TRANSITION TO THE ENDGAME

A great number of games are decided at the point where exchanges (of queens, especially) bring about an ending with only one or two pieces each. This is because certain types of advantage increase as the board clears, whereas other advantages disappear. Also new factors suddenly become relevant.

A king in the centre is exposed to attack in the middle-game. But if the pieces disappear, so that mate is no longer a danger and harassing checks are few, then the centralized king becomes an advantage.

Weak pawns are easier to pick off in the ending, partly because the king is the scourge of isolated pawns. Passed pawns and pawn majorities are easier to advance, because relatively few blockaders are left and because it is less likely that the opponent can take advantage of the unguarded squares left behind by an advancing pawn.

Given open lines, rooks also come into their own in the ending. With their natural enemies, the minor pieces, back in the box the rooks can sweep into the seventh or eighth ranks and attack pawns where they are most vulnerable — from behind. Rooks are also the best supporters of passed pawns.

Knights decline in value in the ending, unless there are no other pieces or unless there are pawns on only one wing. Therefore a player with a knight has to be especially careful about allowing an ending.

Because of these special characteristics of most endings, looking ahead to the endgame is a part of any good positional assessment. Imagine that all the pieces in your position were to vanish, leaving only king and pawns; who would win? Then add a rook each, or bishop versus knight (or whatever piece combination is most likely) and ask yourself the question again.

## Positional judgement

If the endings all look good for you, then you have found the basis for a plan. If some endings will be good, and others not so good, then you can use middle-game threats and manœuvres to steer towards the exchanges you need to get the good ending. If you neglect this long-range aspect of planning you run the risk of being gradually outplayed.

### QUESTIONS

How do you assess 20.4? Should Black choose 8 . . . d6, 8 . . . d5, 8 . . . Be7 or some other move?

How do you assess the position in 20.5? What should Black play?

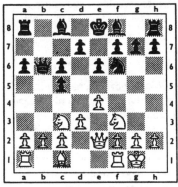

20.4 Black to move

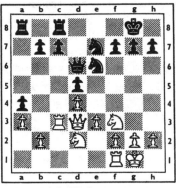

20.5 Black to move

# UNIT 21  GRAND STRATEGY

*MARY'S POSITIONAL MASTERPIECE*

It was the day of the annual 'derby' match between Midlington Chess Club and their rivals from Upcaster. Tom Smith won the toss, so Midlington took White on the odd-numbered boards. As it turned out, the crucial game was on board three between Mary Mashem and one Fearless Fred, who was Upcaster's version of Harry Hacker, only rather more dangerous.

As soon as the team lists were exchanged, before the match could start, Tom took Mary aside to give her some advice about Fred. He warned her of the Upcaster player's love of aggressive openings and middle-game complications, and told her to expect the Sicilian Defence.

Mary decided to keep the game very quiet and just try for some small advantages. If she could exchange into an early endgame, that would be all the less to the liking of Fearless Fred.

So after **1 e4 c5** Mary did not allow Fred to play a Najdorf or Dragon, but instead played **2 c3**. Her opponent had seen this before, and played **2 . . . Nf6** without much hesitation. Mary continued **3 e5 Nd5 4 d4 cxd4 5 Qxd4**, avoiding the sharp line 5 cxd4 and concentrating on centralization. The advanced e-pawn would sooner or later be challenged by . . . d6, leaving her with a Q-side pawn majority: one small advantage on which to build.

Now Black fell in with her plans by **5 . . . e6 6 Nf3 Nc6 7 Qe4 d6** (7 . . . f5!? would have suited Fred better) **8 Nbd2 dxe5 9 Nxe5 Nf6 10 Qa4 Qd5** (10 . . . Bd7 11 Nxd7 with the two bishops) **11 Ndf3 Bd6 12 Bf4** and it was clear that the skirmish for control of the e5 square was ending in White's favour (13 Rd1 was threatened). Mary's eighth move was particularly important, because at that stage she had to foresee this position.

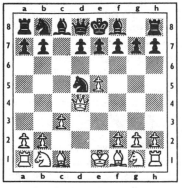

21.1  Position after 5 Qxd4

21.2  Position after 12 Bf4

Black had to go in for exchanges now, which suited Mary very well: **12 . . . Qe4+ 13 Qxe4 Nxe4 14 Bd3 Nxe5 15 Bxe5 Bxe5 16 Nxe5 Nc5 17 Bc2!** White's control of e5 meant that Black had a bad bishop; driving the knight away only leads to weaknesses on Black's K-side. Mary was starting to accumulate new small advantages to add to her Q-side pawn majority.

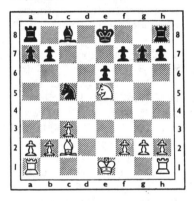

21.3 Position after 17 Bc2!

The games were stopped for tea at this point (this match is always played on a Saturday afternoon), and some of the players talked about their games. It's against the rules, of course, but people still do it.

Harry did not think much of the way Mary was playing. 'Sissy positional play!' he snorted; 'That's the trouble with you women chess players — no fire! No combinations! Just plod, plod, plod.'

'What a male chauvinist you are' she replied irately. 'What's wrong with the way I play, if it gets results?'

Harry shifted his ground. '"Accumulation of small advantages" you call it? How bourgeois can you get! I don't see you getting results from that position, anyway. Instead of playing these boring openings, you should take Mao's advice: "Dare to struggle and dare to win!" Like I do.'

Johnny Brain, hearing this, was very puzzled. He hadn't heard of Mao playing chess.

Mary looked upset, so Tom thought he had better intervene for the sake of team morale. He said he thought Mary was playing well and warned Harry that there is no intrinsic value to sacrifices and combinations.

'Forget Mao-Tse-Tung' said Tom. 'Remember what Nimzowitsch said: "The beauty of a chess move lies not in its appearance but in the thought behind it". Nimzowitsch was a great player.'

'He was a bourgeois, too' mumbled Harry. This was too much; they had to laugh.

Back at the board, Mary's opponent played **17 . . . f6 18 Nc4 Ke7 19 0-0-0 Bd7 20 Nd6** (a new outpost) **20 . . . b6 21 b4** (advancing the majority) **21 . . . Na6 22 Rhe1** (threatens 23 Nf5+) **22 . . . g6 23 Bb3 Rad8 24 f4 Nc7**. See diagram 21.4.

All White's pieces were by now more actively placed than their black counterparts. The e6 pawn, weakened at move 17, now requires constant protection. Mary wanted to force one more concession: an open line for her rooks on the K-side.

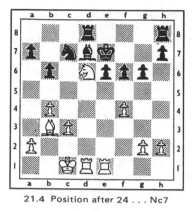

21.4 Position after 24 . . . Nc7

21.5 Position after 34 Rh4

After **25 f5! gxf5 26 Nxf5+**
Mary had succeeded in isolating the
black h-pawn, with a view to winning
it eventually and setting up a
passed h-pawn. She was not
worried about Black's passed e-
pawn, because her pressure on the
centre files and the a2–g8 diagonal
ensured that the pawn could never
be dangerous. Secretly she hoped
Black would blunder by 26 . . .
Kf8?, leaving the Rd8 unguarded.
Then she could show Harry that
she could see combinations too:
27 Bxe6! Nxe6 28 Rxe6! etc.

However, Black played **26 . . .
Kf7**; so she continued with her
plan: **27 Rd3 Bc8** (trying to dis-
entangle himself) **28 Rg3 Ne8
29 Nd4 Nc7 30 Re4**. The threat
now was to double rooks on the
g-file; the time when Black must
lose one of his weak pawns was
not far off: **30 . . . Rdg8 31 Rxg8
Rxg8 32 Nf5!** (with the threat of
Nh6+) **32 . . . Rd8** (32 . . . Rxg2
33 Nd6+ and 34 Nxc8) **33 Rg4
Ne8 34 Rh4.**

Now if 34 . . . Kg6 35 Ne7+
Kg7 36 Nc6 Black loses either his
a-pawn or his e-pawn. So Mary's
strategy was on the brink of success.

Fearless Fred tried to trick her by
**34 . . . h5 35 Rxh5 Kg6 36 Ng3
Ng7 37 Rh4 Bb7** but Mary could
see her g-pawn was not important.
She played **38 Rg4+ Kf7 39 Ne2
f5 40 Rc4!** with a threat to occupy
the seventh rank with her rook.
After **40 . . . Ne8 41 Rd4** Black
could no longer avoid the exchange
of rooks. Fred chose **41 . . . Rd6**
(41 . . . Rxd4 42 cxd4 Bxg2
43 Nf4) **42 Nf4 Bc8 43 Ba4!**
(decisive) **43 . . . Rxd4 44 Bxe8+
Kxe8 45 cxd4** and Black was
given a loss on adjudication. His
backward e-pawn, no longer passed,
only obstructs his bishop. White's
passed h-pawn ties down the black
king to the K-side and the white
king is bound to break through
eventually in the centre. See diagram
21.6.

'I felt I never had a chance
throughout the game' said Fred.

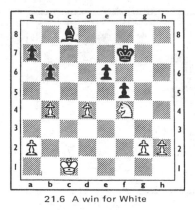

21.6  A win for White

'Tell that to Harry Hacker' Mary replied.

## BLOCKED POSITIONS

Occasionally one gets a position which is almost completely blocked by pawn chains. There are some special problems with these, as Johnny Brain discovered in the same match.

Johnny was Black on board four. His game began  **1 d4 Nf6  2 c4 g6 3 Nc3 Bg7  4 e4 d6  5 Be2 0-0 6 Bg5 c5  7 d5 e5** (he regretted this move later)  **8 Qd2 Na6  9 h4.**

21.7  Position after 9 h4

Normally a wing attack of this kind, with the white king on its home square, would be premature, and would be met by opening the centre files. But in this case Black will have difficulty setting up counter-play in time. To have any chance of opening the game in his favour, Black must play either ... b5 or ... f5 and both of these moves will take time to prepare. So White is right to start his attack without delay, in the hope of opening the h-file and forcing checkmate.

Johnny tried to prevent White opening the K-side files, playing **9 ... h5  10 f3 Qd7  11 Nh3 Nc7 12 a4** (to rule out ... b5 sacrifices) **12 ... Na6?** This move aims to exploit the hole at b4. Such longwinded manœuvres are sometimes all right in blocked positions, but here White has real chances of opening the game up; so Black should have been thinking about his defences.

White now played  **13 Nf2 Kh7** (to prevent Bh6)  **14 g4 Ng8 15 gxh5 gxh5.**

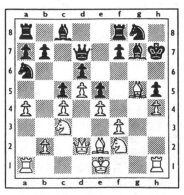

21.8  Position after 15 ... gxh5

Johnny thought he was safe now, thanks to his plan of . . . f6 and . . . Qf7. He had not realized that White has one pawn 'lever' left, with which to prise open new lines. The Upcaster man played **16 f4! f6 17 Bxh5** obtaining a decisive attack. Johnny tried **17 . . . Ne7** (to give the king a flight square) **18 fxe5 fxg5** (else he's a pawn down without compensation) **19 hxg5 Kg8 20 e6 Qd8**. White has three pawns and an attack for his piece. The piece is worth nothing to Black because the centre and Q-side are still blocked, so he cannot organize counter-play. After **21 Ng4! Nc7 22 Qg2 Nxe6** (the only hope) **23 Nf6+ Rxf6 24 gxf6** Johnny had to resign.

After the game, Johnny realized he had made some slight errors in defence, such as his 12th and 14th moves. The real reason he lost, though, was because of the strategic error of blocking the centre by 7 . . . e5. Although you could not prove a win for White from that point by forced tactical means, this was nevertheless the move to blame, for at this point he assessed the position inadequately and so chose the wrong plan. He played . . . e5 because he thought it would lead to a game of manœuvring, where he would have chances based on . . . f5, whereas . . . f5 without . . . e5 would be undesirable (because of the backward pawn on the e-file). He saw the levers that he could exert on the position (. . . f5, . . . b5) but underestimated White's own (h5, f4). He should have remembered that in

closed positions a lot can still happen: with a blocked centre, a pawn storm can often be safely employed on the wing. The player who gets his lever in first usually gets the initiative, and this is decisive because counter-play cannot be organized in time.

## STRATEGIC ERRORS

Johnny's 7 . . . e5? was a strategic error because it was a serious error of planning, a move that should have been avoided on general principles. Let us look at some other examples of strategic errors.

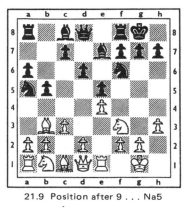

21.9 Position after 9 . . . Na5

Diagram 21.9 is reached by the well-known Ruy López sequence **1 e4 e5 2 Nf3 Nc6 3 Bb5 a6 4 Ba4 Nf6 5 0-0 Be7 6 Re1 b5 7 Bb3 d6 8 c3 0-0 9 h3 Na5**. In this position, White normally plays 10 Bc2, the only move to offer an advantage. This bishop is very important, both for protecting the e-pawn and central white squares, and for creating long-term threats on the K-side; so any move (e.g. 10 d4) which permitted Black to exchange it for a knight would be a serious error. Many strategic mistakes involve exchanging (or permitting the opponent to exchange) key pieces.

After 10 Bc2 Black invariably plays 10 . . . c5, and with best play should reach equality. Other moves for Black would be strategically incorrect, because they would neglect the fight for the centre, e.g. 10 . . . Bb7 11 d4 Nc4 12 b3 Nb6 13 Nbd2 Nbd7 14 b4! as in a game of Fischer's.

Here are a few examples of strategic blunders in the opening.

(a) 1 e4 e5  2 Nf3 Bd6? Black impedes the development of his own Q-side.

(b) 1 e4 e5  2 Nf3 Nc6  3 Bc4 h6? Black wastes time and neglects development.

(c) 1 d4 d5  2 c4 Nf6?  3 cxd5 Nxd5  4 Nf3 Black neglects the centre.

(d) 1 d4 d5  2 e3?! White hems in his queen's bishop.

Types of error to guard against are:

(a) Moves that weaken the pawn structure.

(b) Exchanges that concede control of a file or diagonal to the opponent.

(c) Moving pawns to the same colour square as your bishop.

(d) Making a compromising move when a sound move is available.

# VI. Choosing a move

## UNIT 22   ORGANIZING YOUR THOUGHTS

*THE TASK*

The game is under way. You are out of the opening and must think for yourself. You have some general ideas about the position, but at the moment it is your opponent's turn. You try to guess what he will do.

Then he moves. The spotlight is on *you*. Just how do you set about deciding on your reply?

Choosing a move is after all the most important process in a chess game. Opening and endgame knowledge, tactical vision and positional technique are all very well, but if they do not help you to find the right move most of the time (and adequate moves the rest of the time) you will lose a lot of games, even if you do understand them better than your opponent. In any game, you have to make thirty or more choices of a move, and only a few of those can be entrusted to your reflexes or your memory of variations from an openings manual.

The elements upon which your choices should be based — especially in the middle-game — have all been discussed in the earlier units in this book. Positional judgement, tactical acumen, and long-range strategic ideas can all help you to make your decision. One more thing is needed, though, if you are to be systematic in your approach to the task in hand: a method, or program, for organizing your thoughts.

*THE PROGRAM*

When computers are taught to play chess, they have to be given a long and complicated set of instructions for dealing with every foreseeable contingency — they need a program. A human player does not need a program to see that his opponent can be mated on the move, or his queen captured; all that is needed is a quick safety check, to guard against the human tendency to jump to conclusions.

However, choices of any difficulty need to be handled methodically, and even the easy, 'obvious' ones should not be taken lightly. There was a time when it was 'obvious' that the world is flat.

The process of making a move can be divided into several more or less distinct stages, which will vary in importance from one case to another. These stages, in the order in which they are best tackled, are:

(1) Assessment of the opponent's last move. How have things been changed by it?

(2) What immediate threats must I meet? Find possible defences.

(3) What immediate tactical blows are at my disposal? List the apparently strong moves in the position.

(4) Positional assessment, including long-range considerations.

(5) What moves are suggested by these positional musings? List them.

(6) Compare the 'candidate moves' which derive from 2, 3, and 5 and form a short-list of two, three, or four of them.

(7) Calculate variations based on the short-listed 'candidate moves', and assess the resulting positions that could arise.

(8) Compare these assessments, and so decide on the move you prefer. Write it on your score sheet; do not make it on the board yet.

(9) Have a last look round, to guard against traps and blunders. It should be routine to examine all the opponent's replies which could be tactically awkward: checks, captures, mate threats, threats to the queen or rooks, threats to pieces by pawns, advances of passed pawns.

(10) If you are still satisfied with your choice, make it on the board.

This ten-point program will be illustrated by the examples in chapter 6 (Units 22–6) showing how it applies to the task of finding your best move in all types of position. The process is not really as complicated as it may seem when set out in words as above; a lot of it is probably second nature to you already, or can soon become so.

## EASY MOVES AND 'EASY MOVES'

Some moves really are obvious, and can be handled by an abbreviated form of the program. After the first three steps, if you are already convinced you know the best possible move, you can then leap to number nine and check that you have not overlooked something. When you do make up your mind quickly, step nine is doubly important. Jumping from three directly to ten, or only going through the motions of step nine in a perfunctory way, is a major cause of avoidable blunders.

Diagram 22.1 is a true-life illustration of this, from a London League game played in 1976. White thought his opponent's resignation was long overdue and so was playing by instinct, not really thinking at all. He played

1 Nf5?? and his opponent replied
1 . . . Rd1+! and announced 'Mate'
(anticipating 2 Rxd1 Qxd1). Shocks
like this have induced resignation
countless times, but fortunately White
saw that it was not mate, and replied
2 Qe1, the game eventually ending in
a draw.

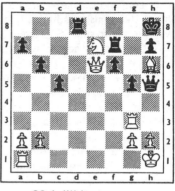

22.1 White to move

So how should White have set about choosing his move in the position?

The first stage, you have seen, is to assess the opponent's last move, to
see how it has changed the situation. The last move was . . . Qg6-h5. White
presumably gave little thought to that — because of the threat to the queen,
it had to go to h5. He did not notice a positive feature of the move.

The second step follows from the first: . . . Qh5 changes the situation to
the extent that . . . Rd1+ has now become a threat. If White has thought of
it at all, he would have immediately rejected any move that did not cope
with this threat — 1 Rh3, and the move chosen (1 Nf5) included. Instead
he would have thought in terms of these moves: 1 h3, 1 Re1, 1 Rf1, 1 Rf3
or 1 Nd5.

As there is a strong black threat to be met, while in the long-term White
has a winning material and positional advantage, stage three (strong blows
for White) is of lesser importance. Nonetheless, considering the above list
of candidates from an active point of view, 1 Re1 and 1 Nd5 would have
sprung to mind.

Stages four and five can be discarded with minimal consideration because
White's material advantage and the insecurity of the black king show that
(with care) a rapid tactical solution can be found.

Stage six is here just a confirmation that 1 Re1 and 1 Nd5 are the most
promising moves. Stage seven, the analysis of these two 'candidates',
follows right away.

1 Nd5 prevents the . . . Rd1 swindle and threatens 2 Re1 and 3 Qe8+
etc. Black cannot leave his back row unguarded, nor his Rf7 nor his pawn
at f6, so clearly has no constructive move. 1 . . . Kg8, when 2 Re1? is met
by 2 . . . Qxh6, is instead answered by 2 Nxf6+! and 3 Nxh5. So 1 Nd5
appears to win by force.

1 Re1 is at least as convincing. 1 . . . Rd1, no longer check, is met by

2 Qc8+ etc., and the desperate throw 1 . . . Qxh6 fails to 2 Qxf7 Rf8
3 Nf5. 1 Re1 is also aesthetically preferable, since it brings the last unmoved piece into play. So, stage eight, write 1 Re1 on the score-sheet.

After all this methodical work, stage nine should not take long. The
only check (1. . . Qxh2+) is brushed off by 2 Kxh2. The captures are just
as hopeless (1 . . . Rxe7 2 Qxe7 threatens the Rd8) and the last attempt
to soften up the back rank (1 . . . Qe2) has no hope here because White has
two major pieces on the e-file. The last look round turns up no surprises,
so 1 Re1 can confidently be played.

Diagram 22.2 is even 'easier',
because there is one outstanding
move. Black, whose piece sacrifice
has misfired, has just played
. . . b7-b6 instead of . . . Bb6 which
would have been relatively best.
The refutation, 1 Bb5!, probably
leaps to your mind right away. But
unless you are in desperate time-
trouble, it pays to run a quick check.

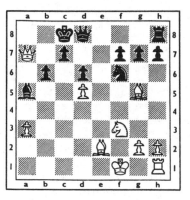

22.2 White to move

You have already done step one — Black's move appears weak because he
does not threaten the white queen, and the squares a6 and c6 are no longer
defended. He threatens no checks and 1 Bb5 does not allow any, while it
threatens mate in one by 2 Qa8. No other moves look half as good as 1 Bb5
(since 1 Ba6+ or 1 Qa8+ lets the king out to d7) and positional play clearly
won't be needed.

Already we are through to stage seven, at which point we calculate the
'variations'. Most of his moves allow 2 Qa8 mate; 1 . . . c6, and 1 . . . Nd7
are met instead by 2 Ba6 mate. So 1 Bb5! forces mate quickly in all variations; nothing could be better than that (end of stage eight). Stage nine is
a quick recap of these possibilities, and then 1 Bb5 can be played.

If you did not see 1 Bb5 instantly, the program could still help you
find it. At stage three, seeing that checks are not immediately decisive, but
are potentially mating threats, it would be natural to look for moves that
cut off the flight square.

The only time you should move more or less instantaneously (the early
part of well-known openings perhaps excepted) is when you only have one
legal move. As soon as you are satisfied there is no alternative, make the

move; otherwise you just give your opponent time on the clock. I have seen players sit for five minutes or more before playing a forced move, just because their opponent's last move had surprised and upset them. Forced moves should be played quickly and confidently, so as not to encourage the enemy by showing fear.

## OTHER SIMPLE MOVES

Clear wins and forced moves are not the only time when you can decide fairly quickly what your move will be. There are also straightforward recaptures of pawns or pieces, and there are situations where you are following a plan; your opponent's move was as expected and so you feel you have already made your decision. Here too you cannot afford to neglect stages two and nine, your safeguards against blunders.

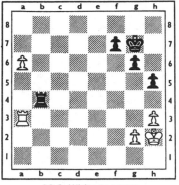

22.3 White to move

22.4 White to move

Diagram 22.3 is about the simplest type of straightforward move. Black, who has just captured something on b4, threatens to blockade your pawn by 1 . . . Rb8 and 2 . . . Ra8. It should not take you long to establish that 1 a7 is safe and wins. Similarly, if that pawn were black (so 1 . . . Rb6 was a threat) it would not take you long to decide on 1 Rxa6. See diagram 22.4.

In 22.4 White has already formed his plan, based on black-square pressure. His last move

(Rd1-d2) has been met by Qd8-e7. The natural and consistent continuation is 1 Rf1-d1, especially as White wants to see how Black will meet the threat of 2 Rxd7 before committing his other pieces or his Q-side pawns to new squares (it would make a difference which rook went to d8). Even so, White sensibly ran through the program before making his move, and saw that 1 Rfd1 can be well met by 1 . . . Qe6. He then spotted a tactical trick that would improve his game: 1 Qc4 and if 1 . . . Nb6 2 Bxf6; e.g. 2 . . . Nxc4? 3 Bxe7 or 2 . . . Qxf6 3 Qxc7. It often turns out, as here, that the routine move is not best.

Hasty captures and recaptures are another danger time for players who do not look ahead and use their 'choice of a move' program conscientiously. Sometimes the apparently 'bad' recapture can be better than the 'obvious' one, and occasionally there is a zwischenzug which is better than any recapture at all.

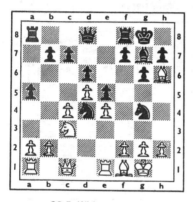

22.5 White to move

Here White's move Bh6 (to exchange dark-squared bishops) has been met by . . . Nf6-g4. If White now plays 1 Bxg7? a nasty surprise awaits him. If Black does not see the refutation at once, he might just recapture (1 . . . Kxg7?) but the move-choice program could help.

At stage three, Black is urged to look for threatening blows at his disposal. What he can do that might outweigh the loss of a bishop? Well, he could threaten checkmate — with 1 . . . Qh4. At stage seven, when he makes his in-depth calcu-

lations of the candidate moves, he finds that 1 . . . Qh4 can be met only by 2 h3. But then Black has at least one forced mating sequence: 2 . . . Nf3+ 3 gxf3 (or 3 Kh1 Nxf2 mate) 3 . . . Qxf2+ 4 Kh1 Qh2 mate. So after making his check at stage nine, Black plays 1 . . . Qh4! and wins. If on the other hand, in diagram 22.5, the white queen stood at d2 (instead of c1) Black would find, at stage seven, that White had f2 adequately guarded and would reject 1 . . . Qh4 in favour of 1 . . . Kxg7.

22.6 Black to move

Diagram 22.6 arose by **1 e4 b6 2 d4 Bb7 3 Nc3 e6 4 Nf3 Nf6 5 Bd3 Be7 6 Qe2**. Castling is so often the correct thing to do, at an early stage of the game, that it can become a habit with players to castle at the earliest opportunity and without deep thought. Yet this, like other reflex moves, will now and then be wrong. As an exercise, in diagram 22.6, should Black castle? If not, what should be play? Try to follow the 10-point program.

# UNIT 23   OPEN POSITIONS

*STRATEGY AND TACTICS*

The examples given in the previous unit were all at the decisive stage. Tactical calculations alone gave a clear-cut answer to the question 'What should I play?' Normally, stages four and five of the ten-point program would have more importance. In some cases, the choice of a move has to be made almost entirely on positional grounds, and there are few in which they do not carry some weight. In units 23 to 26, we shall look at a variety of types of position, classified for convenience into open, complicated, blocked, and simple positions, in the light of the program worked out in the previous unit. In each case, decide what you would play before reading the commentary.

A single move cannot of course stand alone. Nearly always, a move fits into a plan of campaign which may take several moves, or even the whole game, to bring to completion. If something unforeseen happens, a new plan may be needed; this kind of general thinking is often best done when it is the opponent's turn to move. Then you can work out your long-range strategy, without having to deal with the short-range tactical factors, and while your clock is not ticking.

Tactics consist of the specific operations, like threats and captures and combinations, that are employed to further strategic ends. Tactical play without a guiding plan all too easily degenerates into 'play from move to move'; position play without an eye for tactics can mean that one becomes too 'clever', or through incorrect execution spoils a basically good idea. Chess strategy, like politics, is 'the art of the possible'. The tactical interplay of the white and black forces determines what is possible, and what is not. This is why long-range thinking and accurate tactical calculation are no substitute for one another; a grandmaster may have a leaning in one direction or the other (a stylistic matter) but he will be very good at both.

*STRATEGY IN OPEN GAMES*

Cut-and-thrust play is definitely important in positions where the centre and many lines are open. This is because the pieces have great mobility in the absence of pawns, and readily come to grips with one another.

Nevertheless, strategy is still an important part of handling open positions. Even 'attack the enemy king down the h-file' is a strategy. Also, even when engaged on a ferocious attack, you have to think about the future (assuming you don't have a forced mate). It is necessary to think about the centre, the Q-side, and the endgame at all times. Sometimes positional factors will be relevant when you least expect them.

### THE NEED FOR PRECISION

In many situations, good positions and bad, there is a great temptation to play the first good move you think of. Sometimes, that will be all right, but many positions require the absolutely best move — or at least something better than the obvious one. After all, your opponent has probably seen the obvious move some time ago and has prepared something against it.

Diagram 23.1 was reached after the, not very masterly, sequence **1 d4 Nf6  2 Nf3 g6  3 c4 Bg7 4 e3 0-0  5 Be2 c5  6 0-0 Nc6 7 Nc3 cxd4  8 Nxd4 d6  9 Qc2? Bd7  10 a3 Rc8  11 b4 Ne5  12 Ne4 Nxe4  13 Qxe4 Nxc4  14 Bxc4 Rxc4  15 Qxb7.** What should Black play now?

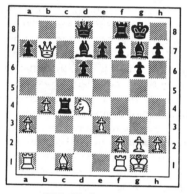

23.1 Black to move

Black works through the move-choice program. First, what did White's last move do? It re-established the balance of pawns, and threatened the a-pawn. On the other hand, it unguarded the d4 square and decentralized the queen.

What does White threaten? Just 16 Qxa7, but that could be serious, because then he would have connected passed pawns on the a- and b-files, a winning factor for the endgame.

What immediate threats do I (Black) have? For one thing, 15 . . . Bxd4 would lead to the win of a pawn temporarily; even 15 . . . Rxd4 might be worth looking into. Also 15 . . . e5, to drive off the knight, and 15 . . . Rc7, attacking the queen, come into consideration at this stage.

At step four, it is time for Black to think about long-range considerations. One has already been mentioned — he does not want to allow Qxa7 unless he can get a strong compensation in material or attack. On the other hand, the control of the c-file, the possession of the two bishops, and the vulnerable look of the white king certainly suggest that an attack may be 'on'. Also, the pin on the white knight may be made use of in some way.

If queens were exchanged, Black would have a lead in development and control of the open lines, but Black would also not mind the queens remaining on the board. So 15 . . . Qc7 (stage five now) might be good, but it loses time after 16 Qxc7; the exchange on c8 would be better because then the KR would come into play. So 15 . . . Qc8 is an idea, although it would have to be analysed carefully in case of 16 Qxa7. On the other hand, long-range considerations lead Black to reject 15 . . . Bxd4, because of the dark-square weaknesses that result (apart from the loss of the a-pawn). 15 . . . Rxd4 16 exd4 Bxd4 is also poor, because of 17 Ra2; the exchange cannot be regained.

At stage six, from the candidate moves we form a short-list of 15 . . . e5, 15 . . . Qc8 and (as a safe move in case the others are flawed) 15 . . . Rc7.

After 15 . . . Qc8 the exchange line 16 Qxc8 Rfxc8 is evidently advantageous to Black, although there is no obvious forced win. If instead 16 Qxa7 e5 would lead to play similar to 15 . . . e5, except that Nb5 is not a possible reply, and the white queen will find it hard to guard the K-side.

15 . . . e5 leads to four distinct variations, which should be analysed systematically: 16 Nb5, 16 Nb3, 16 Ne2, and 16 Nf3. While looking at these, also bear in mind any differences that would follow from the white queen being instead at a7 and the black queen at c8.

15 . . . e5 16 Nb5 is a sharp line. Black could then play 16 . . . Bc6 17 Qa6 Qg5 18 g3 Bf3 and would be bound to checkmate soon. However, 18 e4! turns the tables. Black would have to look for a different seventeenth move and the position would be obscure.

The other knight retreats are not so threatening. However, Black still faces the difficulty that his queen has to attack on the K-side black squares, whereas if it were on c8 it could come to g4 instead and so avoid White's e3-e4 resource.

Comparing the candidates, Black finds that he does not really trust 15 . . . e5 because the d-pawn could be weak in the end, whereas putting the white pieces offside by 15 . . . Qc8 16 Qxa7 e5 is very promising. The only problem is whether White might draw after 16 Qxc8, so Black takes another look at the ending and satisfies himself that he has good winning chances after 16 . . . Rfxc8 17 Bb2 e5 18 Nf3 Rc2 19 Rab1 Bb5 20 Rfc1 Kf8 21 Ne1 Rxc1 22 Rxc1 Rxc1 23 Bxc1 d5; with a symmetrical pawn structure and spatial advantage, the two bishops should be decisive in the end. So Black decides on 15 . . . Qc8, writing this on his score-sheet.

At stage nine, it occurs to Black to wonder what he would do if White just retreated the queen, e.g. by 16 Qd5 e5 17 Nf3. However, Black's pieces then become very active, as after 17 . . . Be6 18 Qxd6 Rd8 19 Qe7 Rd7 20 Qg5 Rg4 the white queen is lost. Finally, Black is satisfied that there are no swindles, and he plays 15 . . . Qc8!

For the record, White took up the gauntlet, only to regret it. After **16 Qxa7 e5 17 Ne2 Rc2 18 Ng3 f5 19 Qb6 f4 20 Ne4 Bc6** (diagram 23.2) Black had a mating attack.

Now 21 f3 Bxe4 22 fxe4 Qg4 23 Rf2 Rxf2 (23 . . . fxe3 24 Bxe3!) 24 Kxf2 fxe3+ 25 Kxe3 Bh6+ 26 Kd3 Qd1+ leads to mate, which is hardly surprising with the king so exposed.

23.2 Position after 20 ... Bc6

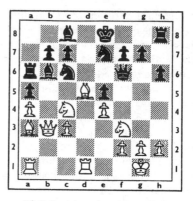

23.3 Position after 15 ... Ra6

White gave up without a fight: **21 Nxd6? Qg4 22 f3 (22 g3 f3) 22 ... Qxg2 mate**, thanks to the support of the Rc2.

## SACRIFICE – OR NOT?

Diagram 23.3 arose from an Evans Gambit as follows: **1 e4 e5 2 Nf3 Nc6 3 Bc4 Bc5 4 b4 Bxb4 5 c3 Ba5 6 d4 d6 7 Qb3 Qd7 8 dxe5 dxe5 9 0-0 Bb6 10 Rd1 Qe7 11 a4 a5 12 Bd5 h6?!** (White has sacrificed a pawn, in return for which he has a lead in development and has chances of attacking the black king in the centre) **13 Ba3 Qf6 14 Nbd2 Nge7 15 Nc4 Ra6.** Black hangs on to the pawn, at the cost of an awkward placement of this rook. What should White play? See diagram 23.3.

Black's move has protected b6 for the second time, so ruling out the move Nxb6 which White was planning. Black has no immediate tactical threats. He cannot even castle without returning the pawn,

because ... 0-0 is met by Bxc6 (and if ... Nxc6, then Bxf8). The weakest point in White's position is f2, because if White's KN moves, Black can take the f-pawn: even that would be no disaster, as White could attack down the f-file perhaps.

On the other hand, White has no good checks, and cannot make progress by any of the obvious exchanges. However, with both black rooks out of play, there ought to be some combinative ideas in the position: 16 Ncxe5 certainly comes into consideration.

From a positional point of view, White obviously stands well. He controls the open d-file and the a3–f8 diagonal, as well as lots of important squares in the centre. Only on the K-side is he a little thin on the ground. So he must look out for counter-play based, say, on the advance of the black g-pawn.

White can consider moves that improve the position of his rooks, e.g. 16 Rd3, 16 Rd2, or 16 Ra2. He could play one of these, manœuvre around to maintain his bind and wait for Black to make an error. However, rather than risk missing the tide, he should calculate the combinative idea first.

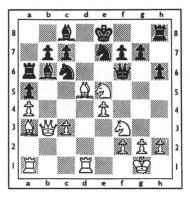

23.4 Position after 16 Nc3xe5

The main point of 16 Ncxe5 (diagram 23.4) is the variation 16 . . . Nxe5 17 Nxe5 Qxe5? 18 Bxf7+ Kf8 19 Rd8 mate. It is not hard to see that Black's only counter-chances lie in capturing on f2 at some point. If 16 . . . Be6 17 Bxe6 Nxe5? 18 Nxe5 Qxe6 19 Rd8+! Kxd8 20 Nxf7+ Kd7 21 Rd1+ etc. winning the black queen.

If 16 . . . Nxe5 17 Nxe5 Qxf2+? 18 Kh1 it is clear that Black has no more threats; so it is the Bb6 which must capture on f2. This leaves two lines to calculate, and White must get them right.

After 16 . . . Nxe5 17 Nxe5 Bxf2+ 18 Kh1 0-0 19 Bxf7+! (or 19 Nxf7 Kh7 20 e5) 19 . . . Kh7 (19 . . . Rxf7 20 Rd8+) 20 Bxe7 Qxe7 it is not really clear that White is winning. He has no material ad-

vantage yet; the black QR may come to f6 and create threats against White's back rank. It certainly does not seem that White's position is better than the one he started with (23.3).

(White must also consider 16 . . . Bxf2+ 17 Kh1 Rb6, but after 18 Qa2 that seems fine for White. The previous variation is the problem.)

Rather than use up all his time trying to improve on 19 Bxf7+, or to find clever wrinkles in the main line, White should go back and compare the waiting moves with the rooks. If the f2 square were guarded by one of the rooks, White's combination would be crushing. With the right preparation, he might be able to play it next move.

23.5 Position after 16 Rd2

16 Rd3 does not guard f2; 16 Ra2 might be met by 16 . . . Bg4 pinning the Nf3. So 16 Rd2 (23.5) looks like the move — what can Black play to avoid the sacrifice next move? 16 . . . 0-0 17 Bxc6, and 16 . . . Nxd5 17 exd5, and

16 . . . g5 17 Nfxe5 all win for
White, which leaves the choice between 16 . . . Be6 and 16 . . . Ba7.

After 16 Rd2 Be6 17 Rad1
White's position continues to improve (17 . . . Bg4 18 Ncxe5! Nxe5
19 Nxe5! Bxd1 20 Bxf7+).

16 . . . Ba7 (to revive the QR)
would be more consistent on Black's
part. Here, too, White has simple or
complicated ideas — he can play
17 Rad1 or 17 Ncxe5 Rb6 18 Qa2
and should win in either case.

So White writes down 16 Rd2
and has a last look around the
board.

At the last minute he sees that
16 . . . Bd7 (23.6) 17 Rad1 0-0
18 Bxc6 Bxc6 19 Ncxe5 is not particularly impressive. 17 Bxf7+ is also
superficially attractive, but after
17 . . . Qxf7 18 Rxd7 0-0! nothing
special is happening.

So White tries his other tactical
idea and it works. After 16 Rd2 Bd7
17 Ncxe5 Nxe5 (17 . . . Nxd7
18 Nxd7) 18 Nxe5 Qxe5 (18 . . .
Bxf2+ doesn't help) 19 Bxf7+ Kd8
20 Rad1 White regains his piece
with a strong attack. So all is well,
and after checking this variation,
White plays **16 Rd2!** and so denies
Black any real counter-play.

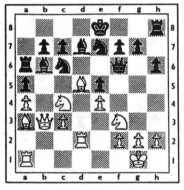

23.6 Position after 16 . . . Bd7

# UNIT 24   COMPLICATIONS

*ANALYSIS AND JUDGEMENT*

In many games, not just in open positions, the in-fighting between the pieces comes to a head. Sometimes there is no better course than to go in for tactical adventures which, however deeply one tries to analyse them, do not seem to lead to any definite advantage for one side or the other. Sometimes there is just too much to calculate — though in postal games that excuse is not really admissible.

Where shortage of time or the difficulty of the position is of this kind, the best analysis you can make of the complications may still leave you in doubt about which is the best move. In that case your positional judgement must be brought into play again — as well as pragmatic judgement that takes into account subjective factors like the time-pressure, and your estimate of the abilities of your opponent.

However, the more complicated the position is, the more you must be sure of your analysis, because one error in calculation can mean a blunder and a humiliating loss. To avoid oversights, at stage seven in the program, it is essential to perform the calculations systematically.

Take one candidate move at a time, and follow it as far as you can, reaching an assessment of the final position in the variation. Repeat this process with other sub-variations from the same candidate move, then move on to the next candidate move. In this way you build up what Soviet Grandmaster Kotov calls 'the analytical tree'. At the end (stage eight) you compare the assessments at the end of the branches and try to select the most favourable one.

It is no good repeating the calculation of one variation over and over again. This will probably result in your seeing fewer possibilities rather than more; you have to develop confidence in your ability to see things correctly the first time round. If, after all, you do make a mistake, either it won't matter because you reject that candidate move on other grounds, or you will pick up the error when you run your check at stage nine.

*CAN I WIN A PAWN?*

When you see a chance to win a pawn — especially a centre pawn — it is often vital to get the calculations right. If the opponent has blundered, then winning the pawn may set you on the road to victory; on the other hand, he may be setting you a trap. If there is any danger of an attack or complications following the pawn win, you cannot be too careful.

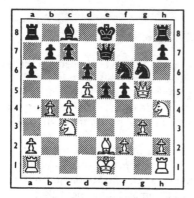

24.1 Position after 15 Qg5

Diagram 24.1 was reached by the unusual opening sequence **1 c4 g6 2 Nc3 Bg7 3 d4 d6 4 e4 e5 5 d5 Nd7 6 Be3 Bh6!?** (to exchange the bad bishop) **7 Qd2 Bxe3 8 Qxe3 a6** (preparing . . . b5 in case White castles Q-side) **9 b4 f5 10 exf5 gxf5 11 Nf3 Ngf6 12 Be2 Qe7 13 g3 Nf8 14 Nh4 Ng6 15 Qg5.** Before reading further, decide what you would play here; take your time about it.

Running through the program, the first things that Black noticed were these. White threatens to win a pawn, either by 16 Nxg6 or simply by 16 Nxf5. Black might be able to exploit White's last move by 15 . . . Nxd5 because the white queen is temporarily unprotected (16 Qxe7+ Ndxe7 or 16 Nxd5? Qxg5). The candidate moves are 15 . . . Nxh4, 15 . . . Ng8, 15 . . . Ne4, and 15 . . . Nxd5!? as a result of the preliminary review of tactical possibilities.

The positional factor that stands out most is that Black has the preferable pawn structure. White's b4 and g3 moves have weakened his position, whereas Black has a potentially mobile central majority. Black's king position is less secure than White's, though, so that after the quiet continuation 15 . . . Nxh4 16 Qxh4 White's game is freer and Black would have to be careful; nevertheless, this line is a stand-by if the alternatives are too risky.

On the other hand, there is a strong positional objection to 15 . . . Ne4. After 16 Qxe7+ Kxe7 (16 . . . Nxe7 allows a nasty bishop check) 17 Nxg6+ hxg6 18 Nxe4 fxe4 19 Kd2 Black has a doubled e-pawn (the one on e4 is very weak) White would eventually get a strong passed h-pawn. So 15 . . . Ne4 has to be rejected.

The task now is to analyse 15 . . . Nxd5. If it turns out to be no good, 15 . . . Nxh4 will have to be played, or possibly 15 . . . Ng8.

It does not take long to see that 15 . . . Nxd5 16 Qxe7+ Ndxe7 is a safe extra pawn for Black, and that 16 Nxd5 and 16 Nxg6 are refuted by 16 . . . Qxg5. Similarly 16 Qd2 Nxc3 is very pleasant for Black. Now there is a temptation for Black to snap the d-pawn off without further thought.

But look at the position after 15 . . . Nxd5 from White's point of view. If he moves his queen to h5 or h6, pinning the black h-pawn, he will be threatening both Nxg6 and Nxd5. So Black must analyse these.

16 Qh6 can be quickly ruled out after 16 . . . Nxc3. If then 17 Nxg6 Qf6 pins the white knight, emerging a pawn ahead, while 17 Bh5 Qf6 (also pro-

tecting the rook) 18 Nxg6 hxg6 19 Bxg6+ Ke7 or 18 Bxg6+ hxg6
19 Qxg6+ Qxg6 20 Nxg6 Rg8 result in Black winning a piece.

So this leaves 15 . . . Nxd5 16 Qh5! to be calculated.

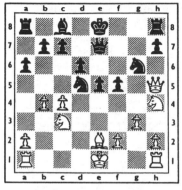

24.2 Position after 16 Qh5!

It does not take long to see that after this move 16 . . . Nxc3 just loses to 17 Nxg6 Qf7 18 Nxh8 (the bishop guards the queen), while protecting g6 allows Nxd5. So is it time to abandon the idea of winning a pawn, and to start comparing the merits of 15 . . . Nxh4 and 15 . . . Ng8. No, not yet.

One good rule of thumb in calculation is to look for 'desperado' moves with attacked pieces. Since the Ng6 cannot move, look at the other moves available to the Nd5. It can attack the white queen from f6 or f4, so these retreats are worth calculating.

The natural move is 16 . . . Nf6, but it should not take long to see that White wins a piece by 17 Nxg6 Nxh5 18 Nxe7 (18 . . . Nf6 19 Nxc8). The attempt to improve upon this by 17 . . . Qf7 is refuted by 18 Nxh8 Qxh5 19 Bxh5+ Nxh5 20 Nd5 etc. This leaves the most

improbable move of all to be considered.

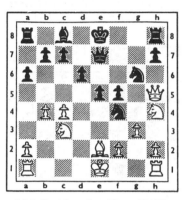

24.3 Position after 16 . . . Ndf4!

After 15 . . . Nxd5 16 Qh5 Ndf4! the subtle difference is that 17 Nxg6 can be met by 17 . . . Nxg6 (17 gxf4 Qxh4 is clearly harmless). Apart from 17 Nxg6 candidate moves for White are 17 Nd5, 17 Qh6, and 17 Nxf5 (a desperado for White). Of these 17 Qh6 can be written off quickly in view of 17 . . . Nxh4 18 gxf4 Ng2+ or 17 gxh4 Be6.

17 Nxg6 Nxg6 18 Nd5 looks at first as if it gives White compensation for the pawn: 18 . . . Qd8 19 Qh6! c6 (19 . . . Be6! is more obscure) 20 Qg7 etc. However, 18 . . . Qf7 is safe enough. If then 19 Qh6 Be6 (or 19 . . . c6!? 20 Nb6 Rb8) 20 Bh5 0-0-0 defends everything, while after 19 Qg5 Be6 (19 . . . h6? 20 Nxc7+!) 20 Nf6+ Kf8 21 Nh5 (or 21 Bh5? Kg7) 21 . . . h6 White is beaten off.

The systematic analysis continues with 17 Nd5. After 17 . . . Nxh5 (17 . . . Nxd5?? 18 Nxg6) 18 Nxe7 Nxe7 (not 18 . . . Kxe7 19 Nxf5+!) Black keeps his extra pawn for the endgame.

The last try for White is 17 Nxf5, trying to get his pawn back. This move sets off a new round of complications.

24.4 Position after 17 Nxf5

Considering that Black has to see all this in his head before playing his fifteenth move, the position is not easy (easier in a postal game). Black has to discipline himself to ask once more what the candidate moves are. They appear to be 17 . . . Bxf5, 17 . . . Nxh5, and (maybe) 17 . . . Qf7. So they must be calculated.

After 17 . . . Bxf5 White has two possibilities: 18 Qxf5 and 18 gxf4. In either case the follow-up move 19 Nd5 looks troublesome. So it is natural to see whether the alternatives offer a simpler solution.

If Black (from diagram 24.4) plays 17 . . . Nxh5 18 Nxe7 Kxe7 (not 18 . . . Nxe7 19 Bxh5+

followed by 0-0 and f2-f4) 19 Nd5+ Kd8 20 Bxh5 Rf8 the ending is messy and quite likely drawn with best play. This will be worth comparing with the outcome of 15 . . . Ng8 and 15 . . . Nxh4 (especially considering the pitfalls for White along the way) but clearly Black cannot shirk the analysis of 17 . . . Bxf5 after all!

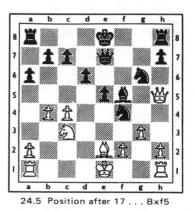

24.5 Position after 17 . . . Bxf5

After 18 Qxf5 Black was at first dismayed to see that 18 . . . Nxe2 did not lead to anything clear, either after recapture or after 19 Nd5 (e.g. 19 . . . Nxg3+ 20 fxg3! Qf7 21 Qxf7+ Kxf7 22 0-0+).

However the intermediate move 18 Qxf5 Rf8! makes a big difference. With f6 protected and the white queen driven back, Black has less to fear from the white knight. Next move he can take the bishop on e2 confident that he has some positional advantage, thanks to his control of the half-open f-file and his better pawns; the king will be safe after the exchange of queens (or after Q-side castling).

This leaves 18 gxf4 to be analysed. Here the threats are 19 Qxf5 and 19 Nd5, with 18 . . . Be6 ruled out because of the fork by 19 f5.

24.6 Position after 18 gxf4

Black's candidate moves are 18 . . . Qf7 and 18 . . . Rf8.

After 18 . . . Qf7 the threat of . . . Nxf4 brings matters to a crisis. 19 fxe5 Nxe5  20 Qxf7+ Kxf7 (e.g. 21 Nd5 Rac8  22 Ne3? Be4), the light-square weaknesses are finally telling against White. Black has good winning chances in the ending.

White's other plausible reply to 18 . . . Qf7 is 19 Nd5, but 19 . . . 0-0-0 should be strong in reply. The white king is then the more exposed of the two.

After 18 . . . Qf7  19 Nd5 a blunder would be 19 . . . Nxf4? because of 20 Nxc7+ exploiting the pin on the queen, while 19  . . exf4 is suspect on account of 20 Nxc7+ Qxc7 21 Qxf5 Rf8 22 Qe6+. Is Black going to fall at the last hurdle?

Black needs to guard c7, since his queen is temporarily overloaded (having to guard f5 too). 19 . . . Rc8 is passive, but revives the threat to the f-pawn. Since the endgames are unpalatable for White, he might then try  20 fxe5 Nxe5  21 Nf6+ Ke7  22 Nd5+ Kd7  23 Nf6+ Ke6 24 Nd5 c6 (25 f4 Ng6). This is not an exhaustive analysis, but sample variations do suggest that Black has the advantage. There are more defenders than attackers in the action zone; White's rooks and bishop cannot do much.

Black should also look at 18 . . . Rf8, planning to meet 19 fxe5? by 19 . . . Qxe5 and most other moves by Q-side castling. White would play 19 Nd5 Qd7  20 fxe5 dxe5 21 Rd1 which could prove awkward. So it finally looks as if the main line after 15 . . . Nxd5 runs 16 Qh5! Ndf4!  17 Nxf5! Bxf5!  18 gxf4! Qf7!  19 Nd5! Rc8!  20 fxe5 Nxe5... Material is level, but the long-term factors are in Black's favour, which should be good enough thanks to his lead in development.

Analysis of the alternative fifteenth moves, 15 . . . Nxh5 and 15 . . . Ng8, show that they do not really put up much of a struggle for the initiative. Black surely cannot hope for more than equality with either of those moves. However, if 15 . . . Nxd5 had not led to an advantage, Black would have had to look into them in greater depth.

In view of the complications, Black must make his stage nine check especially carefully — if the time is left on the clock. At least he should check as far as 17 . . . Bxf5 to make sure that the correct moves are firmly fixed in his mind.

Then he can play **15 . . . Nxd5.**
(In the actual game, White replied
**16 Qxe7+** and Black duly won.
White did not see **16 Qh5** at all!)

This may seem like a lot of hard

work, just to play a combination
which does not even win a pawn if
White is careful. On the other hand,
if Black chickens out of . . . Nxd5,
he cannot hope to get much of a
position. 'There is a tide . . .'

### EXERCISES

In 24.7 White has sacrificed the
exchange for a pawn. How should he
continue?

you do it in your head and get it all
right.

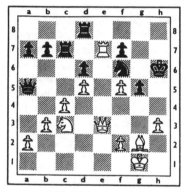

24.7 White to move

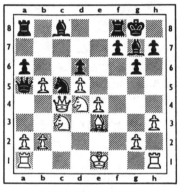

24.8 Black to move

Diagram 24.8 involves a long
piece of calculation. Full marks if

White has just played Qd3-c4.
Black would like to reply 1 . . . Nxe4.
Is this sound?

# UNIT 25   CLOSED POSITIONS

## *BLOCKED OR TENSE STRUCTURE?*

Many middle-game positions are closed positions, in the sense that there are few (maybe no) open or half-open files, and few open diagonals. The pawn structure restricts the action of the pieces, so that the focus of the struggle is positional.

Closed positions may be of two kinds. In blocked positions, rigid pawn chains have come into being and it is hard to see how, short of a piece sacrifice, the position can be opened up. There are also closed structures, however, in which there is tension in the centre (and maybe on the wings too) as the white pawns and black pawns come to grips. Tense structures may persist for a while, but eventually either they become blocked, or pawn exchanges open them up. In this unit we shall examine one position of each type.

## *A BLOCKED POSITION*

Diagram 25.1 shows a position in which Black has erected a barricade on the white squares. How is White to break it down? Black has long-term chances of Q-side attack because White wrongly castled there (the position arose by **1 e4 g6 2 d4 Bg7  3 Nc3 c6  4 f4 d5  5 e5 h5  6 Nf3 Nh6  7 Be3 Bg4  8 Be2 e6  9 Qd2 Nd7  10 0-0-0? b5 11 h3 Bxf3  12 Bxf3 h4** — to fix the K-side pawns — **13 Bf2**). Put yourself in Black's shoes.

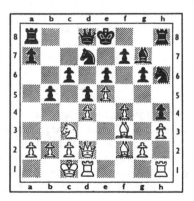

25.1 Position after 13 Bf2

This position is very different from the ones we looked at in the three previous units, but the ten-point program is still applicable. There is little going on tactically; so the positional stages (five and six) of the program carry more weight.

White's latest move, Be3-f2, is not particularly threatening. Black notes that Qe1 and/or g3 at some stage is probably White's intention, but it can hardly be called a threat. As long as Black does not castle K-side, g3 will not lead to much for White, who will incur an isolated h-pawn that would be a liability in the ending. On the other hand, Black has no immediate threats either.

So Black concentrates on his positional assessment. The two bishops, which would be a major advantage for White in an open position, are here a liability. The dark-squared bishop, impeded by its own central pawns, is particularly bad. Black's bad white-squared bishop has been wisely exchanged.

In blocked positions, it can often be good to have two knights. This is especially true here, because each one can reach a promising spot near the centre: the KN goes to f5, and the QN to c4, via b6. The white knight cannot reach a comparable square.

As already hinted, the position of the kings also favours Black. His is in the centre, which is a good thing in this case because it means that it is virtually inaccessible to the white pieces. Black's twelfth move, which prevented any g4+f5 pawn advance, was important in guaranteeing this security.

White's king, on the other hand, is vulnerable to an attack from advancing black pawns in conjunction with the knight at c4, and from the QR and Q also. Black might even be able to use his bishop in the attack — because it is a potentially good bishop, only the two rook's pawns out of eight standing on its own colour.

On the basis of this preliminary assessment, Black can be confident that he possesses a positional advantage, and that he ought to be looking for the best way to build up his attack. A whole string of moves might come into consideration, e.g. . . . Nf5, . . . Nb6, . . . a5, . . . Qa5, . . . b4, . . . Bf8. On what grounds is he to choose between them?

One good rule is to maintain flexibility until the decisive moment of the attack. All the pawn moves and . . . Qa5 are too committal, because they show Black's hand too early to the defender and also rule out alternative methods of attack. It is better to play a move that you definitely want to play sooner or later, and see how White reacts. Also . . . Nf5 can be set aside for a while because it does not contribute to the Q-side attack, and is not necessary at least until White threatens to recapture on g3 with his knight.

So the main candidate moves are 13 . . . Nb6 and 13 . . . Bf8. Black should now turn to the analysis of variations arising from these moves.

Analysing attacking lines in detail at this stage is quite futile, because White has not shown how he will deploy his forces. Quite likely each of the candidate moves would lead quite shortly to the same position as the other. So the choice between them can be made solely on defensive considerations.

Were White to launch a desperation attack after . . . Bg7-f8, with the black knight away on b6 or c4, could it do much damage? Probably not, because the build up (g4, Bxg3, h4, h5) takes a lot of time and forces no serious weakness near the black king. Just the same it is better to move the bishop first, because we know it is doing little good where it is, whereas the knight on d7 could be used to hit back with . . . c5 or . . . f6 if White ever weakened his centre by f5. So **13 . . . Bf8** is Black's choice, and after a last look round, he plays the move.

The master game that we are following continued **14 Ne2 Nf5 15 Kb1 Nb6 16 Bg4 Nc4 17 Qe1?** (shuts out the Bf2 from the Q-side) **17 . . . a5 18 Bxf5 gxf5 19 Ng1?** (another piece away from the war zone) **19 . . . Bb4 20 Qe2?** (better 20 c3 despite . . . Be7 and subsequently . . . b4) **20 . . . a4 21 Nf3.**

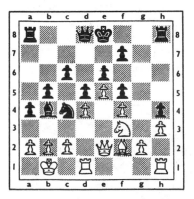

25.2 Position after 21 Nf3

It is clear by now that Black made the correct assessment and move choice at move 13. He has built up a strong attack, and White's disorganized defence has helped that attack to reach decisive proportions. It is now time for Black to look for the tactical breakthrough, and the obvious target is the b2 square. Try to work it out for yourself. The solution is in the back of the book.

## CENTRAL TENSION

Diagram 25.3 arose by **1 c4 g6 2 Nc3 Bg7 3 g3 d6 4 Bg2 c6 5 e4!? e5 6 Nge2 Be6 7 d3 Qd7 8 h3?** (better 8 0-0 despite 8 . . . Bh3) **8 . . . Ne7 9 Qa4 Na6 10 b4 0-0 11 a3 Nc7 12 Bd2.** The position is closed at the moment, but there is a lot of latent energy in the centre this time.

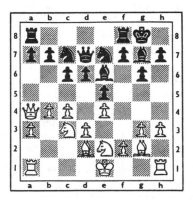

25.3 Position after 12 Bd2

Black has reached the stage where all his pieces apart from the rooks are fairly well placed, and he needs to decide on his plan. This involves making an overall positional assessment, using the ten-point program.

White has no immediate threats. His last move was a developing move, but not a very aggressive one. It defended the Nc3, and prepares either Q-side castling (unlikely) or

Rc1 or Rd1. Certainly White has no initiative, and the fact that he cannot castle K-side without losing his h-pawn suggests that any short-term tactical opportunities should be Black's.

Black has no immediate forcing moves. What he would like to do is open central lines to attack the white king before he can castle. But to do this he must advance at least one pawn to increase the tension in the centre and bring about favourable exchanges leading to the opening of attacking lines.

The obvious move for this purpose would be 12 . . . d5, were it not that the white queen stands at a4. After 12 . . . d5 White can play 13 cxd5 cxd5 14 Qxd7 Bxd7 15 exd5 winning a pawn, so Black must find something more subtle.

Black could also challenge the centre by . . . f5. The trouble with that is that neither . . . f4 nor . . . fxe4 (met by Nxe4) would be much of a threat. So, whichever pawn thrust Black decides to go for, he will need to prepare it in some way. Ideally he would like to use his rooks, but 12 . . . Rad8 would allow 13 Qxa7. After 12 . . . Rfd8 13 Rc1 Black could play 13 . . . d5 but the exchange of queens after 14 cxd5 and 15 Qxd7 would diminish the pressure and allow White to castle. It looks as if the queen should be driven from a4.

Black can drive the queen off by 12 . . . b5 (or 12 . . . Rfd8 13 Rc1 b5) but after 13 cxb5 cxb5 14 Qd1 d5 15 exd5 Ncxd5 16 Ne4 White gets counter-play as

Black has weakened his Q-side. Evidently Black would prefer to recapture on b5 with the a-pawn, which suggests that 12 . . . a6 is a candidate move.

Black compared the two candidates, 12 . . . Rfd8 and 12 . . . a6, and decided to play the rook move first because it is less committal than a pawn move. If White replied with some unexpected move, he might not need to play . . . a6 after all.

After checking for blunders, Black played 12 . . . Rfd8 and the game went on 13 Rc1 a6 14 Qc2 b5 15 Nd1. White refused to open the a-file for the black Ra8. Instead he tried to keep a pawn at c4, to make . . . d5 as hard as possible to force.

25.4 Position after 15 Nd1

It was clear to Black that the game was beginning to take tactical shape. Once he played . . . d5 White would be at a crisis. Unfortunately 15 . . . d5 was out of the question, because of 16 cxd5 cxd5 17 Qxc7, but this variation suggested the natural move — 15 . . . Rac8 which, after the usual precautions, Black played.

After **15 . . . Rac8 16 Ne3 d5** Black threatened to capture twice on c4 and try to cash in on his control of the d-file; alternatively, he could increase the central tension to breaking point by a subsequent . . . f5. So White tried to keep the position closed by **17 exd5 cxd5 18 c5.**

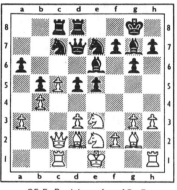

25.5 Position after 18 c5

In this way, White kept the d-file closed and obtained a protected passed pawn on the c-file. However, this transformation of the pawn structure has been foreseen by Black. Since White is still unable to castle, the central pawn majority, giving chances of a breakthrough in a few moves, seemed to Black to outweigh the passed white c-pawn. This was especially so because, with his next move **18 . . . Nc6** Black was able to make the ideal blockade of the pawn, increasing the scope of the knight and rendering White's doubled

major pieces on the c-file quite ineffective.

White is now threatened with . . . f5, followed by a . . . d4, . . . e4, or . . . f4 line-opening advance in due course, and there is little hope of counter-play. White tried **19 g4!?** (probably hoping to castle) but after **19 . . . f5 20 gxf5 gxf5 21 f4** (real desperation) the scene was set for the final attack.

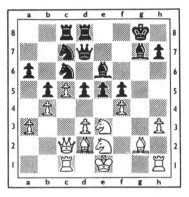

25.6 Position after 21 f4

Black will have good chances with practically any plausible move, but naturally he wants to find the best one. He has to work out what are the most dangerous threats he can create.

Capturing on f4 is clearly what White wants, then the knight from e2 comes into the game. 21 . . . e4, threatening 22 . . . d4 (and if 22 dxe4 fxe4!), looks promising, but why not 21 . . . d4 right away? They may come to the same thing in fact.

After **21 . . . d4** White has to find squares for his retreating minor pieces: **22 Ne1 e4 23 Kd1 Qf7** (threatening . . . Bb3) **24 Rb1 Kh8** (just a precaution, and to show White he has no good moves) **25 Nfg3 Nd5** (this threatens . . . Ne3+) **26 dxe4** (White can no longer prevent lines opening) **26 . . . d3!** **27 Qxe3 Nc3+** and White has to resign.

Note how Black always kept the central pawn situation fluid, so that White could not set up a permanent blockade. With the king as a target, Black knew that eventually he would be able to strike a decisive blow with his pieces. White on the other hand tried to keep the position closed, using his pawns as cover for the king.

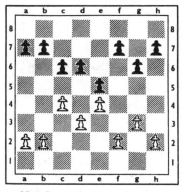

25.7 Pawn structure after 7 d3

Note also that the course of the middle-game struggle was within limits laid down by the pawn structure that arose within the first ten moves. In fact the most important consideration was determined at move 5. With the pawn structure in the centre (see diagram 25.7) including a backward white d-pawn, Black knew that an eventual . . . d5 would cause White difficulties (lest the file be opened against that pawn). After this disadvantage was exacerbated by move eight, compromising the king, White's game was already strategically lost.

The moral is that natural-looking moves in the opening — especially pawn moves — can often have far-reaching consequences. You cannot retract pawns; so damage done by casual advances like 5 e4 and 8 h3 can be permanent.

# UNIT 26   SIMPLE POSITIONS

*LATE MIDDLE-GAMES*

When only about three pieces remain on each side, the position may be not really a true middle-game but not an ending either. The kings can sometimes begin to play an active role, but only cautiously. If neither player has established much of an advantage, after maybe thirty moves play, there is often a temptation to agree a draw rather than suffer the inconvenience of arranging a second session of play.

Yet these 'simple' positions often conceal interesting ideas, and trivial advantages can sometimes be nursed to victory. The extra half-points earned can be vital in winning matches or tournaments, or in getting an improved ELO rating.

Some grandmasters — e.g. Rubinstein, Capablanca, Ulf Andersson — are renowned for their ability to 'make something out of nothing' in simple positions. How do they do it?

In part, their success here depends on their having great patience and determination to win, which manifests itself all the more at the stage when their opponents, confident of having reached a drawish position, start to relax. The great players of simple positions actually enjoy what bores many others.

A player with a fine strategic 'eye' can appreciate subtle points about a particular position, and of course these matter more in the so-called simple positions. There are not too many pieces left to complicate the game, and distract it from the pure positional line. A primarily attacking player, on the other hand, may find it hard to get his bearings.

*RUBINSTEIN IN ACTION*

Diagram 26.1 was reached by Rubinstein against Dr Tarrasch, after moves 1 c4 c5 2 Nf3 Nf6 3 d4 cxd4 4 Nxd4 d5 5 cxd5 Nxd5 6 e4 Nf6 7 Nc3 e5 8 Ndb5 Qxd1+ 9 Kxd1 Na6 10 f3 Bc5 11 Na4 Be7 12 Be3 Bd7 13 Rc1 0-0 14 a3 Rfd8 15 Ke1 Ne8 16 Be2 Nd6 17 Nac3 Nxb5 18 Nxb5 b6. Black was wrong to exchange queens, although it was tempting to prevent White castling, because

he has been on the defensive ever since; his last move was necessary to save the a-pawn. See diagram 26.1.

What would you play here? How would you assess the position?

Rubinstein realized that his knight on b5 was very strong and rejected the good tactical continuation 19 Nxa7!? Rxa7 20 Bxb6 Rda8 21 Bxa7, preferring to increase his bind by ruling out . . . Nc5.

26.1 Position after 18 . . . b6

Rubinstein prevented this by **19 b4!** and the game continued **19 . . . Be6  20 Kf2 Rd7  21 Rhd1 Rxd1** (21 . . . Rad8  22 Rxd7 Rxd7 23 Rc8+ Bd8  24 Nxa7) **22 Rxd1 Kf6** reaching diagram 26.2.

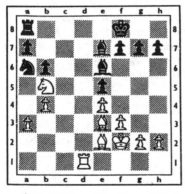

26.2 Position after 22 . . . Kf6

Superficial assessment might suggest that this position is drawish. Material is exactly level, and the pawn structure is symmetrical. But various factors are in White's favour.

The knight on b5 ties down the black rook to the defence of the a-pawn, and also makes it hard for

the black knight to get into play. If Black ever gives up a bishop for the knight, then White would obtain the two bishops — a big advantage in an open endgame.

White needs to induce a second weakness in the enemy position. The ultimate object is to set up a passed pawn on the K-side; the black e-pawn is a likely target. How to attack it?

White can play the manœuvre Be3-c1-b2 to attack the pawn, but then . . . f6 will defend it. So White needs to attack it a second time with the f-pawn, and in such a way that . . . e5xf4 can be met by g3xf4 so obtaining a central pawn majority. This majority would give White the initiative and chances of getting a strong passed pawn.

Rubinstein therefore began his assault on the centre with **23 g3! Ke8  24 f4!** Black now had to face the unpleasant choice between allowing White the central majority, or else having his e-pawn weakened.

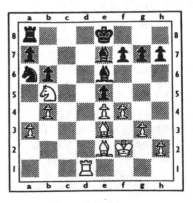

26.3 Position after 24 f4!

Tarrasch played **24 . . . f6** and Rubinstein continued logically with **25 fxe5 fxe5 26 Bc1 Bc8 27 Bb2 Bf6 28 Nd6+ Ke7 29 Nc4!** (avoiding the trap 29 Nxc8+ Rxc8 30 Bxa6 Rc2+ and 31 . . . Rxb2 equalizing) **29 . . . Ke6.** Apparently Tarrasch has succeeded in guarding his e-pawn.

26.4 Position after 29 . . . Ke6

As several black pieces are off-side, it is natural for White to look for a combination to break down the resistance. Checks like 30 Rd6 and 30 Bg4 do not lead to anything clear-cut, but perhaps they can be put together in a more powerful way.

Rubinstein played **30 Nxe5!**, winning the valuable centre pawn (and the game in a few more moves). The point is that after 30 . . . Bxe5 White plays 31 Bc4+ Kf6 32 Rd6+ and the black king can no longer defend e5. Thus a correct plan was carried through logically.

## MAINTAINING UNCERTAINTY

In many positions with diminished material, one or other of the players will be seeking clarification into a true endgame. The other may find it in his best interests to keep pieces on. In that way some middle-game features persist and consequently the uncertainty that remains keeps up psychological pressure on the opponent.

26.5 Position after . . . Rxe7

In this position, the queens have just been exchanged on e7. White is a pawn down, but as that is just a doubled e-pawn he has nothing immediate to fear.

Both sides have several weak pawns; so the activity of the pieces is going to be important. White naturally starts by seizing the open file: 1 Ra1. The game continued 1 . . . Rb7 2 Ra8 Nf6 3 Ra6. (White avoids 3 Rxf8+ Kxf8 4 Nxd6 Rd7.) Now Black could not allow the rook to end up on d6, so he defended with 3 . . . Rd8, reaching diagram 26.6.

White had a difficult decision to make here. On the one hand, he liked the look of 4 Nxd6, but on the

26.6 Position after 3 . . . Rd8

other this was probably what Black was hoping for. Waiting tactics might be appropriate.

White decided that he would have to analyse the endings resulting from 4 Nxd6 in detail. Play might continue 4 . . . Rbd7 5 Nf5 Nxd5 (not 5 . . . Rxd5? 6 Ne7+) and now the choice would be between 6 Rxd5 and 6 Ra5.

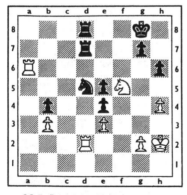

26.7 Position after 5 . . . Nxd5

6 Rxd5 Rxd5 7 Ne7+ Kf7 8 Nxd5 Rxd5 9 Rb6 Rd3 10 Rxb4 Rxe3 certainly did not seem an ending worth exchanging off for. Black

might even have slight winning chances.

6 Ra5 would threaten 7 Rxd5 etc., but Black would not allow that or give White chances like 6 . . . Nf6 7 Rxd7 Rxd7 8 Rb5 Rd3 9 Rb7. He could simply play 6 . . . Kf7 keeping his extra pawn a while longer. So 4 Nxd6 seemed to be a red herring.

Going back to 26.6, White looked at 4 Rxd6. Then Black would win by 4 . . . Rxd6 5 Nxd6 Rd7 6 Nf5 g6! 7 Nxh6+ Kg7 trapping the knight.

White started to look for a waiting move. He had the possibility of moving his king towards the centre. What would Black do then? Did he have a hidden threat?

Possibly Black would have a way of forcing simplification after all — by playing . . . Rb5 he would threaten the white d-pawn a second time, so forcing White to capture on d6 and go into an ending.

White calculated the variation 4 Kg3 Rb5 5 Rxd6 Rxd6 6 Nxd6 Rxd5 7 Rxd5 Nxd5 8 Nxe4 Nxe3 and did not like it much. Then he saw that if his king were on g1 instead of g3, he would have a resource: 7 Nxe4! (instead of Rxd5) 7 . . . Rxd2 (7 . . . Nxe4? 8 Rxd5) 8 Nxd2 and the knight ending is plainly drawn. With the king on g3, Black would of course refute this little combination by 7 . . . Nxe4 check.

So White had found a candidate move, 4 Kg1. As the draw after 4 . . . Rb5 etc. was much clearer than the ending following 4 Nxd6 and

6 Rxd5, White need not fear Black forcing the issue. However, could Black benefit from the continued middle-game?

If Black did nothing but move his king, then the white king would eventually reach e2. Then, with the e3 pawn guarded, he would be able to draw the ending, e.g. 4 . . . Kh7 5 Rxd6!? Rxd6 6 Nxd6 Rd7 7 Nc4 Rxd5 8 Rxd5 Nxd5 9 Kf2! and 10 Nxe5. Finally, 4 . . . Rbd7 would lose the b-pawn after 5 Rb6.

So White played 4 Kg1!, confident that this move was his best line if he wanted a draw. What is more, it gave him chances of winning if Black did not force the ending soon. Black's reply 4 . . . Kf8 showed White that things were going well, so he calmly played 5 Kf2 reaching 26.8.

26.8 Position after 5 Kf2

White was not afraid of 5 . . . Ng4+ because he could always repeat moves by 6 Kg3 etc. Another plausible continuation, 5 . . . Ne8, could even lead to a K-side attack for White after 6 g4. Black's best move would be 5 . . . Kg8 or 5 . . .

Rb5 but White was satisfied that there was nothing to fear from these.

Black in fact blundered by 5 . . . Ke7 into a trap that White had seen when he chose 4 Kg1. White now wins the exchange.

White played 6 Na5, threatening both the Rb7 and the fork on c6. Black replied 6 . . . Rdd7 7 Nxb7 Rxb7 8 Ra5 (to liberate the other rook) 8 . . . Nd7 but White refused to be driven into passivity. After 9 Rxa2 Nc5 10 Ra7 Rxa7 11 Rxa7+ Kf6 12 Ke2 Nxb3 13 Rd7 he set up a strong passed pawn. The final moves were 13 . . . Nc1+ 14 Kd2 Nd3 15 Rxd6+ Kf7 16 Rd7+ Kf6 17 Rb7 and Black resigned. He could have fought on longer, but zugzwang could not be far off: 17 . . . Kg6 18 d6 Kf6 19 Rxg7! Kxg7 20 d7 is a sample of what he has to avoid.

The waiting tactics adopted by White in this game are often appropriate in simple positions. Where the 'obvious' continuation leads to a clear draw, it is always worth looking for a way to improve the king's position, or to improve your pawn structure in some small way, without changing the main features of the situation. Of course you have to be sure that your opponent cannot seize the initiative from you!

*EXAMPLES FOR STUDY*

We conclude with a couple of examples for you to consider. In each case White has some advantage, but not enough to force a win. How

## Simple positions

should he continue? The answers are at the back of the book.

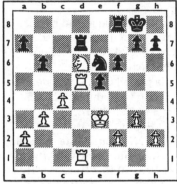

26.9 White to move        26.10 White to move

# VII. Endgames

## UNIT 27   GUIDELINES

### AIMS IN THE ENDING

Your long-term plan in most endings will be to create a passed pawn, advance it and queen it. If there is no hope of doing this, you must prevent your opponent from making a new queen and gradually exchange off the remaining pawns until a draw is inevitable. Checkmate can occur in an ending, but because few pieces remain it is unlikely until the new queen is on the board.

The ending arises after piece exchanges have brought the players down to just one or two pieces each, besides the kings. However, because of the huge number of possible positions, books on the endings can deal only with very simplified positions — usually with just one piece and no more than three pawns each. For practical purposes the club player should ignore these technical treatises and instead concentrate on learning the basic principles of endgames.

When you reach an ending, it is usually a good idea to get clear in your mind right away whether you are trying to win or only to draw the position. This is because the ending is the time when you can least afford risky or over-optimistic play.

When assessing an endgame position you should look first at the material situation. Usually it is the player who has extra material (especially pawns) who has the chances of winning. As a rule only a passed pawn (or preferably connected passed pawns) is a substitute for material advantage in the ending — all this because promoting pawns is the main business of endings.

The pieces you do have left have two jobs to do in the ending — to support your own pawns and to blockade (or capture) enemy pawns. The king, now he need not fear mate, is needed in the centre, or at the main scene of action; more about him in the next unit. The presence of other pieces lends a specific character to the ending, because each type of piece has its own way of dealing with pawns.

### ROOK ENDINGS

Rook endings are probably the kind you will meet most often. The advantage of an extra pawn is often hard or impossible to turn into a win with best play in rook endings, so it is the kind a defender will usually steer for. The factors determining whether a win is possible are: the number and situation of the pawns, relative position of the rooks to any passed pawns or weak pawns, and the placement of the kings.

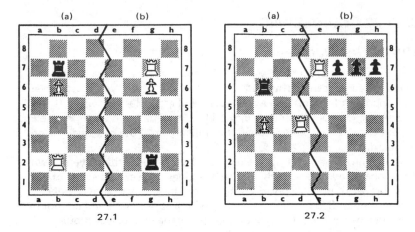

27.1                                        27.2

In 27.1(a), the white rook is well placed behind its passed pawn, supporting the advance, and the black rook is a passive blockader; if the white king can reach c6 it is all up with Black. In 27.1(b) the situation of the rooks is reversed; as the passed pawn advances, the white rook is devalued. This is a much harder position to win.

So rooks belong behind passed pawns — your own, to push them, and your opponent's, to attack them and tie his rook down. If you cannot get behind your passed pawn, a lateral defence (as in 27.2(a)) is the next best thing. Your pawn cannot advance but the rook is still quite active.

In the absence of passed pawns, you should try to infiltrate your opponent's ranks and attack his pawns from behind or from the side, as with the 'rook on the seventh rank' in 27.2(b). A rook on the seventh often keeps the enemy king out of play for some time.

Assuming both sides castled K-side, you have the best chances of winning if your passed pawn is well over on the Q-side. The following example shows the basic plan; note that the game is finally decided by the white king on the K-side after the black king is decoyed away.

See diagram 27.3.

1 Ra4! (behind the passer) 1 ... Kf6 2 Kf3 Ke5 (bars the way to b5) 3 Ke3 h5 4 Kd3 Kd5 5 Kc3 Kc5 6 Ra2! White throws the obligation to move on to his opponent at a time when Black has only moves that harm his cause. This technique, known as *zugzwang*, is common in endgames, and we shall see it again soon.

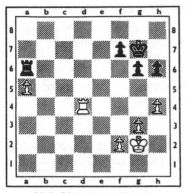

27.3 Distant passed pawn

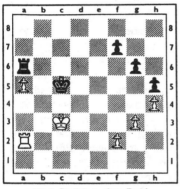

27.4 Position after Ra2!

If Black moves his rook, White plays the pawn on to a6 and Black has to concede ground to the white king. 6. . . Kd5 allows 7 Kb4 Kc6 8 Kc4 etc.; so the lesser evil is to allow the white king to go towards the K-side.

Black played 6 . . . Kb5  7 Kd4 Rd6+ (7 . . . Rxa5 8 Rxa5+ and wins the pawn ending) 8 Ke5 Re6+ 9 Kf4 Ka6 10 Kg5 Re5+ 11 Kh6 Rf5 apparently protecting everything. However, White can now win another pawn by means of *zugzwang*:

12 Kg7! Rf3  13 Kg8 Rf5  14 f4 Rf6 15 Kf8 Rf5  16 Kg7 and Black might as well resign. Black would have had more chances of drawing if there had been only one or two pawns each on the K-side.

When there are pawns on only one side of the board, the defending king is usually there too and the win is well-nigh impossible. Four pawns against three offers some chances, but only if there are weaknesses in the defender's position. The next example shows how knowledge of a 'book' draw enabled Black to save a difficult position.

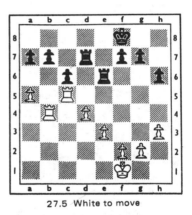

27.5 White to move

Double-rook endings are very hard to play, because of the additional attacking chances offered by the second rook. Black also has here a sorry pawn structure whereas White can force a central passed pawn eventually. After 1 Ke2?! Black decided to give up a pawn rather than suffer in silence. Taking advantage of the temporary pin on the white e-pawn, he played

1 . . . b6! 2 axb6 axb6 3 Rxb6
Rxd4 4 Rbxc6 Rxc6 5 Rxc6 Rd5
reaching diagram 27.6. The extra
rooks and Q-side weaknesses have
disappeared. White can win this
type of position (it has been known
for over fifty years) only if he can
advance his pawn to g5 without
Black being able to exchange it for
the h-pawn; in that case Black would
be cramped, his h5-pawn weak and
White could get a strong passed e-
pawn. But here 6 g4 will be met by
6 . . . h5, thanks to the black rook's
last move, and the resulting three
against two positions are all draw-
able without much trouble.

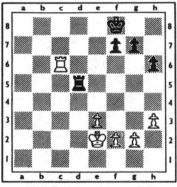

27.6 Position after . . . Rd5

White tried 6 e4 Re5 7 Ke3 h5!
8 f4 Ra5 9 e5 but Black commenced
typical rook harassment by 9 . . .
Ra2 10 Kf3 (10 g4? Ra3+) 10 . . .
Ra3+ 11 Ke4 Ra2! (but not 11 . . .
g6 12 e6! fxe6 13 Ke5 Re3+
14 Kf6) and White agreed to a draw.
The only winning try would be 12 f5
but 12 . . . Rxg2 13 f6 gxf6 14 exf6
Ke8 15 Rc5 Rg6 puts a stop to that.

## MINOR PIECE ENDINGS

An extra pawn generally gives good
winning chances in these endings,
with one exception. That is the
ending with bishops of opposite
colours, which is considered in
Unit 30.

Bishop endings (both on light or
on dark squares) are relatively
straightforward. The relative value
of the kings is more important still
than in rook endings, because a
bishop cannot cut a king off from
a vast area of the board in the way
a rook can. The only other crucial
factor is the colour on which the
pawns stand, if the pawn chains
are more or less fixed. In that case
the player whose pawns are on the
same colour squares as his bishop
is at a disadvantage — they obstruct
his bishop and are vulnerable to
attacks by the enemy bishop.

Knight endings are very much
like king-and-pawn endings. The only
real peculiarity of the knight is its
impotence against a passed rook's
pawn — a factor which sometimes
allows one player to sacrifice his
piece.
See diagram 27.7.

Black is having problems cashing
in his extra pawn, because the white
king holds the centre and it is not
easy to make a passed pawn. The
only hope is to creep down the edge:
1 . . . Kb5! 2 Nd6+ Ka4 3 b5?!
(but 3 Kd4 Kb3 followed by . . . a5
. . . a4 should also win) 3 . . . a5!
(3 . . . axb5? 4 Kd5 Kb3 5 Kc6 etc.)
4 Kd5 Kb3 5 Kc6 a4! Black offers

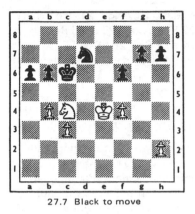

27.7 Black to move

the knight, because White will not be able to stop the a-pawn now.

27.8 Position after 5 . . . a4!

Any other piece would at least be able to sacrifice itself for the pawn, but not the knight. If now 6 Nf5 a3 7 Nd4+ Kb2 etc.

White played 6 c4 a3 7 Kxd7 a2 8 c5 to set up a passed pawn of his own. Black avoided 8 . . . a1=Q? 9 cxb6, and instead headed for a second pawn-versus-knight situation: 8 . . . bxc5 9 b6 a1=Q 10 b7 Qa7 11 Kc8 c4 12 b8=Q+ Qxb8+

13 Kxb8 c3 14 Nf5 c2 15 Nd4+ Kc3 16 Ne2+ Kd2 17 Nd4 c1=Q 18 Nb3+ Kc2 19 Nxc1 Kxc1. The pawn ending is easily won for Black as you can verify for yourself.

Endings of knight versus bishop are more difficult. A knight can dominate a bad bishop and win if there is a way through for the king. With pawns only on one side of the board, a knight should be no worse, though most such positions will be drawn. With mobile pawns on both wings, the bishop is almost always superior. Two bishops against bishop and knight or two knights is even better; often a decisive advantage in itself.

27.9 The Two Bishops

The two bishops need space to work in and to deprive the black knight of support points. So 1 g5! hxg5 2 hxg5 fxg5 3 fxg5 Ne5 4 Bf5 g6 5 Bc8 Nc4 6 Bc1! (6 Bc3 Nd6 and 7 . . . Ne4+) 6 . . . Nd6 7 Bg4 Ke7 8 Kf4 Be6 9 Bf3 Bf5 10 Bxd5 Bxc2 11 Ke5 Bf5.

White allows Black to exchange his isolated pawn to clear the board and gain a tempo for the king.

27.10 Position after 11 . . . Bf5

12 Be3 (threat Bc5) stretches Black's defences to the limit. After 12 . . . Nf7+ 13 Kd4 Nd8 14 Kc5 Bc8 15 b4 Bd7 16 Bd2! (not 16 Bd4 Ne6+) the combined threats to the b-pawn and g-pawn can probably no longer be met adequately.

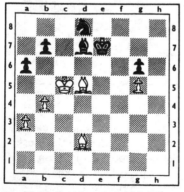

27.11 Position after 16 Bd2!

The final act was 16 . . . Bb5?! 17 Be4 Kf7 18 Kd6 Bc4 19 Kd7

Nc6 20 Kc7 Nd4 21 Bxb7 Nb5+ 22 Kb6 Nxa3 23 Bxa6 Be6 24 Kc5 Bf5 25 b5 Nxb5 26 Bxb5 and White finally won with his extra piece.

## OTHER ENDINGS

Endings with just the kings and pawns will be discussed in the next unit, and endings with unusual material situations in Unit 30. Endings with queens or with a rook and minor piece each are fairly common, though, and are worth a brief mention here.

Queen endings often lead to a draw because the power of the queen on an open board makes perpetual check an ever-present possibility. Where there is no perpetual check, everything depends on passed pawns. One advanced passed pawn can compensate for several extra, but less advanced pawns, on the other side. This is because a queen can force her pawn through against a blockade whereas a rook cannot. Substitute queens for rooks in 27.1(a). White plays 1 Qb5, 2 Qc5, 3 Qc7 and the pawn goes through.

Where rooks are present with minor pieces, the player with a material advantage normally wants to exchange rooks; and his opponent wants to keep rooks on and exchange minor pieces. However, these positions sometimes have an independent character, as in 27.12. Black's rook is a lot better than White's; so it pays him to keep them on and try to force a way in for his king.

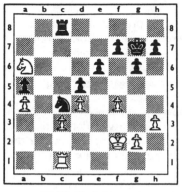

27.12 Black to move

Black has a positional advantage, thanks to the pawn structure and his better-placed pieces. He may not have a won game yet, so it suits him to keep things complicated.

He plays 1 . . . h5! (space-gaining) 2 Ke2 (2 Rb1? Nd2 wins the c-pawn) 2 . . . Rc6 3 Nc5 Rb6 4 Rc2 Rb1 (encirclement) 5 Kf2 Kf6 6 Kg3 Rf1 (6 . . . Kf5 is also promising) 7 Nd7+ (7 Rf2 Rc1 8 Rf3 Nd2) 7 . . . Kf5 8 Ne5 Ke4 9 Nxc4 (9 Nxf7 Kd3) 9 . . . dxc4 and when the black king reaches c3 the game is decided.

The presence of a pair of rooks can also make a difference in opposite-colour bishop endings. They make it all the more important to possess the initiative, as example 30.8 shows.

*EXERCISES*

27.13 Black to move

Diagram 27.13 was an ending played by grandmaster Pachman. How did he win?

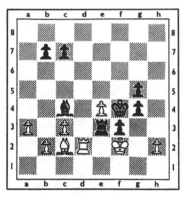

27.14 White to move

Can Black win?

## UNIT 28    USING THE KING

### KING MARCHES

You will have noticed in the examples from the previous unit (especially 27.12) that the king often plays an active role in the endgame. It is not unusual for him to go on long walks to attack enemy weak points or to support his own passed pawns. King marches occasionally occur in blocked middle-game positions, but it is normally in the endgame that king manœuvres come into their own.

In the middle-game the king appears slow and vulnerable, but in the endgame his strong points come into their own. His ability to defend or attack a set of adjacent squares simultaneously often gives him the edge over the bishop (which can only cover squares of one colour) or the knight (with its awkward gait and blind spots). A centralized king can reach any square on the board in three or four moves, and once it gets to close quarters the enemy pawns are often doomed. Even in queen endings, the king is sometimes able to make a positive contribution.

In Unit 1, no value was assigned to the king. In endgames, though, you can reckon that he is a fighting force roughly equal to a minor piece.

### THE OPPOSITION

The two kings often find themselves engaged in a duel for a key square or set of squares. When there are no other pieces left at all, these duels usually decide the game.

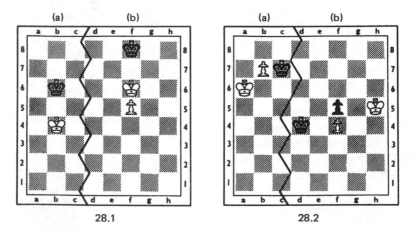

28.1                              28.2

In 28.1(a) the kings face one another, with the square b5 as a no man's land between them. This situation is known as *the opposition*, and it has

Page 194

quite a few applications to practical endgames, taken in conjunction with zugzwang, the compulsion to move.

Look at 28.1(b). If it is Black's move, then we say that White has the opposition. Black must give ground and White queens his pawn: 1 . . . Kg8 2 Ke7 Kg7 3 f6+ etc. From this example there follows a general rule, which is applicable to all positions with king and pawn against king so long as the pawn is on one of the six central files (i.e. not a rook's pawn). The rule is: if the attacking king is in front of its pawn, then the pawn will queen so long as the attacker has the opposition.

The corollary is that if the defender has the opposition he sometimes draws. With White to play the game ends 1 Kg6 Kg8 2 f6 (not 2 Kg5 Kf7) 2 . . . Kf8 3 f7 etc. still winning, but this only works with the pawn on the fifth rank. If the pawn were on f4, the white king on f5 and the black king on f7 then White to play only draws: 1 Kg5 Kg7 2 f5 Kf7 3 Kf6 Kf8! (not 3 . . . Kg8 4 Kg6) 4 Kg6 Kg8 5 f7+ Kf8 6 Kf6 stalemate.

28.2(a) shows the same idea. White to play wins by 1 Ka7. Black to play draws by 1 . . . Kb8.

## TRIANGULATION

We have already seen some examples of zugzwang — situations where it would be better *not* to have the move. Diagram 28.2(b) shows a case where win or loss depends on losing a move.

If White hastily plays 1 Kg5?? he will lose. Black replies 1 . . . Ke4, to protect his own pawn and attack White's. Then White finds himself in zugzwang: his king must move away, and Black snaps up the pawn.

To win, White must go to g5 in two moves instead of one: 1 Kg6! Ke4 2 Kg5 and it is Black who is in zugzwang. This method of losing a move is known as *triangulation*. Here is another example to illustrate triangulation and the opposition.

See diagram 28.3.

An exchange of pieces has just resulted in White capturing with a pawn on e6. He claimed a win on adjudication, in view of the continuation 1 . . . Kxe6 2 Ke4 (taking the opposition) 2 . . . Kd6 3 Kf5 etc.

Black draws, though, because he does not have to take the pawn. After 1 . . . Kf6 (1 . . . Kd6 is the same) 2 Ke4 Kxe6 Black has the

28.3 Black to move

opposition, and it is White who must triangulate: 3 Kd3 (3 Ke3?? loses to 3 . . . Ke5) 3 . . . Ke5 4 Ke3 Kd6 5 Ke4 Ke6 etc.

White can try to be subtle. After 1 . . . Kf6 he can play 2 e7 but then 2 . . . Kxe7 3 Ke4 Ke6 is the draw again. Or if 2 Kf3, still hoping for 2 . . . Kxe6?, Black plays 2 . . . Ke7! 3 Ke3 Kf6! and so on for ever.

any square of the board and the position would still be a draw. Black just plays Ka8-b7-a8 until he is stalemated. See 30.10 for another example of this.

### PASSED PAWNS

In king-and-pawn endings, any passed pawns are naturally important. But the most important are those that can look after themselves.

### ROOK'S PAWNS

It is much harder to win with a rook's pawn than with any other pawn in most endings, because of the possibilities of stalemate created by the edge of the board. Diagram 28.4(a) shows the standard case, and 28.4(b) a rather more unusual form of the draw.

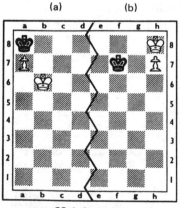

28.5 White wins

This is a simple win for White, whoever is to move. The black king can never go further to the K-side than e6 and e7, nor further down the board than the third rank, without White simply queening his c-pawn. So White has all the time in the world to mop up Black's K-side pawns with his own king. See diagram 28.6.

Passed pawns do not have to be on adjacent files to protect one another from the enemy king. In example 28.6, we see that passed pawns one file apart are also self-protecting, as long as they are not

(a)                    (b)

28.4 Stalemate

Note that in 28.4(a) you could give White a dark-squared bishop on

28.6 Black wins

threatened with capture on the move.
Whichever pawn the black king con-
fronts, the other will advance and
the king must back down.

Pawns two or more files apart are
often stronger. Black is actually
winning 28.6 because his passed
pawns are on the fifth rank. Play could
go 1 Kg2 (1 Ke3? h3) 1 . . . e3 2 Kf3 h3
3 Kxe3 h2 etc. If they were further
back they could not force their way
through like this, but would be safe so
long as they stayed on the same rank
as each other until attacked. For
example, with WKf3, BPe5, h5 White
must wait by 1 Kg3, forcing Black to
move his king. But after 1 . . . K a5
2 c4 Ka4, it's a draw by 3 Kf3 Ka5, etc.

## ZUGZWANG

The idea that it is better to have the
move than not to have it can be
hard to forget — just because it is
almost invariably a correct idea in
the opening and the middle-game. In
the ending, however, and especially
where manœuvres with kings, pawns,
and sometimes knights are concerned, only careful study of the

position will show whether the move
is an advantage — or a decisive disadvantage.

Zugzwang, the case where having
the move is a disaster, crops up in
countless endings. You should always
be on the look-out for it.

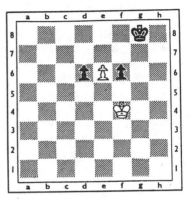

28.7 White to move

First impressions of 28.7 suggests
that White is losing. After 1 Kf5
Kg7 2 e7 Kf7 3 e8=Q+ Kxe8
4 Kxf6 Black plays 4 . . . Kd7
5 Kf5 Kc6 6 Ke4 Kc5 7 Kd3 Kd5
and, because his king is in front of
the pawn, and he has the advantage
of opposition, Black eventually wins.

However, White can draw by putting his opponent into zugzwang.
Instead of 4 Kxf6 the correct move
is 4 Ke6!, reaching diagram 28.8.

If White had to move, he could
not avoid the previous variation, but
Black, having the move, cannot win.
If 4 . . . Kd8 5 Kxd6 or 4 . . . Kf8
5 Kxf6 both pawns are lost, so
Black must move a pawn right away.
However, after 4 . . . f5 (4 . . . d5 is
no different) 5 Kxf5 Black will
never be able to get his king in front

28.8 Zugzwang

of the passed pawn; e.g. 5 . . . Kd7 6 Ke4 Kc6 7 Kd4.

28.9 White to move

In many cases there is a close link between zugzwang and the opposition; the opposition, as an effective device, is really only a special case of zugzwang. In 28.9, White is able to force a win, although going directly for the black pawn would not achieve anything (1 Kb6 Ke4 2 Kxb7 Kd4 or 1 b4 Ke6! 2 Kb6 Kd5).

White puts Black into zugzwang by 1 Kd5! Now if 1 . . . b5 (or 1 . . . b6) 2 b4 followed by Kc6 wins; so Black must move his king, and 1 . . . Kf4 2 b4 etc. is no problem for White.

So after 1 Kd5 Black plays 1 . . . Kf6! and White maintains the opposition by 2 Kd6! At the same time he gains a crucial tempo for approaching the black pawn, and the game ends 2 . . . Kf5 3 b4 Ke4 4 b5 Kd4 5 b6 and the White pawn must queen.

## TEMPO GAINING

A corollary to this idea of zugzwang is that sometimes to lose a move is to gain a move! This is another paradox, but true in those cases where you have to be in the right place at the *right* time.

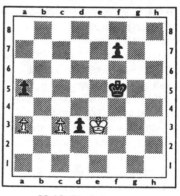

28.10 Black to move

Black first plays 1 . . . d2! 2 Kxd2 Ke4 in order to get his king to the important e4 square, where it can stop the white passed pawn and support his own f-pawn. The question is: can he keep it there or will he have to give ground? After 3 Ke2 Black would put White into zugzwang by 3 . . . a4, but what should he do after 3 a4!

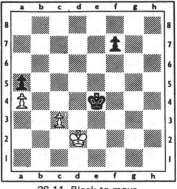

28.11 Black to move

The obvious move 3 . . . f5 fails to win after 4 Ke2 Kd5 (or 4 . . . f4 5 Kf2) 5 Kd3 f4 6 c4+ Kc5 7 Ke4 because of the stalemate draw with a rook's pawn (White's king gets back to c1 in time). It would be good practice for you to work this out for yourself.

The secret is that Black's as yet unmoved pawn possesses a 'reserve tempo' — it has the right to move either one square or two on its first go. White has no reserve tempo left (after a4), because if he plays c3-c4 Black will win both pawns and the white king won't get back in time *unless* (the point of the previous variation) the black pawn is at f4 or f3 or f2.

So 3 . . . f6! puts White into zugzwang. After 4 Ke2 f5 5 Kd2 Kf3 6 Kd3 (6 c4 Ke4! for the reason just given) 6 . . . f4 7 c4 Kg2 8 c5 f3 9 c6 f2 10 c7 f1=Q+ and Black wins.

## 'HARMFUL OPPOSITION'

It is not always good to take the opposition; sometimes it can be meaningless or even positively harmful, as in 28.12 below. Taking the opposition can be useful, as we have seen, on a fairly open board or with certain pawn structures (like 28.3), but there are other pawn structures where the fight between the kings must be carried on in a different way. Remember that the opposition is important when it leads to zugzwang, but only then.

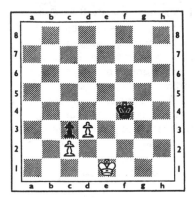

28.12 Black to move

Here White would like to get his king to e2, and so on to e3 and glory. Alternatively he would like to go to b3, and to stop that Black must always be able to meet Ka2 by . . . Kb4. So what should Black play here?

If he takes the opposition, by 1 . . . Ke3, he should lose! This is proved by the variation 2 Kd1 Kf3 (2 . . . Kd4 3 Ke2) 3 Kc1 and White reaches b3.

On the other hand, spurning the opposition by 1 . . . Kf3! draws. If 2 Kf1 Ke3 3 Kg2 (3 Ke1 Kf3 again) 3 . . . Kd2 draws, since both sides make a queen. While if 2 Kd1 Ke3

3 Kc1 Kd4  4 Kb1 Kc5  5 Ka2 Kb4
6 Ka1 (an attempt to triangulate)
6 . . . Kb5! (but not 6 . . . Ka3??
7 Kb1) Black demonstrates that for
every square the white king goes to,
in its attempt to break through on
one side or the other, he can always
find a corresponding square for his
king to keep White out.

## RELATED SQUARES

This endgame analysis by Grigoriev
is a fairly simple example of the concept of corresponding or related
squares, that is essential for solving
a great number of king-and-pawn
endings.

The theory of related squares is
basically quite simple, although its
application to particular endgames
can sometimes be a very challenging intellectual task. When one king
is trying to reach a certain key square

or one or other of two key squares,
while the defending king manœuvres
to try and keep it out, then there
will be a pattern of related squares
in the position.

By discovering where the defending king must be to guard each key
square, you can gradually discover
the complete series of related
squares, as we did in 28.12. Here
there was a one-to-one correspondence, and so long as he kept to the
right squares according to where
White put his king, Black was able
to draw.

In other positions, especially
where the attacking king has more
space for manœuvring, the pattern
of related squares may not be
perfect. Then if he can discover
where the pattern breaks down, the
attacker can perform the appropriate
triangulation and get to one of the
key squares.

# UNIT 29   PASSED PAWNS

## *PROMOTION*

An endgame is often decided by the promotion of a pawn. When, as often happens, both players have chances of getting a new queen, great care is required. There follows a cautionary tale, taken from a grandmaster game played in 1971.

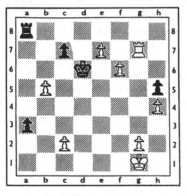

29.1  White to move

With three extra pawns, including two advanced connected passers, White thought he saw a neat way to force a promotion before Black's outside passed a-pawn could reach a1.

He played 1 Rg8??! Rxg8  2 f7 and the game continued 2 . . . a2 3 fxg8=Q a1=Q+  4 Kh2 Kxe7 (4 . . . Qe5+  5 Qg3)  5 Qg5+ and Black resigned, being so many pawns down. Can you see what both players missed in this sequence?

White's combination only worked because his pawn promoted on g8, out of reach of the black king. By 2 . . . Rxg2 check, Black could

have turned the tables on his opponent: 3 Kxg2 Kxe7  and Black stops the e-pawn, while White is unable to stop the a-pawn.

White should have played 1 Rg3! a2 (1 . . . Kd7  2 e8=8+ Kxe8  3Rg8+ or 2 . . . Rxe8  3 Rxa3)  2 Rd3+! Ke6 (2 . . . Kc5  3 Rd1 a1=Q  4 Rxa1 Rxa1+ 5 kf2 Ra8  6 f7, etc.)  3 e8=Q+ Rxe8 4 Ra3 Kxf6  5 Rxa2, and White, a pawn up on each wing, has good winning chances.

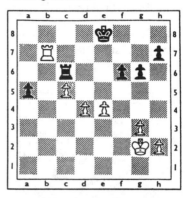

29.2  Black to move

Passed pawns, especially outside passed pawns that the king cannot stop, need to be treated with respect. Ideally, they should be dealt with before they can advance too far. Diagram 29.2 shows the position reached after an example we saw earlier (19.8). White has created a powerful central bloc, and needs only to eliminate counter-play.

Black played 1 . . . Ra6, hoping to drive the white rook into a passive blockading position. But

Passed pawns

White played 2 Rb6! and the game continued 2 . . . Ra8 3 Rxf6 a4 4 Rf2 a3 5 Ra2. So he had to blockade in the end, but having three instead of two connected passed pawns makes the win easy — also there is no f-pawn to keep the king out. The final moves were 5 . . . Kd7 6 d5 g5 7 Kf3 Ra4 8 Ke3 h5 9 h4 gxh4 10 gxh4 Ke7 11 Kf4 Kd7 12 Kf5 and Black resigned, as the white king helps its pawns forward.

But after 1 . . . Ra6 2 Rb6 why did Black not play 2 . . . Rxb6 3 cxb6 Kd7 (of course not 3 . . . a4 4 b7 etc.), when it appears that Black can stop White's pawn, but White cannot stop Black's?

29.3 Position after 3 . . . Kd7

The solution is similar to that in 28.6. After 3 . . . Kd7 White would play 4 e5! a4 (or first 4 . . . fxe5 5 dxe5) 5 e6+! (clearer than 5 exf6) 5 . . . Kxe6 6 b7 a3 7 b8=Q and Black never gets a queen.

Page 202

TYPES OF PASSED PAWN

In most endings, passed pawns will arise sooner or later. This can happen either as the result of advancing a pawn majority created in the middle-game, or by capturing the enemy pawn or pawns that stand in the way of your own.

Some passed pawns are better than others. Outside passed pawns, as we have seen, are primarily useful for their decoy value. Short-range pieces, i.e. knights and kings, are particularly discomforted by the need to capture or blockade passed pawns when the play is about to shift to the opposite side of the board.

For most purposes, though, connected passed pawns are best. They can defend each other if necessary or advance like a steam-roller, forcing even mighty rooks and queens out of their path.

(a)          (b)

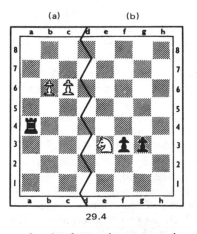

29.4

A pair of passed pawns on the sixth rank can be stronger than a piece or a rook. Even with the move, the rook or knight in 29.4 cannot prevent an enemy pawn from queening: 1 . . . Rb4 2 c7 Rc4 3 b7 Rxc7 4 b8=Q.

Isolated passed pawns generally need the active support of their king or rook, for both defence and attack. It is tempting to advance such pawns as far as you can, but usually you do better to get your king next to the pawn or even ahead of it, to clear its path of blockaders. This is illustrated by the basic theory on rook-and-pawn versus rook.

## THE DRAWN POSITION

Diagram 29.5 illustrates a basic position which Black can always draw with best play. The black king is correctly placed on the file of the pawn (either d7 or d8 would do) and will resist all attempts to be driven off. Note that without rooks White to play wins by 1 Kd6 as in 28.1(b), but Black would draw by 1 . . . Kd7 2 d6 Kd8 3 Ke6 Ke8 etc; this means that White cannot win if he exchanges rooks.

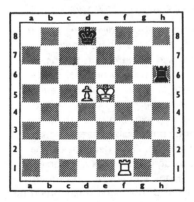

29.5 Draw

Black's plan is to patrol the third rank with his rook to stop White's king from getting ahead of the pawn to the sixth rank. If White marks time, Black does the same: 1 Rg1 Ra6 2 Rg8+ Kd7 3 Rg7+ Kd8. Sooner or later, White will have to try advancing the pawn: 4 d6.

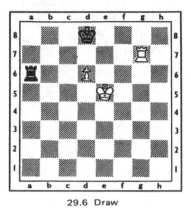

29.6 Draw

White's plan now is to play his king to e6 under shelter of the pawn, and drive off the black king with mating threats. This stratagem can never succeed if Black harasses the white king; so the correct move here is 4 . . . Ra1 (obtaining the maximum checking distance) 5 Rg8+ Kd7 6 Rg7+ Kd8 (not to c6 today, thank you!) 7 Ke6 Re1+ 8 Kd5 Rd1+ and so on until White offers a draw.

This plan always works if you can get the king to the queening square and your rook to the third rank in time to stop the enemy king. It does not matter which file the pawn is on. If you do not have the time to set up 29.5, then you may lose, although bishop's pawns and rook's pawns do offer some extra drawing chances.

### THE WINNING POSITION

Diagram 29.7 shows what Black is trying to avoid. Once the white king

29.7 White wins

reaches the key square d6, it is virtually certain that White can force the pawn forward: 1 Rb2+ Ka7 2 Kc6 etc.

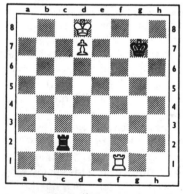

29.8 White wins

When the pawn is on the seventh, and the king stands on the queening square, White's task is to get the king out of the way in order to promote the pawn. Once more, Black has to rely on checks from the rook, but this will save him only if his king is close enough to the pawn to stop it in the event of White interposing his rook to a check.

In 29.8 White can win either by transferring his rook to a8, or by the more general method known as 'building a bridge'. He plays 1 Rf4 Rc1 2 Ke7 Re1+ 3 Kd6 Rd1+ 4 Ke6 Re1+ 5 Kd5 Rd1+ 6 Rd4. Note that this method wins whenever two or more files separate the black king from the white pawn, but that if the king was only one file away Black would exchange rooks and catch the pawn. So if the king is only one file away, it is necessary to drive it further off (as in 29.7) or in some exceptional way to prevent Black's rook getting its necessary checking distance.

### PIECE AGAINST PAWNS

Some of the hardest endgames to play are those where a piece is opposed by numerous pawns. A piece can usually pick off backward or isolated pawns before they become dangerous, but connected passed pawns can often make up for a considerable material disadvantage. A lot depends on the position of the kings of course.

Rook endings not infrequently turn into rook-versus-pawns endings, after one player gives up his rook to stop the enemy passed pawn. This is illustrated by 29.9.

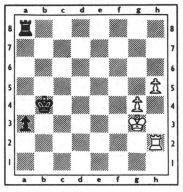

29.9 Black to move

After 1 . . . a2  2 Rxa2 (2 Rh1 loses a tempo here) 2 . . . Rxa2 3 g5! White is winning, because Black needs two moves to get his rook into the optimum position behind the pawns.

The king cannot stop White's pawns: 3 . . . Kc5  4 g6 Kd5  5 g7 Ra8  6 h6 Rg8  7 Kf3 Ke6  8 h7 Rxg7  9 h8=Q and queen versus rook is a win (although it requires care). For similar reasons, 3 . . . Ra8 is no good.

So Black's best try is 3 . . . Ra1 4 g6! Kc5  5 Kf4 Rg1 reaching 29.10. It looks at first sight as if the game will be drawn: 6 Kf5 Kd6 would lead to a stand-off situation where White cannot promote the pawns and Black cannot win them without losing his rook in exchange. See diagram 29.10.

The key move for White is 6 Ke5!, holding the black king at bay. After 6 . . . Kc6  7 Kf6 Kd6 White has gained the tempo for 8 g7, winning

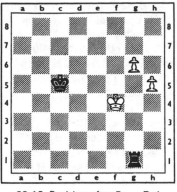

29.10 Position after 5 . . . Rg1

as in the line 8 . . . Rf1+ (else 9 h6) 9 Kg6 Ke7  10 g8=Q Rg1+  11 Kh7 Rxg8  12 Kxg8 Kf6  13 h6.

After 6 Ke5 Black might also try 6 . . . Rg5+  7 Kf6 Rxh5 but after 8 g7 there is another remarkable position in which a pawn is able to beat a rook.

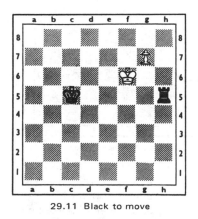

29.11 Black to move

From diagram 29.11 play continues 8 . . . Rh6+ (no other way to stop the pawn) 9 Kf5! It has to be this square, because 9 Kf7 Rh7 pins the pawn and draws, while 9 Kg5

Rh1 10 g8=Q?? loses to the skewer
10 . . . Rg1+. Finally, if 9 Ke5 or
9 Ke7, simply 9 . . . Rg6.

After 9 Kf5 the continuation is
amusing: 9 . . . Rh5+ 10 Kf4 Rh4+
11 Kf3 Rh3+ 12 Kg2 and Black can
resign, because there is no longer a
skewer.

These positions often depend on
small, almost accidental details. In
29.9, the white king controlled the
h2 square for a vital tempo. If instead the king had started at f3,
then 1 . . . a2 2 Rxa2 Rxa2 3 g5
Rh2 would have led to a draw. This
is also why, with the king on g3,
1 . . . a2 2 Rh1? would be a mistake: 2 . . . a1=Q 3 Rxa1 Rxa1
4 g5 Rh1 etc.

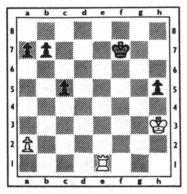

29.12 White to move

Here is a case where the rook
triumphs, so long as White handles
the forces at his disposal with
accuracy. Black cannot improve on
this significantly: 1 Re5 b6 2 Rxh5
Ke6 3 Kg3 Kd6 4 Kf4 (getting the
king within range of the pawns is a
high priority) 4 . . . Kc6 5 a4 (keeping the black king out is another)

5 . . . Kb7 6 Ke4 Ka6 7 Kd5 Ka5
8 Rh4 b5 9 axb5 Kxb5 10 Rc4 a5
11 Rxc5+ Kb4 12 Kd4 a4 13 Rc8
Kb3 (13 . . . a3 14 Rb8+) 14 Kd3
a3 15 Rb8+ Ka2 16 Kc2 Ka1
17 Rb1+ Ka2 18 Rb3 Ka1 19 Rxa3
mate.

So the rook is a powerful piece
and, skilfully handled, is usually
worth a lot of pawns. Nevertheless,
players sometimes panic, or do not
possess the necessary technique to
play these types of position where
they are confronted by an enemy
pawn roller. So when you get into
difficulties in an endgame, it is
worth looking to see whether you
can bring about an ending of
passed pawns against the enemy
piece. This is of course also a good
policy against knights and bishops,
always depending on the position
of the kings and the pawns. It is no
good if your opponent can use his
piece to set up a blockade and
bring his king over at his leisure, or
set up a passed pawn of his own,
but it will not always be possible
for him to do this.

## EXERCISES

In diagram 29.13 White has three
passed pawns for a knight. How
could he now have forced the win,
and why did 1 Ke3 (which he
actually chose) fail?

In 29.14, White has just played
1 Kd2 in reply to a check. Is Black
winning, drawing, or losing? Should
he play 1 . . . Rc6, 1 . . . Rxe6 or
some other move? You should use

29.13 White to move

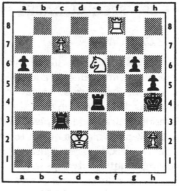

29.14 Black to move

the 10-point program to answer this. (See page 158.)

First, what does White threaten? What can you threaten? What are the long-term considerations in the position? Select your candidate moves and analyse them. Decide which move is best, and check you

haven't made a mistake. Only then look up the comments in the back of the book.

Here are a couple of hints: do not overlook the possibility of White playing Rf4+ in some variations; analyse each line as far as you can — there may be a sting in the tail!

# UNIT 30   SPECIAL CASES

## REVALUATIONS

In Unit 1, the following 'rule of thumb' valuation of the pieces was mentioned: Pawn 1, Bishop and Knight 3, Rook 5, Queen 9. However, as our course has progressed, we have seen quite a few examples which suggest that this scale is an over-simplification.

A more accurate and sophisticated revaluation would count a rook as equal to 4½ pawns, and a queen to 8½. This takes account of the following considerations. One pawn is usually not quite enough for the exchange; two pawns slightly outweigh it. Two rooks are more often than not superior to a queen, and three minor pieces also get the better of a queen. Rook and pawn are not always a match for two minor pieces.

All the same, unbalanced material of any kind is likely to mean exciting play, and exceptions even to the above scale of values can always be found — both in the middle-game and in the ending. In the last resort, there is no substitute for positional judgement and precise analysis.

## ROOK v. PIECES

In Unit 13, we saw a couple of examples of a rook fighting a minor piece, but what of rook against two minor pieces? As a rule, any two minor pieces (3+3) should be superior to rook and pawn (4½+1) because, as we saw back in 1.3, knight and bishop are two independent fighting units.

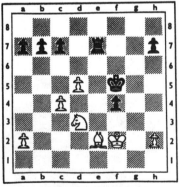

30.1 White to move

Exceptionally, when the rook can find targets, it may be superior to the two pieces. In 30.1, an important factor is Black's passed pawn; with inferior play by White, Black was able to win.

The game continued 1 Nc5 Re3! (essential to activate the rook) 2 Bd3+ (2 Nxb7 Rh3 or 2 . . . Ra3) 2 . . . Ke5 3 Bxh7 Rh3 4 Bb1 (4 Bd3 Kd4) 4 . . . Rxh2+ 5 Kg1 Rd2 6 Bg6 (6 Bh7 would be better) 6 . . . f3 7 Kf1 Kf4. Now White is thoroughly disorganized and faces mating threats; so must give up a piece: 8 Bh5 Ke3 9 Bxf3 Kxf3 10 Ke1 Rb2. With the white king cut off, the rook easily beats the knight: 11 Ne6 Ke3 12 Kf1 Kd3 13 Nxc7 Kxc4 and the white pawns are doomed.

## QUEEN v. PIECES

Three minor pieces, well co-ordin-
ated, should win against the queen.
This is not so rare as you might
imagine; diagram 30.2 arose in a
Botvinnik–Smyslov world championship match game.

30.2 White to move

The black king is much more
safely tucked away than his opposite
number, and this was decisive. The
game ended 1 Qxa7 Be4! 2 a4 (this
pawn is White's only hope of counter-
play) 2 . . . Kg7 3 Rd1 Be5 4 Qe7
Rc8 5 a5 (if 5 Rxd6 Rc1! threatens
rapid mate) 5 . . . Rc2 6 Kg2 Nd4+
7 Kf1 Bf3 8 Rb1 Nc6 and White
resigned. If he defends the a-pawn
by 9 Qc7 d5 10 Qb6 then 10 . . .
Bd4 and 11 . . . Rxf2+ is too strong.

Diagram 30.3 arose in a master
game a few years ago. Can White
win? Probably, although it is not
the easiest thing in the world to
prove! He adopted a plan of using
the knights to shepherd the king
across towards the black king,

30.3 White to move

avoiding perpetual check and
eventually creating mating threats.
After 30 moves, diagram 30.4
came about.

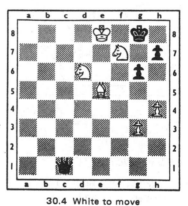

30.4 White to move

Clearly, White has made progress.
Now 1 Nc4! created a zugzwang:
the black queen cannot leave c1
because of Nh6 mate. Therefore a
concession, 1 . . . h6, was forced.
White continued 2 Ncd6 Qe3
3 Ke7 Qa7+ 4 Kf6 Kh7 5 Bf4
Qa1+ 6 Ke7 Qa7+ 7 Kf8 Qa8+
8 Ne8. Black now played in desper-

ation 8 . . . g5  9 hxg5 hxg5
10 Nxg5+ but with a passed pawn
White's win was certain. 8 . . . Qa3+
9 Bd6 Qa8 would have been better,
but 9 Nfd6! instead is decisive, in
view of the variation 9 . . . h5
10 Nf6+ Kh8  11 Be5!

Queen against two minor pieces
in theory should win. Sometimes,
however, the defence can set up an
impregnable wall around the king
and so force a draw, as in 30.5.

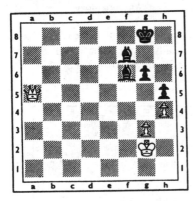

30.5 Drawn

## QUEEN v. ROOK ETC.

Queen against rook and minor
piece happens now and then.
Winning chances normally lie with
the queen, but a lot of these
positions are drawish — depending
on the number and vulnerability of
each player's pawns. Pieces fighting
against the queen need solid pawn
structures to blockade the enemy
pawns and to allow the pieces to
maintain central positions. If the
queen can find targets, or can push

through a passed pawn, then she will
win.

Queen against two rooks is often
a draw, because the rooks protect
one another but cannot achieve anything positive unless they are doubled
on the seventh rank. Here, too, the
number and position of the pawns
(particularly passed pawns or Q-side
majorities) can be a decisive factor.

Queen against just one rook is
not always a win, if the position is
very simplified, and the queen does
not have a passed pawn. With no
pawns at all, the queen should
always win (see below), but a lot of
positions like 30.6 are unwinnable
with correct play.

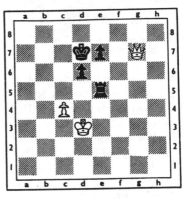

30.6 Drawish

In this sort of position, Black
wants to be entrenched near his
back row (as he is here) so that the
white queen cannot check from
behind and manœuvre the black
king into a bad position. (Alternatively, he should be a long way
forward so that his pawns are a
threat.)

To draw, Black only needs to

move his rook back and forth between c5 and e5 to keep the white king out. However, after 1 . . . Kc7?? (which Black actually played) White was able to make progress.

The game went on 1 . . . Kc7 2 c5! Rxc5 (comparatively best) 3 Qxe7+ Kc6 4 Qe8+ Kc7 ( 4 . . . Kb6 5 Qd7) 5 Kd4 Re5 (5 . . . Rc6 6 Qe7+) 6 Qa8 Rc5 7 Qa7+ Kc6 8 Qb8 Kd7 (8 . . . Re5 9 Qc8+) 9 Ke4 Re5+ 10 Kf4 Rc5 11 Qb7+ Ke6 (11 . . . Rc7 12 Qb5+ and 13 Kf5) 12 Qh7 Rc4+ (12 . . . Re5 13 Qc7 Rc5 14 Qd8 etc.) 13 Kg5 Rc5+ 14 Kg6 Ke5 (14 . . . Re5? 15 Qf7 mate) 15 Qd7.

30.7 Black to move

Now the white king has got into the act, Black's game cannot be saved. A possible continuation is 15 . . . Rc4 (the rook dare not wander far) 16 Qf5+ Kd4 17 Kf6 d5 18 Qd7 Ke4 19 Ke6 Rd4 20 Qh7+ Kf4 21 Qf5+ Ke3 22 Ke5 Rd2 23 Qf1. The pawn lives on, but no longer provides shelter for the black king which will soon be threatened with mate. Because of possible forks and skewers, the rook cannot leave the protection of the king, e.g. 23 . . . Rd3 24 Qe1+ Kf3 25 Kf5!

30.8 Black to move

A typical end could be 23 . . . d4 24 Qf4+ Ke2 25 Ke4 Kd1 (25 . . . d3 26 Qf3+) 26 Qf1+ Kc2 27 Qc4+ Kd1 28 Kf3 Ke1 (28 . . . d3 29 Ke3) 29 Qc1+ Rd1 30 Qb2 Rd2 31 Qb4 Kd1 32 Qb1 mate. The win with queen against rook (no pawn at all) can take thirty or thirty-five moves before mate or win of the rook, but is almost always possible. The technique of close-in manœuvring and use of zugzwang to separate the king and rook is much as in the above example. The defender must try to keep the enemy king away from his own or (if this is impossible) to pull off a stalemate swindle.

One reason for giving the last example in full was to demonstrate how important patience is in endgame play. It is often possible, when you have the initiative or a large material advantage, to try one idea and then, if the correct defence is forthcoming, you can go back to the same position and try a different idea. Manœuvring often achieves results in endings where there is no clear forced win.

## ENDINGS WITHOUT PAWNS

These are very rare, because usually at least one player will have a pawn left. However, computer analysis in recent years has revolutionized theory on some of the endings without pawns. Although there is no space to demonstrate these, it should be helpful to know what the theoretically correct result of a given situation is. Generally speaking:

(1) Queen against Rook or Bishop or Knight — *Win*

(2) Queen against Rook and Piece — *Draw*

(3) Queen against Two Minor Pieces — *Win, sometimes very hard, against two bishops or bishop and knight, but two knights can draw, except for a few special cases*

(4) Rook against Knight or Bishop — *Draw*

(5) Rook and Bishop against Rook — *Many draws, but worth trying to win*

(6) Rook and Knight against Rook — *Draw, almost always*

(7) Queen and Minor Piece against Queen — *Some winning chances, especially with a knight*

(8) Two Bishops against Knight — *The bishops should usually win*

Where one side has only his king, it is of course necessary to have sufficient material left to mate with. Queen or rook is easy; two bishops is quite easy too (not two bishops on the same colour squares, though!). Bishop and knight is hard; three knights (if you ever get them) is not too difficult. King and two knights can only win in special positions where the defender (!) has a pawn left (to avoid stalemate at the crucial moment). This does happen now and then, and a whole book was written (in Spanish) on this type of ending.

## OPPOSITE-COLOUR BISHOPS

Endings in which one side's bishop travels on light squares and his opponent's on the dark present special problems. This is because a bishop can set up a blockade of two (or sometimes more) passed pawns which the other bishop cannot break. Once the situation arises, it tends to be permanent because in the normal way opposite-colour bishops can never be exchanged for one another.

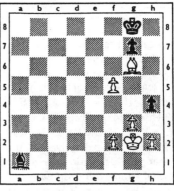

30.9 Draw

This was the final position of one of the 1858 New York tournament games between Morphy (White) and Paulsen; the players agreed to a draw. This was a perfectly reasonable decision in view of the presence of opposite-colour bishops (without the bishops, or with other pieces, White would win).

White is two pawns up, and could win a third pawn by 1 gxh4 (though this would devalue his pawns) but will never be able to queen a pawn. Even if he could get two connected passed pawns (which can always be prevented) he still could not get them past the black-squared blockade on g7.

A general rule for this type of ending is that to win you need to create passed pawns on both sides of the board, so that the enemy bishop cannot cope with both. The following famous endgame combination by Botvinnik shows how this can sometimes be achieved.

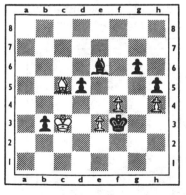

30.10 Black to move

Black won by 1 . . . g5! 2 fxg5 d4+! (so the bishop guards the b-

pawn) 3 exd4 Kg3 4 Ba3 Kxh4 5 Kd3 Kxg5 6 Ke4 h4 7 Kf3 Bd5+ and White resigned. The white king cannot even reach the blockading square h2, and if the bishop tries to help by going to d6, then the b-pawn queens.

More often than not, this type of coup is not available. It would require a strong king position and a material advantage in most cases. There are usually winning tries, but correct defence will block them. So an advantage of even two pawns may not be sufficient to win in many cases with opposite-colour bishops.

If each side also has a rook, then there are usually winning chances for the player who has the initiative. With two pairs of rooks or queens still on, this is even more important; for, as Botvinnik said, the attacker in effect has an extra piece — in the form of his bishop. The enemy bishop is unable to protect those squares which are under attack. The number of pawns can be irrelevant in some positions of this type.

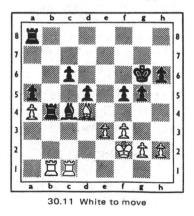

30.11 White to move

Without rooks, this position could well be a draw. As it is, White cannot hold his a-pawn; so goes for complications.

The game continued 1 Bc3 Rxa4 2 Rb7 (going for threats against the king) 2 . . . Ra2+ 3 Kg3 Kh5 4 h4 gxh4+ (4 . . . f4+ first was probably safer) 5 Kf4.

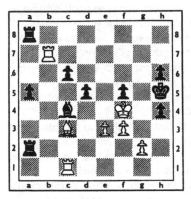

30.12 Black to move

Although he is now three pawns down, White has an attack that should be worth at least a draw. A plausible continuation would be 5 . . . Rxg2 6 Rh1 Rag8 and Black has to go on the defensive, losing his extra pawns eventually.

Black preferred to defend his pawns by 5 . . . Re8 6 Rg7! Re6 7 Rh1 (If 7 Bxa5!? Rg6!, not 7 . . . Rxa5??, 8 g4+ and mates, while 7 g4+?! fails to 7 . . . hxg3ep 8 Rh1+? Rh2.) 7 . . . Rg6. See diagram 30.13.

Now 8 Bf6 fails to 8 . . . Rxg7 and 8 g4+? to 8 . . . fxg4 9 fxg4+ Rxg4+ 10 Rxg4 Rf2+ 11 Ke5 Kxg4.

White's right line is 8 Rxh4+! Kxh4 9 Rxg6 Kh5 (9 . . . h5?

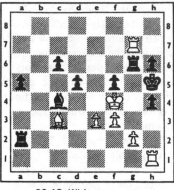

30.13 White to move

10 Be1+) and now 10 Rxc6 Rxg2 (10 . . . a4? 11 Bg7) 11 Bxa5 draws comfortably. White has other possibilities but they risk losing.

## UNUSUAL DRAWS

In some cases it is possible to save apparently lost games in the ending by exploiting certain exceptional circumstances. We have already remarked on the inability of a bishop with the wrong rook's pawn (the one whose queening square it cannot attack) to win against a king which can reach the queening

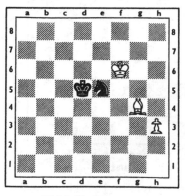

30.14 Black to move

corner. In the 1971 Fischer-Taimanov match, the Soviet grandmaster lost a game he could have drawn, through forgetting this.

Here Taimanov played 1 . . . Ke4?? overlooking 2 Bc8. Now if 2 . . . Nd3 3 Bf5+ or 2 . . . Nf3 3 Bb7+ exchanging the knight, and not giving the king a chance to run to the corner. The final moves were 2 . . . Kf4 3 h4 Nf3 4 h5 Ng5 5 Bf5 Nf3 6 h6 Ng5 7 Kg6 Nf3 8 h7 Ne5+ 9 Kf6 and Black resigned. He never had a chance to sacrifice the knight for the pawn.

1 . . . Nd3! would have been the best move. Then after 2 h4 Nf4 the white king has to come back to chase the knight away — but this allows the black king to slip through: 3 Kf5 Kd6! 4 Kxf4 Ke7 5 Kg5 Kf8 6 Kg6 Kg8 7 Be6+ Kh8 etc.

Sometimes stalemate can save the day — if you can see how to bring it about. A favourite theme of endgame study composers is 'walling in'. Do you see how White draws in 30.15? It's clear he cannot stop Black from queening a pawn.

The amazing solution of this study, composed 120 years ago, is 1 Bd2, followed by 2 Ba5 and 3 b4. Whatever Black does in the meantime, he cannot prevent this stalemate.

Other surprising drawing situations have only been discovered after hundreds of hours of analysis failed to produce forced wins. For example you might imagine that rook and pawn should always win against a bishop? Yet there are positions, at first sight quite ordinary, which are unwinnable. If the pawn is a bishop's pawn, and the defending king is on the queening square, it is a win if the defender's bishop is the colour of the queening square, but a draw if it is the other colour!

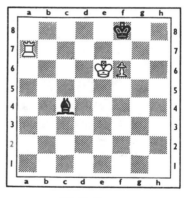

30.16 Draw

This turns out so because only that bishop can prevent the pawn reaching the seventh rank and creating mating threats. See diagram 30.17.

With rook and pawn against bishop and pawn, the pawns blocking one another on the file,

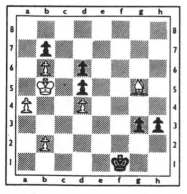

30.15 (by J.G. Campbell) White to move

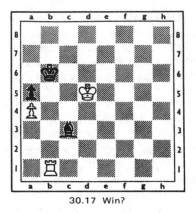

30.17 Win?

and the bishop and pawn mutually defending one another, you can win in most cases but not all. You must drive the enemy king as far away as possible, then sacrifice your rook for bishop and pawn to reach a winning pawn ending. How far the king must be driven depends on how far advanced the pawn is. A rook's pawn on the fifth will win; on the third it will draw. On the fourth (30.17)? People are still arguing about that, fifty years after Rubinstein won such an ending! So it is always worth fighting to the bitter end (the fifty-move draw rule); you learn a lot, and sometimes you score an extra half point.

# Epilogue

## PUTTING IT INTO PRACTICE

If you already belong to a chess club, much of this short final chapter may
be familiar ground to you. Nevertheless there are some aspects of practical
chess-playing which everyone should know about, and may be of special
help to people who have not as yet played much serious chess, or who live
in areas remote from the main chess centres.

### LEAGUES AND TOURNAMENTS

In Britain and Ireland, most chess clubs are affiliated to local or county
leagues, with regular inter-club matches in the winter months, between
September and April. These leagues vary tremendously between small
divisions of five-a-side and the huge London League (established in 1888)
with seven divisions and teams of ten players (twelve teams of twelve
players in the first division). Within these leagues, players of all experience
and abilities are catered for.

Most club chess is played on weekday evenings, with weekends reserved
for tournaments and county matches (although Yorkshire's Woodhouse Cup
is played on Saturdays). Many counties run two or three teams, and most
have junior teams. The advantage of Saturday play is that you can travel
further and still have more time to play (3½- or 4-hour sessions usually),
and that you are not tired after work; so you can give of your best. Evening
sessions are inevitably shorter (2½ or 3 hours), and so usually have to be
played with shorter time-limits, which is where the errors and superficial
play inevitably creep in.

Weekend tournaments, an American phenomenon imported by chess
impresario Stewart Reuben in the '60s, have become a big feature of
the British chess scene. These involve playing a game on Friday evening
(starting about 7 p.m.) then two or three on the Saturday and two on the
Sunday. They provide the most competitive form of chess known to date,
owing to the cash prizes on offer, which are frequently considerable even
in the lower sections (£50 would be a minimum first prize) and run to
£250 or more for first prize in the big Opens.

All these events are run on the Swiss system, in which you are paired in
each round against somebody who has the same score as you. You play in
every round, and as nobody is eliminated you can still catch up and win a
prize, even if you lose your first game.

The disadvantage of a weekend tournament lies in its hectic schedule, which involves adjudications or 'lightning' play-offs of games that do not finish within the allotted time — 48 moves in 2 hours being the customary time-limit. Young players naturally stand up better than veterans to the physical strain of the Opens (the Majors and Minors are less demanding), and many a young talent has been spotted by the junior selectors after a giant-killing exploit at one of these tournaments, and so won a place on a national training scheme.

The more traditional tournaments are held over a week or two, with just one four- to six-hour game each day. Long games are played to a finish in adjournment sessions. These events — such as the British Chess Federation congress in August, or the Jersey Chess Congress in May — are usually held at holiday resorts in the summer; Hastings, just after Christmas, is an exception. Tournaments of this kind give you time to think and play better chess than you perhaps ever realized you could; in between rounds you can relax. The disadvantage of these events is of course that your expenses are higher; you do not get as much chess for your money as you do with weekend congresses or club and league games.

## CORRESPONDENCE CHESS

Postal chess (and its younger brothers, chess by telephone and by fax) is a form of chess particularly suited to people who live in remote areas, or have jobs with unsocial hours (e.g. doctors, policemen, and shift-workers) or who are unable for one reason or another to get to a club or tournament to play 'over-the-board' chess. It also provides a solution for people who find that competitive OTB chess doesn't give them enough time to think, or who find their temperament lets them down. There are postal chess national and world championships, and international matches and tournaments to test the ambitious players — though here one plays for honour and not for cash. Apart from that, postal chess is not really more expensive than going to tournaments, once you compare postal charges with the equally fast-rising cost of petrol or rail fares.

Postal chess also caters for people who wish to play only particular openings. Thematic tournaments, gambit, and counter-gambit tournaments are available; there is even an experimental endgame tournament.

Success at correspondence chess does demand different qualities from OTB. Wild or intuitive play will be ruthlessly punished by the CC expert, who relies on his powers of analysis. In CC you can move the pieces around for hours before deciding on your move, whereas OTB you can't touch the pieces and you only have a few minutes to make up your mind. So the good correspondence player plays sound openings which he has prepared thoroughly in advance; he is patient and precise, always looking for the absolutely best move. This is why he gets into time trouble when you see him play OTB.

## TIME TROUBLE

Handling the time factor in OTB chess is crucial if you want to play better chess. It is no good playing twenty moves of a masterpiece, then finding yourself with only a minute for the last ten moves before the time control. Unless the position has become very easy by then, you are liable to lose on time, or throw away your advantage in the scramble to make the moves.

Although some masters and experts are time-trouble addicts, the majority of strong players have learned by experience how to pace their game through the available time, and only get short of time in exceptionally difficult positions. Also, what counts as time trouble varies from one player to another and from one position to another.

Anything faster than a move a minute may be time trouble if the position presents a problem. Of course it can be hard to say sometimes which is worse — twenty moves in ten minutes, or ten moves in five. In the first case you have more moves to make and may (because of Parkinson's Law) suddenly find yourself with ten to make in two minutes, but also you might win the game or simplify the position so that the last few moves to the control would be easy. It also makes a difference whether your opponent too is racing to make the moves, or whether he has time in hand.

Strong players, especially if they play a lot of five-minute chess, can sometimes make six, eight, or even ten good moves in a minute. If they are winning easily, so that it does not matter much what they play as long as they don't lose on time, then they can manage twenty. You should not underestimate their ability to do this, especially if they have the initiative, or if your moves are forcing their replies. So just because your opponent is running short of time, do not assume you are going to win; you have to set him problems and (if you can) pace the final scramble.

A common mistake is to rush the man who is short of time. Only play quickly if you have prepared a trappy sequence of four or five good moves which you can play instantaneously to prevent him thinking in your time. But making second-best or superficial moves quickly throws away your advantage of having more time than him to think in. Sometimes, if you have a lot of time in hand, it pays to go to the opposite extreme, and move only at intervals of a few minutes. This works because a player in time trouble relies on his body's supply of adrenalin, which enables him to cope with a short period of danger (mental in this case rather than physical) by going into overdrive. But this hormone only remains in the bloodstream for about twenty minutes, and leaves him washed out afterwards; so if you can provoke the opponent's adrenalin response prematurely and then take your time you should win. Opportunities for this ploy probably won't present themselves often, but it remains true that good moves are more effective than quick moves.

## OFFERING DRAWS

Another case where psychology (some would say 'gamesmanship') can help you get better results is over the thorny issue: should you offer draws? Of course nobody says you should not offer the draw when the possibilities are played out, or where the position is hopelessly blocked, but what about those 'grandmaster draws'?

Masters sometimes agree draws in only about ten or fifteen moves — in fact the draw may well have been agreed before sitting down to play — because they want to protect their position in a tournament when they are Black, or because they are playing a friend or compatriot. Most masters have agreed this kind of draw at some time or another, although Fischer and Larsen would not do so. So it is important not to offer an early draw to somebody like them — it will only increase his or her determination to beat you!

What, though, if you have been playing for fifteen or twenty moves and you are not too happy with your game; you feel like offering a draw. Should you do it? If you are playing in a team, you should certainly consult your captain first, but we shall assume you are in a tournament, playing only for yourself.

Although it is tempting to offer a draw when your game is beginning to go downhill, it is a dangerous time to do so. You may alert your opponent to the fact that you are worried; you may be put into a position of obvious psychological inferiority if he refuses. It is also very likely that he will refuse at such a time, unless he has reason to fear you (because of previous defeats you have inflicted on him, or because of your higher rating). About the only time when it can be worth offering a draw is when you have just played a good move, setting him a tricky choice where he may be afraid of going wrong. Exceptionally, if you have a strong and unexpected resource up your sleeve, it may be good timing to offer the draw the move before. Then, if it is declined, you will not go into a psychological decline, because you can confidently produce your surprise move to make it clear that you weren't asking any favours. Your opponent may even offer you a draw then!

Masters sometimes offer a draw when they feel that they have a slight advantage, but that it would be risky for either side to play for a win. Then if the draw is turned down, the man who turns it down has in effect taken upon himself the responsibility, and hence the risks, of front-running. Some players think that they must stand better if they hear a draw being offered — they are particularly susceptible to this kind of strategic peace initiative.

One time when the draw offer stands a good chance of being accepted is after the game has been adjourned, or when time trouble is impending. This is the time to offer when you have been fighting back fairly well from a bad position, and the opponent has played a few inferior moves. If he cannot see a promising continuation, he will probably say yes.

You should not pester your opponent with draw offers; annoying him in this way is against the rules of chess. More than two offers in one session of play is rude and counter-productive. In positions where it is clear that only one player can win, it is up to him to make the offer if and when he decides that he does not want to try and win it any more. In less clear positions, a second offer may be acceptable if the situation on the board has changed a lot since the first offer (e.g. if it has just become a rook ending).

Remember always that you should offer a draw only after you have played your move on the board but before you press your clock. Your opponent may accept right away, tell you he will consider the offer, or he may say nothing. (In any case, press your clock as soon as you have made the offer.) Unless he clearly refuses, your offer remains open until he makes another move. He may, if he wishes, keep you waiting until he has only a second or two left on his clock and you are regretting your offer. You cannot withdraw it unless he moves.

Sometimes people offer a draw while it is their turn to move. It is legitimate to accept such offers, but the reply 'I should like to see your move first' is normal. However this does not bind the first player to offering when he does actually move.

Most draws come about by agreement between the players, but there are some special rules governing draws. Stalemate, rare though it is, is generally clear-cut. If you are not sure, call over an experienced player to arbitrate.

Draws under the 50-move rule can also occasionally occur in endgames. To claim this, you need to keep an accurate score of all the moves in the game, so that if fifty moves are played by each player without a pawn move or capture taking place then the person whose move it is can claim a draw.

Players are often unclear about draws by repetition or perpetual check. Perpetual check (when one player can keep his opponent permanently in check, and decides to do so) is usually obvious and leads to the players agreeing a draw. There is no special rule about 'perpetuals', though; you cannot actually claim a draw until a position has come about three times with the same player to move. So perpetual check is only a special case of drawing by repetition.

A British master not long ago lost the chance of a draw by repetition in an international tournament because he did not know the correct rule for claiming. He made on the board the move that brought about the repetition, and his claim was disallowed. His opponent, who had inadvertently permitted the repetition, played something else then and went on to beat the Englishman.

You must claim *when* it is your turn, and *without moving.* Say to your opponent 'I claim a draw by threefold repetition with *move X* '; if he disagrees, call over the tournament director or some other person to check the claim by playing through the game score. There is a catch: until the claim is verified, your clock is running and if your claim is not upheld you lose clock time (or even the game if your time runs out). If your claim is upheld, it does not matter whether your flag has fallen in the meantime.

Remember it is threefold repetition of the *position* that counts — not the moves that bring it about. Also it must be the same player to move each time, and only the player whose move it is can claim. It is not compulsory to claim, and the same position can occur four or more times without either person claiming. They may both want to win, but repeat moves to reach the time control.

## ADJUDICATIONS

Are these methods (clockmanship, drawsmanship) legitimate? Perhaps it is arguable; at least there are some ploys that are no more ethical.

For example, there is 'pawnupmanship', which is employed by players (or their team captains) in games which are due for adjudication. There is time to play more moves, but they cannot be forced to do so. In that case a player who is a pawn up, but afraid of misplaying the position, will stop play and let the adjudicator win the game for him. What is wrong here is not the behaviour of the player (because if he made an error, his opponent would probably stop the game instead!) but the system of adjudication, which can never be as fair as getting the players to play the game out. The London League rules, which permit no adjudication before move sixty, at least make a reasonable compromise, since most games are decided within that number of moves.

However, the chances are that you will sometimes have to play games where adjudication comes after only thirty or forty moves, and in such a situation it is advisable to take account of the adjudicator's cruel objectivity. It is unwise to go into unclear complications or play risky sacrifices within a few moves of 'time'. This is especially true if you have a good position or a material advantage. The adjudicator will base his decision on concrete analysis of variations or (in quiet positions where analysis is of little help) on general assessment of the position and his deep knowledge of endgame theory. He won't take any account of psychological factors, nor of the relative clock times, nor the grading of the players. So if you have a good position, don't risk spoiling it just before adjudication time. The corollary is that if your position is difficult, it may be best to gamble on a trap or counter-sacrifice while there is still time for your opponent to go wrong, because 'normal' play might lead you to lose on adjudication.

## RATINGS

Many players like a check on whether their results are improving and on how they compare with their main rivals. Also, when entering for chess congresses or other competitions, it is useful to have a guide to what is the best level for you. The various rating systems are designed to meet these needs, among others.

Rating systems operate on various mathematical formulae. The two most important are the British Chess Federation (BCF) grading system and the international (ELO) ratings, versions of which are also operated in many countries (including Ireland and the USA).

The BCF grading list is published each September, based on results of the previous May–April season (two seasons for people who play less than 30 games per year). An average player may be rated anything over 100 and should reach at least 160 (county standard) if he is keen and learns by experience. Expert ratings are 185 upwards and above 210 a player approaches international standard. An International Master should be at least 225 and a grandmaster 240.

The system devised by the American Professor A. Elo is generally considered to be superior to the BCF one. For one thing, its four-figure scale allows for finer discrimination between players closely matched in skill. ELO ratings can be compared with BCF gradings by the formula ELO = (BCF x 8) + 600. Many players have two, widely differing, ratings because of the differences between the systems and because they are based on different sets of results. Only master events of at least nine rounds count towards the international ELO ratings.

No rating system is perfect, however, and they can only be as accurate as the voluntary workers who put in hours of unpaid time to compile the national and regional lists. Important tournaments have been overlooked by the BCF graders more than once. Identification of players with common names (like J. Smith and H. Thomas) and erratic players who play only a few games each season are further sources of errors; so are the notorious band of rapidly improving juniors. So if you are not satisfied with your rating, do not worry too much, lest it bog down your play. Far better to concentrate on winning the game or tournament in hand!

## LIGHTNING CHESS

For many players, lightning chess is an enjoyable way of practising and improving speed of reactions. It can also be played for laughs, since, with little time for thought, bizarre openings and weird combinations have a fair chance of success, and hideous blunders are not uncommon.

The most popular forms of lightning chess are the ten-second and five-minute varieties. Ten-second chess requires a buzzer or other noisy device that marks the time intervals for the players. On the first buzz, White begins the game; on the second buzz Black replies, and so on. When it is your turn, you must move quickly. If your opponent moves before his buzz, you gain extra seconds; you don't have to move on his buzz. If he is slow, you should warn him, and if he persists, claim the game.

For the first few moves, ten seconds will seem much too long, but in the middle-game they are hardly enough to calculate even simple combinations accurately and sound general judgement is essential. Ten-second chess champions can be 'boring' strategic players who are good at endings.

Five-minute chess is just that: each player sets five minutes to the hour on his chess clock, and that is all the time he has to complete the game. This gives it a very different character from 10-second chess; by the time the ending arrives, you may have only half a minute (or less!) so that even large material advantages do not guarantee victory if time is short. Nobody resigns in 5-minute chess if they have a chance of saving the game on the clock. There are special rules to deal with the case where your flag falls but your opponent only has his king, or one minor piece left ('insufficient mating material'). That is a draw, and so is the case where both flags fall before the players notice. An illegal move loses the game.

The advantages of 5-minute chess over 10-second are many. If you are running a tournament of an afternoon or evening, you can be sure that all games in a round will finish more or less simultaneously, whereas a long ending can keep everyone else waiting in a 10-second tournament. Also, there is an objective indication in 5-minute chess when somebody infringes the time-limit.

All you need for 5-minute chess is a clock (though preferably a sturdy one). You can always look to see how much time you have left (with some designs this is easier than others: digital chess clocks, though rare, are best) and pace yourself through the game. Obvious moves and 'book' opening variations can be played instantaneously, leaving you a reservoir of time for spending maybe twenty or thirty seconds on the crucial choices. It's also important not to let your opponent build up too much of a time lead; in level endings these can be converted inexorably into wins on the clock.

Five-minute experts are usually good tacticians, but they are also very quick with their physical reactions of making the moves and pressing the clock (you must use the same hand for both). Strong players can give most people a handicap of two or three minutes and still win, often on time!

Some chess tournaments nowadays provide for an 'allegro finish' as an alternative to adjudication or adjournment. These amount to a kind of lightning chess. Say that the original time-limit was 48 moves in 2 hours. Any game that reaches move 48 without being decided is continued with each player's clock wound back ten (or sometimes fifteen) minutes. Then the game must be completed according to 5-minute chess rules in the time remaining to the players. If you had made your 48 moves in 1¾ hours and your opponent in 1 hr 55 mins, this would mean you would have 25 minutes and he 15 minutes for the rest of the game.

## PROBLEMS AND STUDIES

Everything in this book so far has been concerned with normal competitive chess between two opponents. But there are two forms of chess which aim to be an art rather than a sport — problems and endgame studies.

Problems are often published in the chess columns of newspapers. You see an unlikely looking position, usually with the task: White must force mate against any defence in two moves (or three moves). There are other kinds of problem, but the two- and three-movers are by far the most common. Any two-mover can be solved quite quickly by trial and error, but three-movers can be very challenging. For problem-lovers though, the solving is only part of the appreciation. The interaction of the different mates, defences, and tries that just fail, and the economy of means in the composition are all-important. However, it is a very specialized world, and one that is unlikely to do much to increase your success at normal chess.

Endgame studies are more worthwhile for the practical player, who can hardly fail to learn something about endgame theory if he perseveres with solving them.

In the endgame study world a tension still exists between the realistic-looking compositions of men like Grigoriev and Réti, and the problem-like fantasies devised by a Bent, or a Korolkov. But in all cases the task is 'White wins' where a draw seems inevitable, or 'White draws' where loss appears certain. The trick is to make the impossible come true.

I do not think there could be a better way to conclude this book than by setting a couple of endgame studies as puzzles for you to solve. These are both quite easy, and they may help you to see the relevance of studies to practical chess endgames.

## Putting it into practice

1 White to play and win

2 White to play and draw

# Solutions to puzzles

## Unit 1

1.8    Black played 13 . . . Nxd4?? To his horror the reply was 14 e3xd4!
Rxc1 15 Bxc1 and, having failed to divert the queen from the defence of
a4, he resigned.

This was a reasonable decision as he was now two material units down
with no positional compensation, and furthermore psychologically beaten
as a result of his failure of vision — not seeing in time that the recapture on
d4 with the pawn enabled the bishop on f4 to defend the rook.

1.9    White plays 1 Qe4, threatening mate by 2 Qxh7. However Black
parries this (e.g. by 1 . . . g6 or 1 . . . f5) White will reply 2 Qxc6.

1.10    1 Qa4 threatens the Na5. After 1 . . . c6 (or 1 . . . b6, or 1 . . . c5)
to defend it, 2 Qe4 again threatens mate on h7. Black prevents this by
2 . . . g6 but then 3 Qxe7 wins.

## Unit 2

2.22    White simplifies by 1 Qxf7+! Since the pinned rook cannot capture
the queen, and 1 . . . Kh8 2 Rxg7 costs him a rook, Black has nothing better
than 1 . . . Qxf7 2 Bxf7+ Kxf7 3 Rxg7+ Kxg7 4 Nxe6+ Kf7 5 Nxc7 Ra7
6 Nd5 Rd7 7 Ne3 (unpinning) and with two extra pawns White must win.

2.23    White won by 7 Nxe5 Bxd1 (7 . . . dxe5 8 Qxg4 and White is a
piece up) 8 Bxf7+ Ke7 9 Nd5 checkmate!

## Unit 3

3.15    White should play 1 Kf1 and if 1 . . . Rf8 2 Rd8. Against 1 . . .
Qh3+ 2 Ke1 Qh1+ 3 Ke1 the white king escapes and the extra pawns
should tell. However, White actually played 1 Kf2?? and after 1 . . . Rf8
2 Rd8 Black won by 2 . . . Qh4+! 3 Kg1 Qxf6.

3.16    Black wins material by 1 . . . Rf2+! Now if 2 Kg1 Nxf3+ 3 Kh1
Rh2 checkmate. So White has no alternative to 2 Rxf2 Ne3+ (the point
of the rook sacrifice was to set up this fork) 3 Kg1 Nxg4 4 Rxf7+ Kg8
5 Rxa7 Bc5. Black has now consolidated a material advantage of two
points—enough to win, especially as the remaining white pawns are weak.
The game continued 6 Ra6 Kg7 7 Kg2 Nxe5 8 Kh3 Nxe6 9 Kh4 Kf6 and White
resigned.

## Solutions to puzzles

### Unit 4

**4.14**   One of Black's main ideas in the Benoni is to obtain a Q-side majority of pawns (by 5 . . . exd5) and then advance it in the middle-game, with . . . a6 and . . . b5. White plays 10 a4 to prevent . . . b5, and later he plays a5 with two points. Firstly, the rook may then be developed at c4 via a4. Secondly, if Black eventually does play . . . b5, then axb6 en passant will leave Black with an isolated a-pawn, rather than a mobile front of pawns at b5 and c5.

**4.15**   After 3 . . . b5, White's aim must be to break up Black's Q-side and then pick off the resulting isolated pawns, which will be very weak because of Black's lack of piece development. Play goes 4 a4 c6 (4 . . . a6? 5 axb5 axb5?? 6 Rxa8, while 4 . . . bxa4 falls in with White's plan) 5 e3 e6 (or 5 . . . Bb7, met similarly) 6 axb5! (this brings the QR into play) 6 . . . cxb5 7 b3 a5 8 bxc4 b4 (keeping the pawns united is Black's best chance) 9 Ne5 Nf6 10 Bd3 Be7 11 0-0. White has a very free game in the centre and a useful passed c-pawn. Black's Q-side pawns, although passed, will be lost if they try to advance any further.

### Unit 5

(a) 1 e4 e5 2 Nf3 Qf6?! It is true that this move guards the KP, but the queen occupies a square which rightly belongs to the KN in the early stages of the game. If the knight now goes to e2, what about the bishop? Moreover, the queen, although she looks aggressively placed, is vulnerable to attacks like N-c3-d5 and B-g5, or even d2-d4, and after exd4, then e4-e5. Play can go 3 Bc4 Qg6 4 0-0 Qxe4 5 Bxf7+! Kxf7? 6 Ng 5+. (b) 1 g4? weakens White's K-side, especially the squares f4 and h4, and so makes it unlikely that White can safely castle over there. Moreover, 1 g4 does not contribute much to development (1 g3 is good enough if you want your bishop on g2 in a hurry).

### Unit 6

Harry isn't at his best in positions like this. He played 1 . . . dxc4? but this move really neglects the centre. Tom Smith replied 2 e4; winning the pawn back later will not be difficult. Anxious to make amends and contest the centre, Harry now played 2 . . . c5??, a more serious error because it leaves the Bd6 unguarded. After 3 Nxd7 Black can no longer reply . . . Nxd7 because of Bxd6, while if 3 . . . Bxf4 4 Nxf6+ Qxf6 5 gxf4 Qxf4 6 d5 Black does not have enough for his piece. Harry wriggled hard with 3 . . . Qxd7 4 e5 cxd4 (4 . . . Bxg2 5 Kxg2 Qb7+ 6 Qf3) 5 Ne2 (5 Qxd4 Bc5) 5 . . . Nd5 (5 . . . d3 6 Nc3) 6 exd6 Nxf4 7 Nxf4 Qxd6 8 Rxc4 e5 and put up a fight with his centre pawns, but in the end the piece (against just two pawns) was too much for him. In fact after his bad moves 1 and 2, Harry was lucky to have had any swindling chances at all.

## Unit 7

**7.9** 1 Bxg7+! forces 1 . . . Ke7 (1 . . . Kxg7? 2 Qxe8) but then 2 Qc7+ (not 2 Qe5+ Ne6) 2 . . . Ke6 3 Qe5 mate, or 2 . . . Nd7 3 Qxc4 or 2 . . . Qd7 3 Rxd7+. Even better is 2 Bf6+! Kg8 (2 . . . Nxf6 3 Qxe8) 3 Qxe8+! Kxe8 4 Rd8 mate.

**7.10** White played 13 Nc6, threatening the queen, and also taking control of the e7 square. After 13 . . . Qc7 White has a pretty mate in two: 14 Qxe6+ fxe6 15 Bg6.

**7.11** After 9 . . . Nh5! 10 Qa4+ White must have expected 10 . . . Bd7 11 Qa3. Instead, 10 . . . b5!! won material by force, because if 11 Qa3? b4 12 Qa4+ (or 12 Bxg7 bxa3 13 Bxh8 f6) 12 . . . Bd7. White tried 11 Qxb5+ Bd7 12 Qxd5 but after 12 . . . Bxb2 13 Qxa8 Qxa8 14 Bxa8 Bxa1 15 Rd1 (15 c3 Bf5) 15 . . . Bg7 Black went on to win.

## Unit 8

**8.20** 1 Qf8+! If 1 . . . Rxf8 2 Ne7 mate. If 1 . . . Kxf8 2 Rh8 mate. Who said you need a queen?

**8.21** 1 . . . f4! 2 Bxf4 g5! The pretty point is: 3 Be3 Qxe3+! 4 Kxe3 Bd4 mate. (Black had to get control of f4 first, hence move 1.) White actually tried 3 e4 and the game ended 3 . . . gxf4 4 exd4 Qh3 5 Nf1 Bd4+ 6 Ke2 Rae8+ 7 Kd1 Rxe1+ 8 Kxe1 Re8+ and White resigned.

## Unit 9

**9.11** Black plays 1 . . . c4! 2 Bxc4 Nxe4 3 Nxe4 Bxe4. At a stroke, Black takes control of the long white diagonal a8–h1, and also the square f5, and obtains a half-open c-file down which his heavy pieces can attack.

**9.12** 1 . . . a4! is the move. Black threatens 2 . . . axb3 and if 3 Nxb3 Nxc4. 2 b4 is no good because of 2 . . . cxb4 3 cxb4? Bxb2; Black's previous move had been . . . c6–c5!

White can avoid the loss of a pawn in the short run, but the a-file is an avenue for the black rooks and the c4 pawn is very weak once it loses its pawn protection. The bad bishop at b2, tied to the defence of the c3 pawn, makes matters worse. Relatively best for White would be either 2 bxa4 Rxa4 3 Rxa4 Nxa4 4 Ba1 or 2 Ra3 Ra6 3 Rca1 Rca8 4 bxa4 Rxa4 5 Rxa4 Rxa4 6 Rxa4 Nxa4 7 Ba1 when Black still has to work to make his advantage tell in the endgame.

## Unit 10

**10.15** White played 1 Rxf5! exf5 (1 . . . Ng8 2 Rxh5 or 1 . . . e5 2 fxe5) 2 Nd5+ Kf8 (2 . . . Nxd5 3 Re1+ Kf8 4 Qh8 mate, or 2 . . . Ke6 3 Re1+ Ne4 4 Rxe4+) 3 Nxf6 Rb7 4 Qd5 (4 Nxh5 also wins) 4 . . .

Rcb6 5 Qxf5 (threatening Re1) 5 . . . d5 6́ Nxd5 Rh6 7 Ne3! Qe8
(7 . . . Qe7 8 Qc8+ Kg7 9 Nf5+) 8 Qc5+ Kg8 (8 . . . Re7 9 Nf5;
8 . . . Qe7 9 Re8+ Kg7 10 Nf5+) 9 Qg5+ and Black resigned. If 9 . . . Kh7
(9 . . . Rg6 10 Rd8) 10 Rd8 Qxe3 11 Qg8 mate.

**10.16** After 1 Nxe5! Black should cut his losses by capturing the knight;
then 2 Bxh5 leaves White just a pawn up. The game instead went 1 . . .
Bxe2 2 Nxd7 Bxf1 3 Nb6! (3 Nxf8? Bb5! and the white knight is trapped)
3 . . . Qc2 (3 . . . Qb8? 4 Nxf1 Ra6 5 Nd7) 4 Nxa8 Bd3 (desperation;
White is a pawn ahead with new targets in the black a- and b-pawns)
5 Nb6 Nf7 6 Nf3! Bxe4? 7 Ne1 and White wins a piece.

**10.17** This position arose after **1 e4 c5 2 Nf3 d6 3 d4 cxd4 4 Nxd4
Nf6 5 Nc3 a6 6 Bg5 e6 7 Qd3 Nbd7 8 0-0-0 Be7 9 f4 Qc7 10 Qg3 b5
11 Bd3 b4 12 Nb1 Bb7 13 Rhe1 g6?** (better 13 . . . Nh5) **14 e5 dxe5
15 fxe5 Nh5 16 Qe3! Nc5 17 g4 Ng7 18 Bf6 0-0 19 Qh6 Bxf6** (19 . . .
Ne8 20 g5 threatening Re1-e3-h3) **20 gxf6 Ne8.**
    White played **21 Nf5!**, threatening 22 Ne7+ and 23 Qxf8 mate. If
21 . . . exf5 22 Rxe8 (and g7 cannot be defended) or if 21 . . . gxf5
22 gxf5 with Rg1+ to follow.
    After 21 Nf5! Black played **21 . . . Nd7**, protecting the Rf8, and White
answered with **22 Rxe6! fxe6** (22 . . . Ndxf6? 23 Ne7+ wins the queen)
**23 Ne7+ Kf7** (23 . . . Kh8 24 Nxg6+) **24 Bxg6+** (probably clearer than
Qxh7+) **24 . . . Kxf6** (24 . . . hxg6? 25 Qxg6 mate) **25 Qh4+ Kg7**
(25 . . . Ke5 26 Bxe8 and if 26 . . . Raxe8 27 Qg3+ Kf6 28 Qxc7)
**26 Qxh7+ Kf6 27 g5+ Ke5 28 Bxe8 Be4** (both Qg7+ and Ng6+ were
threatened) **29 Ng6+ Bxg6 30 Bxg6 Rad8 31 Qg7+ Kf4 32 Qd4+ Kxg5
33 Rg1+ Kh6 34 Qh4+ Black resigned** (34 . . . Kg7 35 Qe7+ or Be8+).
Although the final checkmate took a long time to administer, Black was
doomed by the wide-open state of his king on e5, and the disharmony
among his pieces (Qc7 and Nd7 underprotected; Ra8 not developed).
White did not even need his QN!

*Unit 11*

**11.12** Black played **14 . . . e5!**, chiefly to open the a1–h8 diagonal for
his bishop. White played **15 Bxc6 bxc6 16 dxe5** (16 Bxe5? f6) **16 . . . c5!**
(suddenly the crippled Q-side pawns have become powerful) **17 0-0 f6
18 Nf3 Rfe8!** because if 19 exf6 Bxf6 the white Q-side would be indefensible. White tried instead **19 e6 g5 20 Bc7 Ra6 21 Rfd1** but after
**21 . . . Bxe6** Black had restored material equality, with a clear positional
advantage based on his bishop pair and stronger pawns.

**11.13** Black played **12 . . . g5!?  13 fxg5 hxg5** so that control of e5 is
now firmly in his hands. After **14 Bxg5** it would be risky to get the pawn

back by 14 . . . Rxh2 because of 15 Bf4 Rh8 16 Bxb5!? axb5 17 Ndxb5, another standard type of Sicilian sacrifice. However, **14 . . . b4 15 Nb1** (15 Na4 Qa5!) **15 . . . Ne5 16 h3** (16 Rf1 Nfg4) **16 . . . Rg8!** brings about complications in which Black's chances are not at all bad. If 17 Qe3 Nxe4! 18 Qxe4 Bxg5+ or 18 Bxe4? Bxg5 etc.

## Unit 12

**12.15**    After 1 Nf5 Bxc1, White played 2 Rxd7! Qxd7 3 Qg4. This carries the double threat of 4 Qxg7 mate, or (after 4 . . . Bg5 for example) 5 Nxh6+ and 6 Qxd7. Black gave up the queen by 3 . . . Qxf5 4 exf5 Bg5 but soon lost. The remaining moves were 5 h4 Be7 6 Rd1 Rad8 7 Rd5! Bf6 8 Rxd8 Rxd8 9 Qh5 Rd7 10 g4 e4 11 g5 Bd8 12 Qg4 Kf8 13 gxh6 and Black resigned.

**12.16**    The first piece offer was 1 Nxh6+! (This has to be accepted, in view of 1 . . . Kh8 2 Nf7+ Kg8 3 Qh5 threatening Bh7 mate.) After 1 . . . gxh6 2 Qg4+ Kh8 White offered the second piece by 3 Bxh6! Now if 3 . . . Bxh6 4 Qg6! and 5 Nh5. So the second sacrifice must be declined. Black played 3 . . . Re7 and play continued 4 Bxf8 Qxf8 5 Qh5+ Kg8 6 Rxe7 Qxe7 7 Nf5 Qd7 8 Qg6+ Kf8 (8 . . . Kh8 9 Re1) 9 Qxf6+ Qf7 10 Qh6+. Although Black is still a piece up, he has no answer to the introduction of the rook into White's attack. The final moves were 10 . . . Ke8 11 Re1+ Kd7 12 Re7+ Qxe7 13 Nxe7 Kxe7 14 Qg7+ Kd6 15 Qe5+ Kd7 16 Bf5+ Kd8 17 Qf6+ Ke8 18 Be6 Resigns.

## Unit 13

**13.14**    White met 1 . . . Bd7? by 2 Rxf6 gxf6 3 Nd5. Then if 3 . . . Qd8 4 Nxf6+ Kh8 5 Qh5 Re1+ 6 Kd2 and mate cannot be prevented.

**13.15**    White starts by 1 Rxg7! — not a hard move to see, but its justification requires precision in the follow-up. After 1 . . . Kxg7 2 Rg3+ Kh7 White still has to capture h6. He does this by 3 Bg6+! Kg7 (3 . . . fxg6 4 Rxg6 and 5 Qxh6 mate) 4 Bh7+! Kxh7 (4 . . . Kh8 5 Qxh6) 5 Rh3 Rxc3 6 Qxh6+ and mate next move.

## Unit 14

**14.12**    After 1 Nxe6 Black replied 1 . . . fxe6 2 Bxh6 Rxf6! This possibility had been overlooked by White, who had calculated 2 . . . gxh6?? 3 Qxh6 mate, or 2 . . . gxf6 3 Be3+ winning the queen, or 2 . . . Bxf6 3 exf6 (3 Be3+ Qh4) 3 . . . Rxf6 4 Be3+ Rh6 5 Bxh6 with the better game. Instead after 2 . . . Rxf6! 3 Be3+ (3 exf6 Bxf6) 3 . . . Rh6! 4 Bxh6 gxh6 5 Qxh6+ Kg8 6 Qg6+ Kf8 Black has a piece more than in the previous variation, and wins.

**14.13** White played 1 Nxb3! axb2+ 2 Rxb2! (because of 2 . . . Nxb2? 3 Qxa6). There followed 2 . . . Qb5 3 Rb1 Na3 4 Qxb5 Rcxb5 5 Rd1 and Black had been refuted.

## Unit 15

**15.15** The forced winning line is 1 Rxd7! Qxd7 2 Nf6! answering 2 . . . gxf6 by 3 Qg2 (or 3 Qg4). If the second sacrifice is declined, e.g. by 2 . . . Qc7, then White mates by 3 Bxh6! gxh6 4 Rg8.

On the other hand, 1 Nf6? is met by 1 . . . Nxf6! and the attack is indecisive. Also 1 Bxh6!?, though dangerous, is less clear-cut, and indeed 1 . . . g6! may enable Black to defend successfully.

**15.16** After 1 Rxf5? Black played 1 . . . Rb3!! unpinning, and exploiting the fact that White's last move unguarded the first rank. White had to resign, in view of 2 Qxa5 Rxb1+, 2 Qc1 Rxb1 3 Qxb1 Qxf5, or (relatively best) 2 Rxb3 Qxd2.

## Unit 16

**16.13** After 1 Rf1!! d1=Q, White forces a draw by 2 Qe6+! Kh7 (2 . . . Qxe6 3 Rf8+ Kh7 4 Rh8 mate) 3 Nf8+! Qxf8! (or 3 . . . Kh8 4 Ng6+) 4 Qg6+! Kg8 5 Qe6+ etc.

**16.14** Black plays 1 . . . Nd4!, protecting the Bf5. If 2 Rxc5 then 2 . . . Nb3+ and 3 . . . Nxc5. Or if 2 b4 Be7! 3 Rxd4 Bxf6 and 4 Rf4 (to skewer the bishops) fails to the counter-pin 4 . . . Bg5.

## Unit 17

**17.13** 1 Qg5 Bxf3 2 f5 met with unexpected success after 2 . . . exf5??, for White played 3 Qh6, threatening mate on g7, or (after 3 . . . Bf8) on h8. Black was not lost, however. Recovering from the shock reversal of fortune, he played 3 . . . Qxd2+ 4 Qxd2 Bf8 5 gxf5 Be4 and a draw was agreed, since White cannot get through the barricades.

Black should have played 2 . . . Kh7, e.g. 3 fxg6+ fxg6 4 gxh5 Bxh5 5 Rg2 Qe4 and White has nothing for his lost piece.

**17.14** Evidently 1 . . . Bxd5 is hopeless, and 1 . . . e4? 2 dxe4 is just as bad. 1 . . . Nd8 comes into consideration, but after 2 Qb5 Black will soon be in an endgame a pawn down. He has better chances of confusing White in complications. 1 . . . Nc7 was eventually rejected on the grounds that 2 Qxc6! (or 2 Nxc7 Rxc7) 2 . . . Nxd5! (2 . . . Qxc6 3 Ne7+ is worse) 3 Qxd7 Rxd7 4 Rfc1! Rff7 5 Bd6 simplifies too much. 'Playing the man' (and the clock) to some extent, Black chose 1 . . . Rd8!?, counting on the wide choice of possibilities to make life harder for his opponent. If then 2 Qxc6 Qxc6 3 Ne7+ Rxe7 4 Bxc6 Rc7 Black has good chances of regaining his pawn — both a2 and d3 are weak. 3 e4 Nd4 would give Black positional compensation. 2 Nec3 would admittedly have given problems, but what can you expect in a lost position? With so much material still on the board, one pawn down need not be an overwhelming disadvantage, and 2 . . . f4!? might give some attack.

White actually met 1 . . . Rd8 by 2 Rfc1 Bxd5 3 Bxd5 Qxd5 4 Rxc6 Qxd3 5 Qxd3 Rxd3 6 Bc5 (6 Rc8 Rxa3) 6 . . . Rfd7 7 Rc8 Kf7 8 Ra8 Rd2 9 Nc1, but Black obtained adequate play by 9 . . . e4! 10 Rxa7 Rxa7 11 Bxa7 Nd6! and in fact eventually won, after White blundered in time trouble.

## Unit 19

**19.12**   White should not have given up his light-squared bishop. Instead of 4 Bxe4, he could have played 4 Nxe4 dxe4 5 Bg4 e.g. 5 . . . Rxc1 (to escape the pin on the knight) 6 Rxc1 f5 7 exf6 Nxf6 8 Be6+. Black still controls e4, but White's pieces are more actively placed than in the game, so that he probably has some advantage.

5 Nc4!? also helped Black to get his queen into play. The more con-servative 5 Nc2, heading for d4, should have been preferred. Notice how the capture of the black pawn at e4 did not reduce the pressure greatly, because . . . f5 regained control of that point for Black. White should not capture en passant, because exchanges lead to an ending in which White is weak on g2, f4, and b2. 10 Nc3, remaining in the middle-game, probably draws if White is careful.

**19.13**   White played 1 b6! Rxc6 (1 . . . Qxc6 2 Qxc6) 2 b7 Re6 3 b8=Q+ Kh7 4 Qf3 and won quickly.

**19.14**   White won by 1 d6+ Kh8 2 Qf7! (back-rank motif: if 2 . . . Rxf7 3 b8=Q+ Rf8 4 Qxf8 mate) 2 . . . Qxd6 3 Bxe5! Black is defenceless. If 3 . . . fxe5 4 Qxf8+! Qxf8 5 Ra1! and 6 Ra8, promoting the b-pawn. Or if 3 . . . Qxb4 (to continue the defence of f8) then once more 4 Qxf8+ and 5 Ra1 is decisive.

## Unit 20

**20.4**   This position arose after 1 e4 c5 2 Nf3 Nc6 3 Bb5 e6 4 0-0 Qb6!? 5 Qe2 Nf6 6 Nc3 a6 7 Bxc6 bxc6 (7 . . . Qxc6 8 d4!) 8 d3. Black has the two bishops but an irregular pawn structure. 8 . . . d6 fails because of 9 e5! Nd5 10 Ne4 and Black's doubled c-pawns become isolated too. 8 . . . Be7 9 e5 Nd5 10 Ne4 f5 is possibly playable; difficult problems arise for both players. But 8 . . . d5 is simplest, and equalizes: if 9 exd5 cxd5 or if 9 Bg5 Qxb2 or if 9 Rb1 Be7.

**20.5**   Black has virtually no weaknesses, because practically every square

## Solutions to puzzles

is controlled by a pawn. White on the other hand has a glaring hole at b3, which cannot be removed by advancing the b-pawn, since Black would capture en passant and then occupy the weak squares at a4 and c4. Black should therefore find a plan based on controlling and occupying those weaknesses in the white camp, e.g. by 1 . . . b6  2 Rfc1 c5  3 dxc5 bxc5 when Black's 'hanging pawns' are well compensated for by his pressure down the b-file.

Instead, Black played 1 . . . b5? This was a serious misjudgement, because White was able to control b4 and build up pressure against Black's self-inflicted wounds on c5 and c6. Play went 2 Qc2 (2 Rfc1 is also good, but not 2 Qxb5? Rcb8 and . . . Rxb2) 2 . . . Rcb8  3 Ne1! Nc8 (3 . . . b4 would have been more consistent, and would have minimized Black's disadvantage) 4 Rc6 Qe7  5 Nd3 Nb6  6 Nb4 Rd8  7 Qf5 Rd6  8 Rfc1 Rxc6 9 Rxc6 Rd8  10 Rxb6! cxb6  11 Nc6 Qc8  12 Nxd8 Qxd8  13 Qc2 and White is virtually a pawn up in the ending. This was a game between Botvinnik and Keres!

## Unit 22

**22.6**    White played 6 Qe2 in order to answer 6 . . . 0-0 by 7 h4! followed (after e.g. 7 . . . d5) by 8 e5 Nfd7 (the queen on e2 covers e4)  9 Bxh7+ Kxh7  10 Ng5+ etc. winning. Therefore Black must not castle, but should hit back in the centre with 6 . . . c5 or first 6 . . . d6.

## Unit 24

**24.7**    Here 1 h4!? looks good but it is a red herring. White has a clear-cut win by 1 b4! for if 1 . . . Qxb4  2 Rxc7 leaves White a piece up, as does 1 . . . Qb6  2 Qxb6 axb6  3 Rxc7. If 1 . . . Rxe7  2 Qxe7 Qb6 (or 2 . . . Ng8 3 Qxf7 threatening mate on g6 as well as the queen) 3 Qxf6+ and White wins comfortably.

**24.8**    Black played 1 . . . Nxe4? and was duly refuted. Black cannot improve on the following: 2 Nc6! Bxc3+ (else the knight is lost) 3 bxc3 Qxc3+  4 Qxc3 Nxc3  5 Ne7+ Kg7  6 Bd4+ f6 (or 6 . . . Kh6  7 Bxc3 Re8  8 Bf6) 7 Bxc3 Re8  8 0-0 and Black resigned in view of 8 . . . Rxe7  9 Bxf6+ Kf7  10 Bxe7 etc.

## Unit 25

**25.2**    Black won by 21 . . . Bc3!  22 bxc3 Qe7  23 Be3 b4  24 Qe1 b3 25 cxb3 axb3  26 Bc1 Rxa2  27 Rd2 Qa7 and White resigned.

*Page* 234

## Unit 26

**26.9**    Botvinnik (White) played 1 Nb5! He rejected 1 Nf5 (which denies e7 to the black rook) because after 1 . . . Rc7 2 Rd6 Re8 3 Rd7 Rec8 4 R1d6 Nc5 White has no good continuation.

With 1 Nb5 he pursued the policy of advancing on the wing where he had a majority of pawns. After 1 . . . Re7 2 Rd7 Rff7 3 Rxe7 Rxe7 4 Rd6 Kf7 (4 . . . Nc7 5 Nxa7 Ne8 6 Rd8) 5 Rc6 Rd7 6 Rc8 (threatening Ra8) 6 . . . Nc5 7 b4! Nd3 8 c5! and White had made definite progress (8 . . . Nxb4? 9 c6!) although some drawing chances remained.

**26.10**    White has good central pawns, yielding him a space advantage and great scope for his pieces. He also has chances of play down the a- and b-files and on the a2–g8 diagonal. Black has no threats, and therefore White should not be in a hurry. With a move like 1 Rb1 or 1 Qb3, he could quietly improve his position; Black is likely to create more chances for his opponent because 'in a bad position you only have bad moves'. White instead played 1 d5!? exd5 (1 . . . Nb8 is unthinkable) 2 exd5? Ne5 3 Nxe5 dxe5 and suddenly realized how dangerous Black's play against f2 might become. If 4 Be4 Bc5 5 Rf1 (5 Bxh7+ Kh8 6 Re1 is risky) 5 . . . Bh3 6 Bg2 Bf5 draws (7 Qb2? Bd3) while 4 Bxe5 Bc5 5 Rf1 Bf5 gives Black good chances for the pawn sacrificed.

## Unit 27

**27.13**    Pachman played 1 . . . c3! to meet 2 Rxh6? by 2 . . . b3 3 cxb3 c2, and the game actually ended 2 Rh2? Rd2 3 Rxh6 Rxc2 4 e6 Rf2+ 5 Kg5 c2 6 Rh1 b3 (but not 6 . . . fxe6? 7 Kg6!) 7 e7 Re2. White's best try would have been 2 e6! Against that, 2 . . . fxe6+? 3 Kg6 would win for White (Rxh6, f7+ etc.) but Pachman intended 2 . . . Rf1+! 3 Ke5 fxe6! (here 3 . . . b3? 4 e7 Re1+ 5 Kd4 bxc2 6 Rh1! leads to a draw) 4 g5! hxg5 5 Rxb4 Re1+ 6 Kd4 Kf7 7 Rc4! (7 Kxc3 Rd1!) 7 . . . e5+! 8 Kxc3 Rd1! 9 Rb6 Rd8! 10 Kb4 Kg6 and Black's pawns, supported by their king, should win.

**27.14**    White lost on adjudication, If 1 Bd1 Bd3! (clearer than 1 . . . Rxe4 2 Bc2 Re2+ 3 Rxe2) or if 1 Bb1! Bb5! 2 Bc2 Bc6 Black wins the e-pawn (3 Rd4? Re2+) and eventually the rook ending.

## Unit 29

**29.13**    White could have won by 1 Rc5! (not 1 Rb5? Ne6 2 Rb8 Nxc7) 1 . . . Rc8 2 Rb5! (if 2 e8=Q Rxe8 3 c8=Q Rxc8 4 Rxc8 Ne6! Black reaches the draw of N versus R) 2 . . . Ng6 3 e8=Q! Rxe8 4 Rb8 etc.

Instead 1 Ke3? was played and Black replied 1 . . . Nd5+! 2 Kd4

(2 Rxd5 Rxe7+ 3 Kf4 Rxc7 is another book draw) 2 . . . Nxc7 3 Kc5 Ra8 4 Kc6 Ne8 5 Kd7 Ng7 and Black has an adequate blockade.

**29.14** Apart from Kxc3 White's main threat is to promote his c-pawn. Black's threats are to win the knight, or the passed pawn, and then win the ending with either his a-pawn or his h-pawn.

Candidate moves are 1 . . . Rc6, 1 . . . Rxe6 and 1 . . . Rec4. If 1 . . . Rcc4 2 Kd3! and all other moves lose material immediately.

If 1 . . . Rxe6 (hoping to win by 2 c8=Q? Rxc8 3 Rxc8 Kh3 etc.) White has the combinative coup 2 Rf4+! Kg5? 3 Kxc3 Rc6+? 4 Rc4. Black can improve on this by 2 . . . Kh3 (reckoning that 3 Rf3+?! Rxf3 4 c8=Q Rxf2+ 5 Kd3 Rff6 is fine for him) 3 Kxc3 Re8 4 Rc4 Rc8 and scramble a draw thanks to his rook's pawns, but can't he do better than this?

1 . . . Rc6 looks more reliable. Then 2 c8=Q Rxc8 3 Rxc8 Rxe6 should win for Black, and 2 Rf4+ loses to 2 . . . Rxf4 3 Nxf4 Rxc7. But White can play other moves. Not 2 Ra8? Rexe6 3 Rxa6 Rxa6 4 c8=Q because of 4 . . . Rad6+ and 5 . . . Rc6+ but 2 Rf6! g5 (or 2 . . . Rexe6 3 Rxe6 Rxc7 4 Rxa6 with a straightforward draw) 3 Nxg5! Rxf6 4 c8=Q Kxg5 5 Qg8+ and a draw is virtually inevitable.

The third possibility is 1 . . . Rec4 when once more 2 Rf6 should lead to a draw (2 . . . g5 3 f4 Rc2+ or 3 . . . g4 4 f5 Rxc7). If instead 2 Rf4+!? Kh3! (here 2 . . . Rxf4 fails to 3 Kxc3 Rf3+ 4 Kd4) 3 Rxc4 Rxc4 4 Kd3 Rc6! (4 . . . Rc1 5 Kd4 Kxh2 6 Nc5 Rd1+ 7 Kc4 Rc1+ 8 Kd5 Rd1+ 9 Kc6) 5 Kd4 Kxh2 (5 . . . Rxe6?? 6 c8=Q) and it's Black who wins because if 6 Kd5 Rxc7 (6 . . . Rc1? 7 Nc5) 7 Nxc7 h4 8 Ke4 Kg2 9 Ne6 a5! and White cannot stop both the widely split passed pawns.

Which should Black choose? In theory all three moves draw with best play, and each contains traps for both players. Criteria for making the choice should be: choose the line that gives the best practical chance of winning, or choose the line which you are most confident that you have calculated correctly! Black actually played 1 . . . Rc6 and a draw was agreed; perhaps 1 . . . Rec4 would have been worth trying, but the variations were not easy to analyse exhaustively — it looked too much like brinkmanship. Against a weak opponent 1 . . . Rxe6 might be best, hoping that he does not see 2 Rf4+. The final choice must sometimes be made on subjective grounds!

## *EPILOGUE*

1 (study by H. Rinck)  White wins by 1 h7! (not 1 a7? Rg8! and draws) 1 . . . Rh1 2 a7 Ra1 3 Rd1!! This is the point: one or other rook will be deflected from its duty of preventing pawn-promotion. If 3 . . . Raxd1 4 a8=Q+, 3 . . .

Rhxd1 4 h8=Q Rxa7 5 Qh5+, or if Black moves his king or pawn then 4 Rxa1 Rxa1 5 h8=Q wins.

2 (study by F. Simkhovitch) Black threatens 1 . . . Rb1 and 2 . . . Rxb2 winning; so White must play 1 Bg4+ Kd6 2 Bf5! but then 2 . . . Ra2! looks strong. Yet White can allow this: 3 Nxa2 bxa2 4 Kc1 a1=Q+ 5 Bb1! Kd5 6 Kc2 Ke4 7 Kc1 etc. Black cannot bring his queen out of the corner, so long as White plays Kc1-c2-c1. When the same position occurs for the third time, or earlier if Black recognizes that he cannot win and offers a draw, White has saved the game.

A CATALOG OF SELECTED
**DOVER BOOKS**
IN ALL FIELDS OF INTEREST

# A CATALOG OF SELECTED DOVER
# BOOKS IN ALL FIELDS OF INTEREST

CONCERNING THE SPIRITUAL IN ART, Wassily Kandinsky. Pioneering work by father of abstract art. Thoughts on color theory, nature of art. Analysis of earlier masters. 12 illustrations. 80pp. of text. 5⅜ x 8½.                    0-486-23411-8

CELTIC ART: The Methods of Construction, George Bain. Simple geometric techniques for making Celtic interlacements, spirals, Kells-type initials, animals, humans, etc. Over 500 illustrations. 160pp. 9 x 12. (Available in U.S. only.)     0-486-22923-8

AN ATLAS OF ANATOMY FOR ARTISTS, Fritz Schider. Most thorough reference work on art anatomy in the world. Hundreds of illustrations, including selections from works by Vesalius, Leonardo, Goya, Ingres, Michelangelo, others. 593 illustrations. 192pp. 7⅛ x 10¼.                    0-486-20241-0

CELTIC HAND STROKE-BY-STROKE (Irish Half-Uncial from "The Book of Kells"): An Arthur Baker Calligraphy Manual, Arthur Baker. Complete guide to creating each letter of the alphabet in distinctive Celtic manner. Covers hand position, strokes, pens, inks, paper, more. Illustrated. 48pp. 8¼ x 11.     0-486-24336-2

EASY ORIGAMI, John Montroll. Charming collection of 32 projects (hat, cup, pelican, piano, swan, many more) specially designed for the novice origami hobbyist. Clearly illustrated easy-to-follow instructions insure that even beginning papercrafters will achieve successful results. 48pp. 8¼ x 11.                    0-486-27298-2

BLOOMINGDALE'S ILLUSTRATED 1886 CATALOG: Fashions, Dry Goods and Housewares, Bloomingdale Brothers. Famed merchants' extremely rare catalog depicting about 1,700 products: clothing, housewares, firearms, dry goods, jewelry, more. Invaluable for dating, identifying vintage items. Also, copyright-free graphics for artists, designers. Co-published with Henry Ford Museum & Greenfield Village. 160pp. 8¼ x 11.                    0-486-25780-0

THE ART OF WORLDLY WISDOM, Baltasar Gracian. "Think with the few and speak with the many," "Friends are a second existence," and "Be able to forget" are among this 1637 volume's 300 pithy maxims. A perfect source of mental and spiritual refreshment, it can be opened at random and appreciated either in brief or at length. 128pp. 5⅜ x 8½.                    0-486-44034-6

JOHNSON'S DICTIONARY: A Modern Selection, Samuel Johnson (E. L. McAdam and George Milne, eds.). This modern version reduces the original 1755 edition's 2,300 pages of definitions and literary examples to a more manageable length, retaining the verbal pleasure and historical curiosity of the original. 480pp. 5³⁄₁₆ x 8¼.                    0-486-44089-3

ADVENTURES OF HUCKLEBERRY FINN, Mark Twain, Illustrated by E. W. Kemble. A work of eternal richness and complexity, a source of ongoing critical debate, and a literary landmark, Twain's 1885 masterpiece about a barefoot boy's journey of self-discovery has enthralled readers around the world. This handsome clothbound reproduction of the first edition features all 174 of the original black-and-white illustrations. 368pp. 5⅜ x 8½.                    0-486-44322-1

# CATALOG OF DOVER BOOKS

ANIMALS: 1,419 Copyright-Free Illustrations of Mammals, Birds, Fish, Insects, etc., Jim Harter (ed.). Clear wood engravings present, in extremely lifelike poses, over 1,000 species of animals. One of the most extensive pictorial sourcebooks of its kind. Captions. Index. 284pp. 9 x 12. 0-486-23766-4

1001 QUESTIONS ANSWERED ABOUT THE SEASHORE, N. J. Berrill and Jacquelyn Berrill. Queries answered about dolphins, sea snails, sponges, starfish, fishes, shore birds, many others. Covers appearance, breeding, growth, feeding, much more. 305pp. 5¼ x 8¼. 0-486-23366-9

ATTRACTING BIRDS TO YOUR YARD, William J. Weber. Easy-to-follow guide offers advice on how to attract the greatest diversity of birds: birdhouses, feeders, water and waterers, much more. 96pp. 5³⁄₁₆ x 8¼. 0-486-28927-3

MEDICINAL AND OTHER USES OF NORTH AMERICAN PLANTS: A Historical Survey with Special Reference to the Eastern Indian Tribes, Charlotte Erichsen-Brown. Chronological historical citations document 500 years of usage of plants, trees, shrubs native to eastern Canada, northeastern U.S. Also complete identifying information. 343 illustrations. 544pp. 6½ x 9¼. 0-486-25951-X

STORYBOOK MAZES, Dave Phillips. 23 stories and mazes on two-page spreads: Wizard of Oz, Treasure Island, Robin Hood, etc. Solutions. 64pp. 8¼ x 11. 0-486-23628-5

AMERICAN NEGRO SONGS: 230 Folk Songs and Spirituals, Religious and Secular, John W. Work. This authoritative study traces the African influences of songs sung and played by black Americans at work, in church, and as entertainment. The author discusses the lyric significance of such songs as "Swing Low, Sweet Chariot," "John Henry," and others and offers the words and music for 230 songs. Bibliography. Index of Song Titles. 272pp. 6½ x 9¼. 0-486-40271-1

MOVIE-STAR PORTRAITS OF THE FORTIES, John Kobal (ed.). 163 glamor, studio photos of 106 stars of the 1940s: Rita Hayworth, Ava Gardner, Marlon Brando, Clark Gable, many more. 176pp. 8⅜ x 11¼. 0-486-23546-7

YEKL and THE IMPORTED BRIDEGROOM AND OTHER STORIES OF YIDDISH NEW YORK, Abraham Cahan. Film Hester Street based on Yekl (1896). Novel, other stories among first about Jewish immigrants on N.Y.'s East Side. 240pp. 5⅜ x 8½. 0-486-22427-9

SELECTED POEMS, Walt Whitman. Generous sampling from Leaves of Grass. Twenty-four poems include "I Hear America Singing," "Song of the Open Road," "I Sing the Body Electric," "When Lilacs Last in the Dooryard Bloom'd," "O Captain! My Captain!"–all reprinted from an authoritative edition. Lists of titles and first lines. 128pp. 5³⁄₁₆ x 8¼. 0-486-26878-0

SONGS OF EXPERIENCE: Facsimile Reproduction with 26 Plates in Full Color, William Blake. 26 full-color plates from a rare 1826 edition. Includes "The Tyger," "London," "Holy Thursday," and other poems. Printed text of poems. 48pp. 5¼ x 7. 0-486-24636-1

THE BEST TALES OF HOFFMANN, E. T. A. Hoffmann. 10 of Hoffmann's most important stories: "Nutcracker and the King of Mice," "The Golden Flowerpot," etc. 458pp. 5⅜ x 8½. 0-486-21793-0

THE BOOK OF TEA, Kakuzo Okakura. Minor classic of the Orient: entertaining, charming explanation, interpretation of traditional Japanese culture in terms of tea ceremony. 94pp. 5⅜ x 8½. 0-486-20070-1

THE MALLEUS MALEFICARUM OF KRAMER AND SPRENGER, translated by Montague Summers. Full text of most important witchhunter's "bible," used by both Catholics and Protestants. 278pp. 6⅝ x 10.　　　　0-486-22802-9

SPANISH STORIES/CUENTOS ESPAÑOLES: A Dual-Language Book, Angel Flores (ed.). Unique format offers 13 great stories in Spanish by Cervantes, Borges, others. Faithful English translations on facing pages. 352pp. 5⅜ x 8½.

0-486-25399-6

GARDEN CITY, LONG ISLAND, IN EARLY PHOTOGRAPHS, 1869–1919, Mildred H. Smith. Handsome treasury of 118 vintage pictures, accompanied by carefully researched captions, document the Garden City Hotel fire (1899), the Vanderbilt Cup Race (1908), the first airmail flight departing from the Nassau Boulevard Aerodrome (1911), and much more. 96pp. 8⅞ x 11¾.　　　　0-486-40669-5

OLD QUEENS, N.Y., IN EARLY PHOTOGRAPHS, Vincent F. Seyfried and William Asadorian. Over 160 rare photographs of Maspeth, Jamaica, Jackson Heights, and other areas. Vintage views of DeWitt Clinton mansion, 1939 World's Fair and more. Captions. 192pp. 8⅞ x 11.　　　　0-486-26358-4

CAPTURED BY THE INDIANS: 15 Firsthand Accounts, 1750-1870, Frederick Drimmer. Astounding true historical accounts of grisly torture, bloody conflicts, relentless pursuits, miraculous escapes and more, by people who lived to tell the tale. 384pp. 5⅜ x 8½.　　　　0-486-24901-8

THE WORLD'S GREAT SPEECHES (Fourth Enlarged Edition), Lewis Copeland, Lawrence W. Lamm, and Stephen J. McKenna. Nearly 300 speeches provide public speakers with a wealth of updated quotes and inspiration—from Pericles' funeral oration and William Jennings Bryan's "Cross of Gold Speech" to Malcolm X's powerful words on the Black Revolution and Earl of Spenser's tribute to his sister, Diana, Princess of Wales. 944pp. 5⅜ x 8⅜.　　　　0-486-40903-1

THE BOOK OF THE SWORD, Sir Richard F. Burton. Great Victorian scholar/adventurer's eloquent, erudite history of the "queen of weapons"—from prehistory to early Roman Empire. Evolution and development of early swords, variations (sabre, broadsword, cutlass, scimitar, etc.), much more. 336pp. 6⅛ x 9¼.

0-486-25434-8

AUTOBIOGRAPHY: The Story of My Experiments with Truth, Mohandas K. Gandhi. Boyhood, legal studies, purification, the growth of the Satyagraha (nonviolent protest) movement. Critical, inspiring work of the man responsible for the freedom of India. 480pp. 5⅜ x 8½. (Available in U.S. only.)　　　　0-486-24593-4

CELTIC MYTHS AND LEGENDS, T. W. Rolleston. Masterful retelling of Irish and Welsh stories and tales. Cuchulain, King Arthur, Deirdre, the Grail, many more. First paperback edition. 58 full-page illustrations. 512pp. 5⅜ x 8½.　　　　0-486-26507-2

THE PRINCIPLES OF PSYCHOLOGY, William James. Famous long course complete, unabridged. Stream of thought, time perception, memory, experimental methods; great work decades ahead of its time. 94 figures. 1,391pp. 5⅜ x 8½. 2-vol. set.
Vol. I: 0-486-20381-6　　　Vol. II: 0-486-20382-4

THE WORLD AS WILL AND REPRESENTATION, Arthur Schopenhauer. Definitive English translation of Schopenhauer's life work, correcting more than 1,000 errors, omissions in earlier translations. Translated by E. F. J. Payne. Total of 1,269pp. 5⅜ x 8½. 2-vol. set.　　　Vol. 1: 0-486-21761-2　　　Vol. 2: 0-486-21762-0

LIGHT AND SHADE: A Classic Approach to Three-Dimensional Drawing, Mrs. Mary P. Merrifield. Handy reference clearly demonstrates principles of light and shade by revealing effects of common daylight, sunshine, and candle or artificial light on geometrical solids. 13 plates. 64pp. 5⅜ x 8½. 0-486-44143-1

ASTROLOGY AND ASTRONOMY: A Pictorial Archive of Signs and Symbols, Ernst and Johanna Lehner. Treasure trove of stories, lore, and myth, accompanied by more than 300 rare illustrations of planets, the Milky Way, signs of the zodiac, comets, meteors, and other astronomical phenomena. 192pp. 8⅜ x 11. 0-486-43981-X

JEWELRY MAKING: Techniques for Metal, Tim McCreight. Easy-to-follow instructions and carefully executed illustrations describe tools and techniques, use of gems and enamels, wire inlay, casting, and other topics. 72 line illustrations and diagrams. 176pp. 8¼ x 10⅞. 0-486-44043-5

MAKING BIRDHOUSES: Easy and Advanced Projects, Gladstone Califf. Easy-to-follow instructions include diagrams for everything from a one-room house for bluebirds to a forty-two-room structure for purple martins. 56 plates; 4 figures. 80pp. 8¾ x 6⅜. 0-486-44183-0

LITTLE BOOK OF LOG CABINS: How to Build and Furnish Them, William S. Wicks. Handy how-to manual, with instructions and illustrations for building cabins in the Adirondack style, fireplaces, stairways, furniture, beamed ceilings, and more. 102 line drawings. 96pp. 8¾ x 6⅜. 0-486-44259-4

THE SEASONS OF AMERICA PAST, Eric Sloane. From "sugaring time" and strawberry picking to Indian summer and fall harvest, a whole year's activities described in charming prose and enhanced with 79 of the author's own illustrations. 160pp. 8¼ x 11. 0-486-44220-9

THE METROPOLIS OF TOMORROW, Hugh Ferriss. Generous, prophetic vision of the metropolis of the future, as perceived in 1929. Powerful illustrations of towering structures, wide avenues, and rooftop parks–all features in many of today's modern cities. 59 illustrations. 144pp. 8¼ x 11. 0-486-43727-2

THE PATH TO ROME, Hilaire Belloc. This 1902 memoir abounds in lively vignettes from a vanished time, recounting a pilgrimage on foot across the Alps and Apennines in order to "see all Europe which the Christian Faith has saved." 77 of the author's original line drawings complement his sparkling prose. 272pp. 5⅜ x 8½. 0-486-44001-X

THE HISTORY OF RASSELAS: Prince of Abissinia, Samuel Johnson. Distinguished English writer attacks eighteenth-century optimism and man's unrealistic estimates of what life has to offer. 112pp. 5⅜ x 8½. 0-486-44094-X

A VOYAGE TO ARCTURUS, David Lindsay. A brilliant flight of pure fancy, where wild creatures crowd the fantastic landscape and demented torturers dominate victims with their bizarre mental powers. 272pp. 5⅜ x 8½. 0-486-44198-9

Paperbound unless otherwise indicated. Available at your book dealer, online at **www.doverpublications.com**, or by writing to Dept. GI, Dover Publications, Inc., 31 East 2nd Street, Mineola, NY 11501. For current price information or for free catalogs (please indicate field of interest), write to Dover Publications or log on to **www.doverpublications.com** and see every Dover book in print. Dover publishes more than 400 books each year on science, elementary and advanced mathematics, biology, music, art, literary history, social sciences, and other areas.